Praise for
Finding Freedom in Jesus

Many books have tackled the topic of our identity in Christ, but *Finding Freedom in Jesus* stands above the rest because of its rich biblical depth, powerful personal stories, and psychological and scientific insights. This is a must-read—one of the best books you'll read this year.

MARGARET FEINBERG, author of *The God You Need to Know*

Transformed into freedom is the watchword of this wonderful new book. JP Foster and Matt Williams are not offering yet another theory of transformation into a new creation life that transforms us into confident and hopeful freedom based on what we have done or some new spiritual practice for us. Rather, they present the glorious message of the gospel that in Christ we are loved and shown grace, restored, and set free. This book offers a gospel-based concentration on who Jesus is and what he has done for you and for me.

DR. SCOT MCKNIGHT, visiting professor of New Testament, Houston Theological Seminary and Westminster Theological Centre (UK)

Drs. JP Foster and Matt Williams invite you to the rarely visited intersection of the scholar and the shepherd. This project takes you to the crossroads where biblical theology converges with spiritual practicality and bids you well on the path of empowerment, encouragement, and inspiration, armed with a more profound revelation, not only about who Christ is, but also about who you are in Christ.

KENNETH C. ULMER, PhD, DMin, senior advisor to the president, Biola University

Ground zero for the Christian life begins with identity—knowing who we are in Christ. Our enemy works overtime every day at his job of being the accuser of God's children, unleashing words of condemnation and critique, all in an effort to discourage and limit us. To counter this, we have to become our favorite podcast preacher, where we turn up the volume on what Jesus and God's Word says about us and then live in those truths. This is where *Finding Freedom in Jesus* becomes an essential resource in our journey into transformation. If you're looking for freedom and transformation, this book is a must-read.

DR. BRYAN LORITTS, author of *Grace to Overcome*

So many people want their identity to be found in their achievement, financial gain, or popularity, only to be dissatisfied with their life and relationships. *Finding Freedom in Jesus* reorients your soul to the real life-transforming, life-sustaining, God-given identity found only in Christ.

JOANNE JUNG, PhD, associate dean and professor
of biblical and theological studies, Talbot School
of Theology, and author of *Knowing Grace*

Finding Freedom in Jesus is a fantastic book about the ancient truths of a believer's position in Christ written for twenty-first-century readers (including links to YouTube video extras!). Christians are created in Christ who have been restored by Christ and can live with confidence in Christ, finding freedom from the tyranny of life's hardships, sins, and distractions by the power of Christ. Highly recommended.

DR. DOUGLAS S. HUFFMAN, professor of New Testament
and dean of the school of theology at the University of
Northwestern–St. Paul; theological advisor for *The Chosen*

In an age that has endless answers to the question "Who am I?," *Finding Freedom in Jesus* offers a timely, biblically based, and practical guide to finding your identity in Christ. Chapters are short, and yet they are packed with stories and biblical insight. It is ideal for personal study, a small group, or in a classroom. I can confidently say that reading this book and taking the truths and reflective exercises seriously will be transformative.

SEAN MCDOWELL, PhD, professor of apologetics, Talbot School
of Theology; YouTuber; and author of *A Rebel's Manifesto*

Drs. JP Foster and Matt Williams have written a must-read primer for anyone seeking to find their true identity in Christ. Read this book, and within weeks it will change your life.

BISHOP ULESES C. HENDERSON JR., team
chaplain for the Los Angeles Lakers

There are few practitioners/scholars I trust as much as Drs. JP Foster and Matt Williams to shepherd readers with true pastoral care and deep Christian wisdom. Toward your journey of knowing Christ, this one-two punch from the pastor at one of Los Angeles's significant pulpits and from among the more sought-after professors where I serve is a gift. Foster has counseled me in profound ways as a leader and follower of Jesus, and Williams's wisdom has impacted me through our personal interactions and his thoughtful scholarship. I know firsthand that they live what they write. Dive into this book with seriousness, and you will find it life-shaping.

BARRY H. COREY, president, Biola University

Like physical structures, our lives—and ultimately their stability—are determined by the foundation on which they are built. In this book, Drs. Foster and Williams address one of the principal issues of our existence—namely, identity. Their carefully crafted substratum of truth offers the biblical bedrock needed to fortify the believer's sense of self and eternal purpose. This timely work is a requisite read for all who desire to faithfully follow our Lord and want to confidently answer the question "Who am I?"

WAYNE CHANEY JR., senior pastor of Antioch Church,
Long Beach, California, and media personality

This book is oxygen for the soul. It provides fresh insights to strengthen our spiritual walk by resting in our identity in Christ. In an age of busyness where we too easily focus on the externals, it calls us to the internals of who we are in Christ.

BRYAN CARTER, senior pastor, Concord Church, Dallas, Texas

Finding Freedom in Jesus is a powerful and practical guide to help believers embrace their true identity in Christ. It is rooted in Scripture, rich with personal stories, and designed for real-life transformation in churches, classrooms, and small groups alike.

BRIAN MOORE, lead pastor, Crosspointe
Church, Anaheim and Brea, California

I am delighted to stand behind such a needed text. I unequivocally believe that this timely and prophetic book will help usher a divided body into unity and understanding of God's will for us to thrive without using Saul's armor.

BISHOP MICHAEL J. FISHER, Greater Zion
Church Family, Compton, California

As a pastor who has experienced the radical freedom found in Christ, I believe *Finding Freedom in Jesus* is one of the most important books you can read. Many people in our churches walk in fear, shame, and ungodly guilt, unaware of the powerful truth of who they are in Christ. This book is a road map to healing, transformation, and discovery of the true riches of heaven. Whether you're a leader looking for a discipleship pathway or someone feeling stuck and searching for hope, this book will help you reclaim your true identity and walk in the freedom Jesus has already won for you.

AJ BONCORE, campus pastor, Saddleback Church, Brea, California

We have few trustworthy resources today to help us bridge the gap between solid biblical truth and wise, real-life application. Many resources go one way or the other, leaving believers to figure out by themselves how truth and life work together. In their timely book *Finding Freedom in Jesus*, JP Foster and Matt Williams provide just what we need—wisdom for living into biblical truth—and all this wisdom circulates around the question of the century: *Who am I?* I enthusiastically applaud their gift to the church.

J. SCOTT DUVALL, PhD, Fuller Professor of Biblical Studies,
Ouachita Baptist University, Arkadelphia, Arkansas

Have you ever heard or read a message and wondered how much further along you'd be in your life in every way had you read it years ago? That's what *Finding Freedom in Jesus* did for me. The good news? It's not too late. You and I can still internalize this message, exercise the recommended spiritual muscles, and truly find our freedom in Jesus.

SAM CHAND, leadership consultant and author of *Leadership Pain*

I have long believed that one of the primary issues in the body of Christ is crisis of identity. Identity theft is not only one of the fastest-growing crimes in the world; I see it as one of the biggest challenges believers face. Misplaced identity is a root cause of many other issues that keep believers in bondage, yet Galatians 5:1 is clear: "It is for freedom that Christ has set us free." Real, transformative, and lasting freedom happens when we discover our identity in Christ. Along with the Bible, this book is the manual we all need to get free, stay free, and live free. Read it and be transformed.

DR. VAN MOODY, pastor and bestselling author of *The People Factor*

One of the fundamental crises we face in our culture today is a lack of purpose. Our world robs us of meaning and value. But the crisis of identity that we face in our world today is just as tragic as lack of purpose and meaning. Drs. Foster and Williams masterfully connect us to who we are in Christ and give us a road map to 2 Corinthians 5:17: "If anyone is in Christ, the new creation has come." By meditating on the terms in this book, you will begin walking in newness of life and claiming your identity in Christ with greater clarity and understanding. You will be truly blessed.

ELDER CHARLES E. BLAKE II, pastor, West
Angeles COGIC, Los Angeles, California

In working through an early copy of *Finding Freedom in Jesus*, I found my own self-evaluations being transformed to what Scripture teaches about who I am in Jesus. I look forward to the morning exercises found in each chapter, and I feel such lightness in my spirit and confidence in Jesus. This book is laying foundational groundwork, shifting the focus from my insufficient self to an all-sufficient Savior.

JACOB SHAFFER, film and Bible student, Biola University

finding freedom in Jesus

finding freedom in Jesus

the 21 attributes of your identity in Christ

Dr. JP Foster & Dr. Matt Williams

ZONDERVAN
REFLECTIVE

ZONDERVAN REFLECTIVE

Finding Freedom in Jesus
Copyright © 2025 by John-Paul C. Foster and Matt Williams

Published by Zondervan, 3950 Sparks Drive SE, Suite 101, Grand Rapids, MI 49546, USA. Zondervan is a registered trademark of The Zondervan Corporation, L.L.C., a wholly owned subsidiary of HarperCollins Christian Publishing, Inc.

Requests for information should be addressed to customercare@harpercollins.com.

Zondervan titles may be purchased in bulk for educational, business, fundraising, or sales promotional use. For information, please email SpecialMarkets@Zondervan.com.

ISBN 978-0-310-17105-8 (audio)

Library of Congress Cataloging-in-Publication Data

Names: Foster, John-Paul C., 1984- author | Williams, Matthew C. author
Title: Finding freedom in Jesus : the 21 attributes of your identity in Christ / JP Foster and Matt Williams.
Description: Grand Rapids, Michigan : Zondervan Reflective, [2025]
Identifiers: LCCN 2025007087 (print) | LCCN 2025007088 (ebook) | ISBN 9780310171034 paperback | ISBN 9780310171041 ebook
Subjects: LCSH: Self-perception—Religious aspects—Christianity
Classification: LCC BV4598.25 .F67 2025 (print) | LCC BV4598.25 (ebook) | DDC 248.4—dc23/eng/20250801
LC record available at https://lccn.loc.gov/2025007087
LC ebook record available at https://lccn.loc.gov/2025007088

Cover design: Studio Gearbox
Cover photo: Shutterstock
Interior design: Denise Froehlich

Printed in the United States of America

25 26 27 28 29 LBC 6 5 4 3 2

Contents

Created in Christ

Restored by Christ

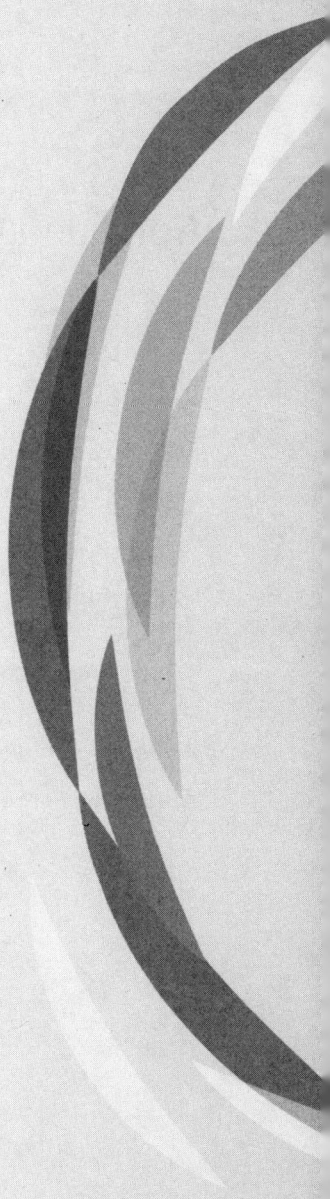

Confident in Christ

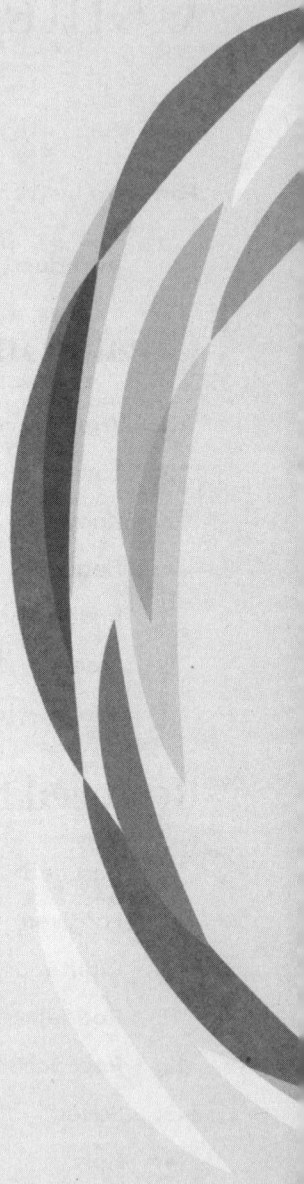

Foreword

In a world where identity can often feel fragmented and transient, the quest for a solid sense of self is more vital than ever. Dr. John-Paul Foster and Dr. Matt Williams have provided a powerful and timely resource in *Finding Freedom in Jesus*. This book invites readers into a transformative journey that centers on understanding and embracing one's identity and finding freedom through the lens of faith, offering a profound exploration of what it means to be truly rooted in Christ.

At its core, this book addresses a fundamental question: *Who am I?* In an age when external influences often dictate our sense of worth and belonging, Foster and Williams guide us back to the source of our true identity and freedom—our relationship with Jesus. They deftly weave together personal anecdotes, scriptural insights, and theological reflections, creating a rich tapestry that speaks to both the head and the heart.

The authors begin by unpacking the concept of identity as it is often perceived in contemporary culture. They highlight the pitfalls of defining ourselves by our achievements, our social status, or even our struggles. Instead, they invite us to consider a more profound truth: Our identity is not a product of our circumstances but rather a gift from God. This perspective shift is not merely academic; it has practical implications for how we live, love, and interact with the world around us.

Throughout the book, Foster and Williams articulate the gospel's transformative power in shaping our understanding of self. They emphasize that in Jesus we are forgiven and adopted as children of God, heirs of a glorious inheritance. This foundational truth lays the groundwork for a life of security, purpose, and joy. The authors provide us with tools to navigate the struggles of self-doubt and insecurity, encouraging us to ground our identity in Christ rather than in fleeting worldly validations.

Moreover, *Finding Freedom in Jesus* is not just a theological exploration but also a call to action. The authors challenge us to live out our identity and find freedom in tangible ways, cultivating a community that reflects the love and grace of Christ. They emphasize the importance of being part of the body of Christ, where we can support one another in our faith journeys. This communal aspect of identity is pivotal, as it reminds us that we are not alone in our struggles and that our identity is enriched through relationships with fellow believers.

As we delve deeper into the pages of this book, we encounter practical exercises and reflective questions that encourage introspection and application. Foster and Williams understand that embracing one's identity in Christ is not instantaneous; it requires time, patience, and grace. They provide a road map for this journey, inviting us to engage with our own stories while anchoring them in the unchanging truth of Scripture.

The authors' insights are bolstered by their personal experiences and backgrounds, which lend authenticity to their message. Dr. Foster's and Dr. Williams's theological expertise and practical wisdom create a dynamic synergy that resonates throughout the text. Their compassionate voices guide us gently yet firmly, fostering a space where each of us can wrestle with our identity and ultimately find peace in who they are in Christ.

Finding Freedom in Jesus is more than just a book; it is an invitation to a deeper relationship with Christ and a challenge to find freedom in our daily lives. Dr. Foster and Dr. Williams have crafted an inspiring and practical resource, equipping us with the tools we need to embrace our authentic selves as defined by the Creator.

As you embark on this journey through these pages, may you find clarity, hope, and a renewed sense of purpose in your freedom in Jesus. This book is a gift, and I encourage you to receive it with an open heart and a willing spirit.

Welton Pleasant II, pastor, vice president
of the Far West Region of the National Baptist
Convention

Introduction

*Do not conform to the pattern of this world, but be
transformed by the renewing of your mind.*

ROMANS 12:2

From Knowledge to Practice to Transformation

Physical therapy. I (Matt) have had a bad back for three decades. In the
summer of 2019, I finally decided to see a physical therapist. Would
it have been enough to help my back if the doctor explained how the
muscles worked so that I intellectually understood why my back hurt?
No, of course not. Would it have been enough to help my back if he only
demonstrated exercises and stretches? No, of course not. I needed to
practice the exercises. I needed to put this knowledge into practice. And
that is what I did. I stretched and exercised for about twenty minutes
a day, every day. Little by little, physical therapy helped my back pain
go away until it was completely gone. After thirty years of pain, little
incremental changes over time transformed my back.

Spiritual therapy. This book is set up like a *spiritual* therapy session. We will examine the intellectual truth of who we are in Jesus through examining twenty-one biblical terms that describe our identity in Jesus. Then we will do exercises to move this theory from our brains to our hearts and lives. The discipline of doing *physical* therapy for my back every day was hard, but it led to a transformed back. If I would have chosen *not* to do those exercises because they were too hard or I was too lazy, my back would still hurt today. I chose to do the exercises and got freedom from pain in return.

The same is true for finding freedom in Jesus. You need to consistently do *spiritual* therapy if you are going to see any real transformation in your life. It will be hard work to do the exercises found at the end of each chapter, but if you do them, your thought patterns and life will be transformed. On the other hand, it will also be hard if you do *not* do these exercises, right? The cost is to not experience the full and abundant life that Jesus offers. Which "hard" will you choose? There is a hard choice either way. We urge you to pick the hard that will give you something *good* in return. Bottom line: If you don't do anything, nothing will change.

Transformed. Jesus came to proclaim "good news" and "freedom" (Luke 4:18). In our experience, as we've taught men and women their identity in Christ through the terms described in this book and given them time to reflect on the terms, we've seen huge transformational improvements in their lives. We can grow in faith, overcome past traumas, break free from destructive habits, overcome fear and anxiety, and unlock a life of hope, purpose, and service. Embracing our true identity in Jesus can boost our confidence and self-image, empowering us with spiritual authority to experience deeper wholeness, freedom, and emotional and spiritual healing. It will also help us love others more deeply.

After reading an early version of this book and doing the exercises, one friend wrote, "I've discovered a renewed strength in knowing my identity in Christ and standing firm against the Enemy's attempts to undermine my faith. This has translated into a more vibrant prayer life and a greater awareness of God's presence in every aspect of my life."

Those who embrace the truth of their identity in Jesus can be transformed. We've seen it happen hundreds and hundreds of times.

Your transformation won't happen overnight; spiritual formation is a journey, not a light switch. But little by little, your thinking will change, and you will become a more confident son or daughter of God, better able to love Jesus and serve others.

Truth versus feelings. We need to experience the *truth* of our identity in Christ. So often we rely on our feelings instead of the truth. That is why these exercises are so important. They will help transform our lives, with the help of the Holy Spirit. Confess this truth out loud right now: "I am who God says I am, regardless of how I feel about myself. I am fully forgiven, fully saved, fully redeemed. My feelings cannot change the absolute truth of God's Word about my identity in Jesus." We need to see ourselves in the truth and light of God's Word.

What about you? Do *you* know who you are in Jesus? Do you know your identity in Christ? If you don't, you've found the right book. Dr. John-Paul Foster has been ministering in the church for more than two decades and teaching at a Christian university for nearly a decade; Dr. Matt Williams has been teaching students at Christian universities and ministering in the church for nearly four decades in both Spain and the United States. One might expect Christian students and churchgoers to have it all together. Some do, but many don't. Many are struggling, and that's why we wrote this book. We are writing for those who are tired of a mediocre Christian experience, for those who are not experiencing the transformed and abundant life that Jesus offered, for those who desire more in their relationship with Jesus.

Negative Self-Talk

Why is it that many Christians don't know who they truly are in Jesus? Let's be honest, the world is a tough place. We have made some poor choices and done some bad things, and we have been wounded, degraded, and mistreated by others, right? Our families, friends, and others have not always been kind to us or spoken truth to us. Parents. Friends. Teachers. Pastors. Neighbors. Coaches. Coworkers. Bosses. Their negative words and actions dirty up our self-image like stains on a carpet. And just like stains on a carpet, these words and actions are hard to remove. Many of us have allowed these lies to float around in our memory, allowing Satan to distort our self-image.

As a result of these bad experiences, our self-talk is often negative and destructive. We say things to ourselves that we wouldn't say to our worst enemy. How do we know this? Because we've asked people to share their self-talk with us. At the beginning of a class at Biola University in which we examined the terms found in this book, we asked students to keep track of their thoughts throughout the day and jot them down, unfiltered. Here is a short list of the destructive thoughts and lies constantly swimming in the minds of Christians:

- I am not enough.
- I deserve to be belittled.
- I am not good enough for God to work through me.
- I don't know if I'm worth people's time.
- I will let people down.
- I am easily disposable.
- I am so messed up.
- I wish I was someone else.
- I wish I was different.
- I don't belong in the church.
- I am exhausted.
- I'm a failure.

Can you hear and feel the pain in each line? These kinds of repeated lies have crippling and long-lasting consequences. Do any of these statements sound familiar to you?

Spiritual warfare. Not only are we tough on ourselves, but the devil uses our pain and these lies against us. Not only are we in an *intellectual* war about our identity as Christians; we are also engaged in spiritual warfare. We have a powerful enemy who accuses, tempts, and deceives us. Satan deceives Christians into believing that the lies are true. Our low self-esteem, our lack of understanding our true identity in Jesus, and our tendency to believe his lies exact a crippling toll on too many Christians and weaken our churches and our mission in the world.

Embracing Our True Identity in Jesus

How would your life be transformed if you embraced your true identity in Jesus, renounced Satan's lies, and walked in confident freedom? This question is the foundation of this book. After just twelve weeks of reading about these twenty-one terms, praying truth, and doing the exercises found in this book, the same students were again asked to reflect on their self-talk:

- I am able to give myself more grace.
- Going back and reading the thoughts I had in my head three months ago and comparing them to my thoughts now is unbelievable. It's devastating to read how hurtful and shameful my thoughts were. I now can see myself as my Creator sees me. I see my intrinsic worth. I am healthier than ever physically and mentally and truly more in love with God than ever before.
- My view of myself changed. My mindset is much less negative. I wouldn't exactly say that it's all happy, and I'm still learning to put on my identity in Christ, but my negative self-talk reel does not play nearly as often.
- I have a better understanding of who I am in Christ and my purpose in life.
- My mental tape was very self-critical, negative, and toxic. It was harmful for me. Now, the mental tape is practically gone. If it does start to play, I don't believe it anymore, and I usually switch over to my identity in Christ.

- I am a lot more confident. I doubt myself a lot less, and the hate-filled self-talk has really diminished. I still struggle in certain aspects with my view of myself, but I have grown in my confidence and the grace I give toward myself.
- After learning these terms, I'm so much more confident in where my identity lies—in Jesus.

These transformational improvements came as a result of knowing, believing, and living the spiritual truth of our identity in Jesus. Are you ready to see the same kind of transformation in your life?

Who am I in Jesus? Jesus said, "You will know the truth, and the truth will set you free" (John 8:32). *Who am I?* The answer to this question should come neither from our feelings nor from the world's definition of self-fulfillment. The answer must come from the Bible. Instead of asking, *Who am I?* we must ask, *Who am I* in Jesus? If we know who we are *in Jesus,* everything changes! When we know and experience the biblical truth of our identity in Jesus, our lives are transformed from negative self-talk and lack of confidence to confidence, hope, joy, and love through Jesus. We are empowered to fight against our negative self-talk and the devil's lies and better love and serve those around us.

How to Be Transformed Through This Book

This all sounds good, but is transformation really possible? Yes! We have seen it happen hundreds of times. That is why we begin each chapter with a link to a videotaped testimony of a transformed life. Be sure to watch these. They will motivate and inspire you by showing that Jesus can transform your life as well.

There are two main steps to transformation. First, we must *know* the truth of our identity in Jesus, and second, we must *practice* the truth. How do we do this? Let's take a quick look at these two steps:

Know the truth. First, we must *know* the truth of who we are in

Jesus. That's why each chapter contains a biblical overview of each term. Have you seen the movie *The Help*? Do you remember how the nanny spoke truth to little Mae Mobley: "You is kind. You is smart. You is important"? Just as the little girl in the movie needed to hear the truth of who she was, we Christians need to hear God's truth spoken to us every day because the world is a tough place in which to live. We need to hear the truth about our identity in Jesus. The twenty-one terms in this book paint a picture of a reality we don't always feel to be true about ourselves. Because of Jesus' death on the cross, God sees you as righteous, adopted, forgiven, and all the terms we're examining in this book. This is who you are through faith in Jesus.

Practice the truth. Second, we must put this knowledge into *practice*. In every chapter, you will find testimonies, stories, applications, and exercises to help you put into practice the truth of these terms. If we hope to replace the lies and negative self-talk, we must meditate and work to put this knowledge into our hearts and lives. It's like working out in a spiritual gym—it's spiritual therapy! Reading the chapters intellectually is not enough. You might get 100 percent on an exam that asks you to define the terms, but until they are felt and experienced in your life, something will be missing.

Transformation comes as a result of consistent effort, empowered by the Holy Spirit. There is no transformation without dedication. We encourage you to read, meditate, worship, and breathe in the truth about each term. It's not easy to change your way of thinking, but transformation is possible in just fifteen minutes per day. The apostle Paul wrote these words:

> Finally, brothers and sisters, whatever is true, whatever is noble, whatever is right, whatever is pure, whatever is lovely, whatever is admirable—if anything is excellent or praiseworthy—think about such things. Whatever you have learned or received or heard from me, or seen in me—put it into practice. And the God of peace will be with you. (Philippians 4:8–9)

From Identity to Calling

In every chapter, you will see a pattern. When we embrace our identity in Jesus, it leads to action. Loved people love. Rescued people rescue. Forgiven people forgive. We are following the pattern found throughout the Bible. We receive grace from God, and we respond to that grace in obedience. We don't earn our salvation from works, but we do work out our salvation (Philippians 2:12). Faith always leads to faithfulness.

This book is not just a self-help book, though it is that. It is not just about our personal transformation, though it is that. Our goal is much bigger. Once we are transformed through embracing our identity in Jesus, we will respond with a deeper love for God and for others. Seeking personal growth is important, but it's not the final goal. The ultimate goal is to participate with God's community in God's mission to reach the world with the good news of the gospel. Personal growth leads to mission and service.

How to Use This Book

Twenty-one days. There are twenty-one terms in this book. Like John-Paul's and Matt's churches, those that begin each calendar year with twenty-one days of prayer and fasting will find this book especially useful. One term can be covered each day. What better way to start a new year than to embrace the biblical truth of our identity in Jesus, knowing and experiencing who we are in him! Our churches will be transformed as we experientially pray through these terms.

Twenty-one weeks. The book can also be used for twenty-one weeks of transformation, taking one term each week. This allows time to deeply digest and meditate on each word, worshiping and reflecting on its truth over and over again.

Twenty-one days and *twenty-one weeks.* Of course, those churches that use the book to begin the year with twenty-one days of prayer and fasting can also take the next twenty-one weeks to cover one term per week. Wouldn't it be great if we examined all the terms in twenty-one days to start the year right and then dove deep for twenty-one weeks to digest each term?

Small groups. Since the contents section divides the terms into three groups of seven ("Created in Christ," "Restored by Christ," and "Confident in Christ), it's easy to use the book for small groups that meet for seven weeks at a time. We designed the exercises at the end of each chapter for both personal reflection and group discussion.

Pastors. Since I (John-Paul) am a pastor who preaches each week at my church, I see another use for this book. There is enough biblical content about each term that a pastor can easily formulate twenty-one sermons. Maybe your church could do a twenty-one-week series in which the pastor covers one term each week, while the small groups work through the book chapter by chapter, in alignment with the preaching schedule. Can you imagine the transformation that would be seen in our churches and in the communities we serve? That's exciting!

Overview of Book's Contents

We believe you will be transformed through the contents of each chapter, which include:

- videotaped personal testimonies from twenty-one men and women who have struggled with various issues, such as alcoholism, loneliness, pornography, greed, broken relationships, guilt, addictions, racism, sexual assault, and the like (see the appendix for a list of all the problems examined in the book).
- a brief summary of how each term is used in our culture to help us understand why we often misunderstand the true biblical meaning of the term.
- a summary of the Old and New Testaments' teachings on each term.

- final biblical thoughts about the overall biblical meaning of the term.
- a practical appeal for "finding freedom in Jesus" that will help us apply and fully embrace the term in our lives.
- a videotaped encouragement and prayer by the authors.
- reflective exercises for individual or group use that will help us fully embrace and personally experience the truth of our identity in Jesus, through breathing, worship, and reflective exercises.

We pray that a deeper understanding of your identity in Christ will transform your negative self-image and self-talk so you become more aware of your value and dignity as a child of God. We are also praying that you will be moved to love God and serve others as we participate together with the church to fulfill God's mission in the world. And finally, we pray that the Spirit will empower you to be dedicated as you learn, grow, and do the exercises for each term. There is no transformation without dedication and the Spirit's empowerment.

Encouragement and Prayer by John-Paul and Matt: Point your phone's camera at the QR code and follow the link or go to youtube .com/@FindingFreedomInJesusBook.

To join the Finding Freedom family, please use the tag #findingfreedominjesusbook.

Our true identity as children of God was lost due to sin in the Garden of Eden. The seven terms unpacked in this section will show the way we were created to be. We need truth reminders about our identity as God's beloved children. Remember that the goal of this book is to embrace our true identity and find freedom in Jesus.

In Jesus, I am:

created in Christ

1. Transformed
2. Loved
3. Known
4. Beautiful
5. Image Bearer
6. Free
7. Shame-Free

Don't forget to practice the breathing and reflective exercises at the end of each chapter. There is no transformation without dedication, empowered by the Holy Spirit.

CHAPTER 1

Transformed

*We all, who with unveiled faces contemplate the
Lord's glory, are being transformed into his image
with ever-increasing glory, which comes from the
Lord, who is the Spirit.*

2 CORINTHIANS 3:18

We all have imperfections; we're not finished products. In the late
seventeenth century, a famous philosopher named Blaise Pascal
wrote, "This [emptiness] he tries in vain to fill with everything around
him, seeking in things that are not there the help he cannot find in
those that are, though none can help, since this infinite abyss can be
filled only with an infinite and immutable object; in other words, by
God himself."[1] All of us have a God-shaped vacuum in our hearts that
can be satisfied only by God the Creator, made known through Jesus
Christ. We all know there is something lacking or missing in us.

The term *transformed* is the solution because it tells us that we can change, that we can become better. This is the biblical story, right? God takes ordinary men and women and transforms them into extraordinary. The weak become strong, the shy lead, and the lame walk. God takes ordinary humans, even prostitutes and murderers, and transforms them into leaders, evangelists, missionaries, prophets, and kings.

We begin the book with biblical examples showing that transformation is possible because our prayer is for you to be transformed through reading this book. God takes the least, the lost, and the last and transforms them into mighty warriors for Jesus' mission in the world. Do you feel that your ordinariness makes you underqualified? Be encouraged—you qualify to be transformed by God's supernatural power into something extraordinary!

Who am I? I am transformed in Christ.

Testimony: Point your phone's camera at the QR code for a video testimony from David or go to youtube.com /@FindingFreedomInJesusBook.

I am currently studying to be a pastor, but when I was younger, I wanted to be a professional video game player. When I lost every single video game for eighteen straight hours, it destroyed me . . .

Transformed in Our Culture

"People change, but not much" is a popular slogan in our culture. Sometimes it's used as an excuse to continue an unhealthy pattern of living. "That's just the way I am. I'm just like my parents. I can't help it." Psychological research and experience, though, have shown that we *can* change.[2] While it is true we are born in a certain culture with certain tendencies, we can change if we are willing to work at it. It's not easy, but all humans have the capacity to grow, learn, and develop.

We both have wives who are licensed therapists. Change and transformation form the foundation of their practices. If people can't change, all strained marriages would end, all abusive parents would continue to abuse, and all angry people would always be angry. We all know that this is not true. We've all seen strained marriages restored, abusive parents stop, and angry people become kind. Change and transformation are the keys to human growth and potential.

We also see transformed individuals throughout the Bible, but there is one key difference between transformation in our culture and among Christians—Christians are transformed through the Spirit's power.

What Does the Bible Say About Being Transformed?

Let's take a look at what the Bible says.

Transformed in the Old Testament

Transformation is the story of the entire Bible—from Adam and Eve in Genesis all the way to the last chapter of Revelation. Spiritually speaking, the weak became strong, the blind became able to see, and the poor became rich. The Bible is filled with transformation stories. The term *transformed* is used only a few times in the Bible, but the concept is found everywhere because God is in the business of changing people's lives. Let's look first at several examples in the Old Testament.

Abraham was transformed from being pagan and childless to a faithful man of God and the father of many nations. At age seventy-five, he left his country and his culture with only a promise from God. He waited twenty-five years, experiencing hurt, doubt, and disappointment along the way, before Isaac was born and the promise began to transform into a reality.

Sarah was transformed from a skeptical, barren woman to a joyful mother. Like Abraham, she laughed in disbelief when she heard God's promise that she would give birth because she was "past the age of childbearing" (Genesis 18:11). When she saw God's promise fulfilled in the birth of her son, she was filled, not with scornful laughter, but joyful laughter.

Joseph was transformed from servitude and prison to leadership. His brothers sold him, and he became a servant in Potiphar's home, one of Pharaoh's officials. Because of a false accusation, Joseph was thrown into prison. God gave him the ability to interpret dreams, and eventually Pharaoh himself released Joseph from prison and made him second in command in all of Egypt, saving the country from famine.

Moses was transformed from Egyptian royalty and murderer to a leader who courageously guided the Israelites out of Egypt. Abandoned in a river by his Hebrew parents, he was adopted by Pharaoh's daughter and raised to become royalty. After murdering an Egyptian, Moses fled from Egypt, leaving behind his wealth and royal power. God appeared to him in a burning bush and called Moses to courageously and miraculously lead the Israelites to freedom.

Rahab was transformed from a pagan prostitute to help the Jewish spies conquer Jericho. When the spies entered Jericho to take the land promised to them, the king wanted to kill them. The pagan prostitute Rahab hid the spies and helped them escape, faithfully acknowledging God as the true God. Matthew included Rahab in Jesus' genealogy (Matthew 1:5).

David was transformed from a shepherd to become the king of Israel. Despite David's many faults, God used him to lead the nation because David repented of his sins and worshiped God.

The prophet Elijah was transformed from a man snared in fear and despair to someone who fully trusted God's plan. He anointed Jehu as king and Elisha as prophet and eventually was taken to heaven in a whirlwind without ever physically dying (1 Kings 19; 2 Kings 2:11).

Transformed in the New Testament

Let's look at some New Testament examples to see how God transformed ordinary people into extraordinary.

Mary was transformed from teenage virgin to mother of our Lord Jesus. Becoming pregnant through the Holy Spirit while engaged to Joseph brought shame to Mary, since few believed the truth of the miraculous conception. Despite the shame, she willingly accepted and trusted the Lord, saying, "I am the Lord's servant" (Luke 1:38). "Mary's Song" gives one of the best testimonies of faith in all of Scripture (Luke 1:46–55).

Peter was transformed from fisherman to fearless evangelist. After Jesus' call, Peter left his father and boats to follow Jesus. Yes, Peter was emotional and impulsive—walking on the water and then sinking, being called Satan by Jesus, cutting off Malchus's ear at Jesus' arrest, and denying three times that he knew Jesus. But after receiving the Holy Spirit, Peter boldly preached on the Day of Pentecost and witnessed the conversion of three thousand people, healed a lame beggar, was imprisoned for his faith, and, according to tradition, was crucified upside down as a martyr in Rome for preaching about Jesus.

Matthew was transformed from a selfish and corrupt tax collector to a disciple of Jesus who generously opened his home for an evangelistic dinner and then wrote the inspired and influential Gospel of Matthew. According to Christian tradition, Matthew was martyred as a missionary in Ethiopia.

Nicodemus was transformed from wealthy, powerful Jew to faithful follower of Jesus. We see the slow transformation and conversion of Nicodemus in the Gospel of John, as he first had a long discussion with Jesus at night about the meaning of being born again, and eventually went with Joseph of Arimathea to ask for Jesus' dead body from Pilate, anoint him with spices, and lovingly place him in a tomb. Nicodemus's story reminds us that not all transformations are immediate.

The Samaritan woman was transformed from unclean, sinful outsider to the New Testament's first missionary (John 4). Samaritan women were considered unclean by Jewish people in the first century. This woman had five former husbands and was living with a sixth man. But Jesus broke Jewish protocol by speaking to her and declaring that he was the Messiah. She was transformed and came to faith in Jesus and then led the entire town to faith.

The bleeding woman was transformed from hopeless outcast with incurable bleeding to recipient of a miraculous healing (Luke 8:40–48). Since blood was unclean in Jewish culture, she was never clean, which meant she could not go to the market, to other people's homes, or to worship times in the synagogue. Everything she touched would become unclean. When she touched the edge of Jesus' cloak to indicate she had faith, though, she was healed. She was transformed from unclean to clean and was socially and religiously restored. She could worship in the synagogue and touch other people for the first time in twelve years. Jesus transformed her physically, spiritually, and socially.

Mary Magdalene was transformed from demon-possessed woman to one of Jesus' closest and most faithful supporters (Luke 8:2–3). After her remarkable release, she was often found at Jesus' side. She traveled with him, waited at the cross with Jesus' mother, was the first to find the empty tomb, talked with the resurrected Jesus, and shared the news with the disciples that Jesus' tomb was empty (John 19–20).

The thief on the cross was transformed at the very last minute from thief to heavenly citizen. Two criminals were hung next to Jesus. One of them taunted Jesus, but the other defended him and asked Jesus to remember him, to which Jesus replied, "Truly I tell you, today you will be with me in paradise" (Luke 23:43). The thief's story is a great reminder that it's never too late for conversion. It inspires us to keep on praying and keep on evangelizing. No one is beyond the transforming power of Jesus.

Paul (originally known as Saul) was transformed from persecutor of Christians to powerful missionary. After a miraculous conversion where he became blind, Saul recognized that Jesus was the expected Messiah. Instead of traveling to various locations to persecute the church, Paul led three missionary trips to start churches, preached the gospel and suffered for Jesus throughout the Roman Empire, and wrote about one-fourth of the New Testament.

The Philippian jailer was transformed from a man consumed with fear and a desire to commit suicide to a man who came to believe in Jesus. When a miraculous earthquake opened all the prison doors to allow Paul and Silas to escape, the jailer knew he had failed and was about to end his own life when they stopped him. The jailer asked Paul and Silas how he could be saved. He was instantly transformed. He washed Paul's and Silas's wounds and invited them to his house for dinner, where his entire household came to faith (Acts 16:25–34).

Jesus was transformed. The term *transformed* occurred in Jesus' transfiguration when he went up on a mountain and was "transfigured before them. His face shone like the sun, and his clothes became as white as the light" (Matthew 17:2). Jesus' face and clothes were "transfigured" or "transformed" (NLT). They glowed and gleamed. This transformed illumination was a foreshadowing of Jesus' eternal and even more glorious light show when the city of Jerusalem will come down out of heaven at the end of time. No sun will be needed because "the glory of God gives it light, and the Lamb is its lamp" (Revelation 21:23). Jesus is the "light of the world" (John 8:12) who will exude light to eternally illuminate the whole city.

We will be transformed. Our own transformed identity will resemble Jesus'. Just as Jesus has a gloriously resurrected body, so will we. Jesus "will transform our lowly bodies so that they will be like his glorious body" (Philippians 3:21). We have the promise that "we will all be changed—in a flash, in the twinkling of an eye, at the last trumpet. For the trumpet will sound, the dead will be raised imperishable, and we will be changed" (1 Corinthians 15:51–52). We *will* be transformed in Christ. That gives us hope to fight on—even in difficult times.

We are transformed. Want to hear more good news? Not only *will we be* transformed completely in Christ at his return, but we are being transformed in Christ *right now* here on earth. As we continue to live out our faith in Jesus, we "are being transformed into his image with ever-increasing glory, which comes from the Lord, who is the Spirit" (2 Corinthians 3:18). This inward and spiritual transformation takes place now through the Spirit's power.

God transforms the lowly, the least, and the lost. He transforms them from sinful to holy, death to life, joyless to joyful, ordinary to extraordinary, and hopeless to hopeful. God transforms sinful people. No matter how bad you think you are, you are not outside of God's reach. He can and will transform you. Our God is a transforming God.

Final Biblical Thoughts on Transformed

Abraham, Sarah, Joseph, Moses, Rahab, David, Elijah, Mary, Peter, Matthew, Nicodemus, the Samaritan woman, the bleeding woman, Mary Magdalene, the thief on the cross, Paul, and the Philippian jailer were all transformed through God's power to become leaders, servants, evangelists, missionaries, prophets, and kings.

Despite our ongoing struggles, we can be hopeful because God loves to take the lowly, the least, and the lost and transform them for his glory. After a long list of sins, Paul concludes, "That is what some of you were. But you were washed, you were sanctified, you were justified in the name of the Lord Jesus Christ and by the Spirit of our God" (1 Corinthians 6:9–11).

The transformation process empowers us to follow God's ways and resist the world's ways. Our transformation in Christ consists of renewing our minds, which means we change our way of thinking. We reject the thought patterns of selfishness, greed, lust, and hatred and dedicate ourselves to kindness, unselfishness, love, and compassion.

It is not just our thoughts that change; our actions are also transformed so that we do good works, even for our enemies. Our thought patterns *and* our behavior come into alignment with the way of Jesus. We seek ways to care for others by pursuing justice, feeding the poor, sharing the good news with others, and serving our neighbors. These changes occur as we cooperate with the Spirit's power to help us fix our eyes on Jesus (Hebrews 12:2).

Even though God has and is powerfully transforming us, we will still struggle in this life, just as Abraham, David, and Peter did. Thankfully, as the saying goes, "God's not done with me yet!" The transformation process continues all the way until we reach heaven, when we will be transformed in an instant to be like Jesus' glorious body.

In one sentence, to be transformed means that the Holy Spirit increasingly changes our thoughts and behaviors—in fact, the entirety of who we are—to become more and more like Jesus.

Finding Freedom in Jesus

Throughout the Bible, we see radical transformation stories of ordinary individuals who played pivotal roles in God's plan for humanity. These transformations not only impacted their own lives but also influenced countless others who came to faith through their ministries.

It's easy to think these people were special and conclude, *I'm not special like they were.* Did you not read their stories? They were prostitutes, criminals, doubters, scoffers, and even murderers. They were suicidal, impulsive, corrupt, and emotionally immature. God transformed *these* men and women. God chose the foolish, the weak, and the lowly to carry out his plan so that no one could boast in themselves, but only in God's transforming power through the Holy Spirit (1 Corinthians 1:27–29).

Your transformation story. God's transformation stories didn't end when the Bible ended. They continued throughout history all the way to *you.* God's desire is to transform *your* life—your thoughts and your behaviors—to be more like those of Jesus. He desires to empower *you* to feel love, peace, and joy, and to embrace your value as an image bearer.

He desires to transform *you* to become a leader, evangelist, missionary, servant, shepherd, pastor, or teacher. He desires to transform *you* into a person known for their kindness, love, joy, peace, patience, self-control, and compassion. God wants to transform *your* life so that you feed the hungry, clothe the naked, fight for justice, house the homeless, and give hope to the hopeless, life to the dead, and sight to the blind. He wants you to be kind to yourself in your self-talk, and he wants you to be kind to other people.

Is transformation automatic? It would be easier if transformation were automatic, but Jesus asks us to cooperate with him in this transformation process. Paul says, "Do not conform to the pattern of this world, but be transformed by the renewing of your mind. Then you will be able to test and approve what God's will is—his good, pleasing and perfect will" (Romans 12:2). Transformation requires a new way of thinking achievable only through the Spirit's power.

Transformed thinking. Neuroplasticity means that when we think the right thoughts, our brains actually change so that we think in new patterns. We can rewire the brain by means of the breathing and reflective exercises in this book. For example, for those of us who struggle with pride in our thoughts, we can memorize Scripture verses about humility and practice humbly serving others. When we do these things, the brain's thought pattern transforms to the point where we more easily think about being humble rather than prideful. Our thoughts can be transformed by the Spirit's power, which is great news for those of us stuck in "stinkin' thinkin'."

Transformed behavior. Renewing the mind will take more than just thinking correctly. Transformation requires a change in behavior. First, we dedicate ourselves to resisting the world's ways. We oppose selfishness, greed, lust, and hatred. Second, we dedicate ourselves to following God's ways. We practice goodness, kindness, selflessness, love, evangelism, and service. These changes require work and dedication. There is no transformation without dedication. For example, if we are thinking about being more thankful, we might practice telling the people in our lives that we're thankful for them or writing them a thank-you note.

Remember that you are not alone in this process. You have a community of brothers and sisters who can encourage you in your transformation. You also have the power of prayer and the Spirit's empowerment working through you. We hope you're reading and working through this book with others in community. If not, who could you ask to read it with you and encourage you to do the exercises consistently?

Embracing your identity. Transformation starts with embracing our identity in Christ. When we embrace who we truly are in Christ, we are free to become what God desires for us. Out of all the transformation stories of men and women in this chapter, which ones do you most relate to? Spend some time praying that God will powerfully transform your life in both your thinking and your actions as you read and do the exercises in this book.

It doesn't matter what our past is, as was illustrated in these stories; it matters what our future is. Why? Because God transforms our past to make us into new creations in Christ—"The old has gone, the new is here!" (2 Corinthians 5:17). He desires to transform your life, but not just *your* life. He desires to use your story to reach others. Are you ready?

Encouragement and Prayer by John-Paul and Matt: Point your phone's camera at the QR code and follow the link or go to youtube.com /@FindingFreedomInJesusBook.

Reflective Exercises for
Personal or Group Discussion to Embrace That You Are Transformed

1. Practice breathing exercises for three or four minutes each day. Breathe in: "Spirit, transform me"; breathe out: "to be like Jesus." The video by John-Paul and Matt explains how to do the breathing exercise. If you're in a small group, someone can set a timer, and the group can do the breathing together.

2. Go to YouTube, find a worship song with the theme of "transformed," and listen to it several times each day. If you're in a small group, sing the song together.

3. Looking back at the chapter, what did you learn that you didn't know previously?

4. Take some time to ponder the biblical definition of *transformed*: To be transformed means that the Holy Spirit increasingly changes your thoughts and behaviors to become more and more like those of Jesus. What part of the definition really speaks to you?

5. *Living out transformed*:
   a) Transformation begins with a renewal of the mind, a change in the way we think. As you begin to dive into this book, spend some time in prayer, asking the Lord to transform your thinking from negative self-talk to biblical and truth-filled thinking. Be sure to pay attention to your self-talk and ask the Spirit

to help you to stop the negativity. You could ask someone to hold you accountable for your reading, meditating, and breathing exercises.

b) Transformation is a renewing not just of our thinking but also of our actions. Spend some time in prayer, asking the Lord to transform your actions as you read through the book. Keep in mind that your actions in the world are a witness for Jesus. Pray that you are conformed to the likeness of Jesus so that no one can accuse you of hypocrisy. Pray for patience because change and transformation typically take time.

6. Take time to meditate and pray through Matthew 17:2; Romans 12:2; 1 Corinthians 15:51–52; 2 Corinthians 3:18; and Philippians 3:21. Allow the Lord to open your heart to the truth that you are transformed in Christ. You may want to choose one of these passages to memorize.

CHAPTER 2

Loved

God demonstrates his own love for us in this: While
we were still sinners, Christ died for us.

ROMANS 5:8

Growing up, my (Matt's) dad rarely told me he loved me. It was hard growing up without the stability of knowing that my dad really loved me and was in my corner. I wasn't quite sure how he felt about me. But when my dad was diagnosed with cancer at the age of seventy-five it was as if he couldn't say "I love you" enough. My dad wanted me to know I was loved while he still had the chance to express it.

Have you experienced something similar? Maybe your family told you they loved you, but their actions didn't show it. Maybe a friend or a spouse shattered your belief that you are worthy of love. A lack of love can lead to scary consequences. Research shows that if you withhold love from a baby, chances are they won't fully develop emotionally, and their overall well-being can be harmed. As these babies grow up, they typically struggle to connect with people, have limited empathy, and low self-esteem. Those who have not experienced love will often seek to fill the emptiness with other people or things.

We need love; we need connection with people. Without love, we can feel lonely, isolated, or worthless. Have you ever been loved? Truly loved? Only God's love can bring true joy and fulfillment.

Who am I? I am loved in Jesus. I can be transformed when I embrace that truth.

Testimony: Point your phone's camera at the QR code for a video testimony from Ann or go to youtube.com /@FindingFreedomInJesusBook.

I was depressed, hated myself, and exhausted. The Lord loved me when I didn't love myself . . .

Loved in Our Culture

Our world offers a superficial meaning of the word *love*: "to feel deep affection," or "to like or enjoy very much." We can "love" a TV show, a car, a spouse, or a steak. Surprisingly, though, no matter where you look in our culture—social media, movies, books, shows, you name it—commitment is rarely a part of what it means to love. When divorced people are surveyed, 75 percent say they got divorced because of a lack of commitment. Is it any wonder that marriages fail, given our fickle definition of love? We fall *in* love as quickly as we fall *out of* love. In the mid-1990s, the idea of a "starter marriage" began— first marriages that last about five years, and the partners move on. That kind of love is fickle, fading; it's just a feeling. When the feelings are gone, so is the love, so you move on to the next person, hoping to find true love.

When I (Matt) was a missionary in Barcelona, I talked with a Portuguese woman about the meaning of love. In the same sentence, she said she loved her husband and she loved her boyfriend. Shocked and confused, I asked her about it. She said, "Yes, I love them both." There was no contradiction in her mind.

We think love means more. Let's turn to the Bible for answers.

What Does the Bible Say About Being Loved?

Loved in the Old Testament

God is love. God is a God of love: "You, Lord, are a compassionate and gracious God, slow to anger, abounding in love and faithfulness" (Psalm 86:15). The Hebrew term *hesed* is used just shy of 250 times in the Old Testament to refer to God's "loving-kindness" or "unfailing love." God has had *hesed* for those in covenant relationship with him "to a thousand generations" (Deuteronomy 7:9). His love does not end.

Love is an action. God's love is not just a feeling, but it is active. God showed his love in many ways—protecting from danger, appointing kings to maintain justice, forgiving sins, rescuing from enemies, freeing the Israelites from slavery in Egypt, and rejoicing and singing over his people (Deuteronomy 23:5; 1 Kings 10:9; Psalm 51:1; 57:3; 136:11; Hosea 11:1; Zephaniah 3:17). God's love acted to protect and care for the Israelites. God has always had his people's best interests in mind. That is biblical love.

God's love is committed. God's love is a committed love—the kind of love that is lacking in our world today. Even when his people were sinful, God continued to love them. He didn't give up on the Israelites or leave them: "They became stiff-necked. . . . But you are a forgiving God, gracious and compassionate, slow to anger and abounding in love. Therefore you did not desert them" (Nehemiah 9:17). In our culture, love seems to be temporary because many of us have been abandoned by parents, spouses, boyfriends or girlfriends, pastors, or friends. God doesn't abandon. He doesn't leave. We can count on his everlasting love.

Hosea and Gomer. To model his committed love, God told the prophet Hosea to love Gomer, his wife, even though she had affairs with other men: "Love her as the LORD loves the Israelites, though they turn to other gods" (Hosea 3:1). We know this command sounds outrageous, but God wanted to show Israel that he loved her even when she was sinful: "While you were doing all these things, declares the LORD, I spoke to you again and again, but you did not listen; I called you, but you did not answer" (Jeremiah 7:13). By demonstrating patient love, God hoped that the Israelites would repent and return to him.

Living Loved Today

When I (Matt) was in college, I repeatedly shared the gospel with a good friend, but she always said no. Ten years later, she told me, "I knew that what you were telling me was true, but I just didn't want to follow Jesus. I'm now a Christian. Jesus never gave up on me. Thank you for sharing the gospel with me all those times. It was not lost on me." What a great reminder! I had given up hope, but God hadn't.

The Suffering Messiah. Isaiah 53 prophesied that the Messiah would experience horrible suffering—being despised, rejected, afflicted, pierced, wounded, oppressed, and crushed. This prophecy was fulfilled in Jesus' cruel death on the cross. How much does God love you? He loves you so much that he was willing to suffer in order to save you: "God so loved the world that he gave his one and only Son" (John 3:16).

Responding to God's love. Just because we are loved by God doesn't mean we can do whatever we want or do whatever feels good or right to us. Israel was called to love God in response to the love they had received. Jewish people recite the *Shema* twice daily: "Hear, O Israel: The LORD our God, the LORD is one. Love the LORD your God with all your heart and with all your soul and with all your strength" (Deuteronomy 6:4–5). True love responds to God's love.

How do we show God our love? Love for God is expressed through faithful obedience: "And now, Israel, what does the LORD your God ask of you but to fear the LORD your God, to walk in obedience to him, to love him, to serve the LORD your God with all your heart and with all your soul" (Deuteronomy 10:12). God lavishly loved us first, and we respond to him with loving obedience.

God also asked the Israelites to "love your neighbor as yourself" (Leviticus 19:18). They were to love even the unlovable, even those who didn't "deserve" love (after all, do any of us "deserve" love?). Israel was asked to love even those who were overlooked or despised, in the hope that they would also experience God's love.

Remaining in God's love. Given that so many of God's beloved Israelites left God and turned to idolatry, how can we remain in God's love and not turn away or abandon him? Perhaps we can learn from the psalmist, who instructed us to meditate on God's unfailing love (Psalm 48:9), and to give thanks to the God of gods whose love endures forever (136:2). That's good advice!

Loved in the New Testament

God is love. The love shared within the Godhead between Father, Son, and Spirit overflowed and was generously shared with humans. Jesus prayed that the love God has for him would also be in us (John 17:26). The result of God's overflowing love brings us into his family: "See what great love the Father has lavished on us, that we should be called children of God" (1 John 3:1). God's love makes it possible for us to experience true love.

The surprising truth is that God loves us in the midst of all the ugliness of our sin: "God demonstrates his own love for us in this: While we were still sinners, Christ died for us" (Romans 5:8; see also Ephesians

2:4–6). We don't earn love or clean ourselves up in the hope that God will then love us. He already loves us, even in our sinfulness.

What does love mean? The New Testament writers did their best to define love but admitted it was impossible to fully understand God's love because it is a "love that surpasses knowledge" (Ephesians 3:19). Paul's definition is profound:

> Love is patient, love is kind. It does not envy, it does not boast, it is not proud. It does not dishonor others, it is not self-seeking, it is not easily angered, it keeps no record of wrongs. Love does not delight in evil but rejoices with the truth. It always protects, always trusts, always hopes, always perseveres.
>
> Love never fails. (1 Corinthians 13:4–8)

This is more than a passage to be read at weddings; it is a profound description of God's love for us and the kind of love we should share with others.

God and Jesus actively love us. God's love is not a vague sentimental feeling but is intimately connected to acts of love: "God so loved the world that he gave his one and only Son, that whoever believes in him shall not perish but have eternal life" (John 3:16). Jesus' love is seen in every action done to bring life to the lost. He demonstrates his love in every miracle, teaching, act of compassion, raising of the dead, driving out of demons, and prayer. His entire ministry was founded on love. Here are a few examples of his active love:

JESUS' LOVE TEACHES. Jesus taught the truth of the gospel because he loved people and wanted them to find eternal life. When the rich man asked Jesus how to inherit eternal life, "Jesus looked at him and loved him." Jesus wanted him to find life, so Jesus told him this: "Go, sell everything you have and give to the poor.... Then come, follow me" (Mark 10:21). Jesus loved the rich man.

JESUS' LOVE HEALS. Jesus did every one of his miracles out of his compassionate love, including healing the blind, lepers, deaf, and mute:

"When Jesus landed and saw a large crowd, he had compassion on them and healed their sick" (Matthew 14:14). When Jesus healed the invalid near a pool called Bethesda (John 5:1–15), he told the Jewish leaders that his healing flowed out of love for humanity (vv. 19–20). Jesus healed two blind men because he compassionately loved them: "Jesus had compassion on them and touched their eyes. Immediately they received their sight and followed him" (Matthew 20:34). Jesus loved them.

One of Jesus' most impressive healing miracles was the raising of Lazarus from the dead. Why did he do that? Because he "loved Martha and her sister and Lazarus" (John 11:5). Martha and Mary were distraught when their brother Lazarus died. Their pain caused Jesus to be "deeply moved," even to weep (John 11:38, 35). Jesus raised Lazarus from the dead, restoring him to life. Jesus loved this family.

Living Loved Today

I (John-Paul) recently preached a sermon based on James 5:14: "Is anyone among you sick? Let them call the elders of the church to pray over them and anoint them with oil in the name of the Lord." I asked any who were ill to come forward for prayer. I told them I was praying that God's will would be done—whether or not they were healed. Prayer is not magic. I prayed for a man with stage 4 liver cancer. The following week, his wife excitedly called the church office to tell us he had been healed. She was so thankful and amazed at God's love for her husband.

JESUS' LOVE DRIVES OUT DEMONS. Jesus also drove out demons as an expression of his love. If Satan's goal was to "steal and kill and destroy" (John 10:10), Jesus' goal was to release people from Satan's grip by driving out demons and bringing them freedom and life. A father once came to Jesus and told him that his son "often falls into the fire or into the water" (Matthew 17:15). Satan was trying to kill this boy. But "Jesus rebuked the demon, and it came out of the boy, and he was healed at that moment" (v. 18). Jesus' desire was for everyone to be released from the influence of demonic powers. Jesus loved that father and that boy.

JESUS' LOVE WASHES FEET. If you had infinite power, what would you do? Be honest. Would you do something selfish? What did Jesus do? At the Last Supper, as the disciples argued about who was the greatest among them, Jesus "loved them to the end" when he picked up a basin of water and washed their feet—their dirty, stinky, poop-covered feet (John 13:1–17)! Only servants washed feet in that culture because feet would have walked through the animal waste and human waste that was dumped into the streets every day. Jesus lovingly stooped down and sacrificially served the disciples by washing their feet. Jesus loved his disciples.

JESUS' LOVE SHARES FELLOWSHIP WITH ENEMIES. At that same dinner, after washing Judas's feet, Jesus shared bread with Judas, even though he knew Judas would betray him, an act that led to Jesus' death (John 13:18–30). I don't know about you, but I try to stay away from those who want me dead! Jesus approached Judas, washed his feet, and shared a meal with him. It's almost as though Jesus was saying, "Judas, there is always a way back. Return to me. I love you." By the way, he says the same thing to us every time we stray from him. Jesus loved Judas.

JESUS' LOVE PRAYS. One final example of Jesus' love at the Last Supper is seen when he prayed that Peter's faith would not fail (Luke 22:31–32; John 13:38). Jesus knew Peter would disown him three times. Despite the fact that Jesus had discipled Peter for three years, when Jesus was in his time of greatest need after his arrest, Peter denied knowing Jesus. Jesus didn't give up on Peter. He powerfully and emotionally restored him to leadership and ministry after the resurrection (John 21:15–17). These examples of love at the Last Supper were some of Jesus' last actions before his death on the cross. Jesus loved Peter.

JESUS' LOVE NEVER ENDS. We should never question whether we are passionately loved by Jesus. There is nothing that "will be able to separate us from the love of God that is in Christ Jesus our Lord" (Romans 8:39). Although we continue to sin, nothing can separate us from his love. He will never leave us or forsake us, as so many humans have done. If you ever question Jesus' love for you, just look at the cross. Jesus' cruel and painful death was his greatest act of love, proving that you are loved. You. Are. Loved.

RESPONDING TO GOD'S LOVE. Those whom God loves should love him in return. Jesus said, "'Love the Lord your God with all your heart and with all your soul and with all your strength and with all your mind'; and, 'Love your neighbor as yourself'" (Luke 10:27). We are called to love God and our neighbor, which includes those we formerly hated because of racial differences (Luke 10). In Jesus' day, Jewish people hated the Samaritans, but Jesus instructed them to love the Samaritans. This changed everything. The "new command" to "love one another" (John 13:34) means we are asked to love everyone, not just those who are our same race, same religion, or same political party. We even love our enemies: "Love your enemies and pray for those who persecute you" (Matthew 5:44). When a Christian loves even the most difficult people, it's a sign that they have experienced God's love.

Living Loved Today

In eighth grade, a girl did something mean to me. I (Matt) didn't talk to her again. Four years later, I met Jesus, and he transformed my life. The week after becoming a Christian, I ran into the girl in a high school hallway. I said, "Hi." She was stunned. After meeting Jesus, I knew I couldn't continue to hate her. Jesus had shown me love and commanded me to love others. I had no other option than to restore our broken friendship, right?

Empowered to love. This call to love the outsider and enemy is very difficult. I mean, come on, this world contains a lot of mean and cruel people. Is it possible to love them? No, it's not—not on our own strength, which is why "God's love has been poured out into our hearts through the Holy Spirit" (Romans 5:5). We have been empowered with a supernatural power through the Spirit that enables us to love even the unlovable.

Love is sacrificial. Because we possess a supernatural power enabling us to love, we can love sacrificially. Love is not just an emotion; it always leads to actions. John gave a practical example of love:

> This is how we know what love is: Jesus Christ laid down his life for us. And we ought to lay down our lives for our brothers and sisters. If anyone has material possessions and sees a brother or sister in need but has no pity on them, how can the love of God be in that person? Dear children, let us not love with words or speech but with actions and in truth. (1 John 3:16–18)

We are called to lovingly help the needy; we can't just ignore them. Like Jesus' love, our love is demonstrated in sacrificing for others: "Love each other as I have loved you. Greater love has no one than this: to lay down one's life for one's friends" (John 15:12–13).

It's no surprise that love stands first in the list of the fruit of the Spirit (Galatians 5:22). As Paul says about the virtues of faith, hope, and love, "the greatest of these is love" (1 Corinthians 13:13). God's expression of love toward us, and our response of loving him and neighbor through the empowering work of the Holy Spirit, is the foundation of the Christian life. You are loved in Jesus.

Final Biblical Thoughts on Loved

God is love—unfailing and unending love—and that love overflows to us. His love is affectionate, seen in his rejoicing and singing over his people. It is also active, seen in his rescuing, forgiving, and caring for his people, even when they are disobedient. Jesus demonstrated love by sacrificially serving others during his lifetime and ultimately by dying on the cross. We are loved by God, and this love requires a response: Love God and love people. We express our love for God through following his commands for righteousness and justice, and we express our love for people by sacrificially caring for the needy and hurting.

In one sentence, to be loved in Jesus means that God loves us with an unconditional, unending care, compelling us to love God and neighbor in response.

Finding Freedom in Jesus

Can you see the differences between the world's and the Bible's definitions of love? Is it any wonder that divorce, broken homes, and violence are so prevalent in our world? As a result of their experience of a broken home, many teen and young adults see love as a pipe dream. Many end up settling for "love" in all the wrong places—sex, alcohol, even marriages that they're quite sure will end in divorce. The world's definition of love is changing, temporary, and fickle—it's a feeling that can end. God's love, though, is sacrificial, enduring, perfect, abundant, and relational—and it leads to loving actions. Do you think Christians have a warped definition of love? If we misunderstand the definition of love in the church, almost any behavior can be justified under the label of "love."

When we grasp and accept that we are infinitely loved by God in Jesus, it affects everything about us—our confidence, self-image, character, and actions. The lies the world tells us no longer hold the same weight. As Ann said in her video testimony, "If I am loved by God, nothing else really mattered. All I have to do is keep my eyes on Jesus." We can rest and be confident in God's love. We will find true joy and fulfillment as we experience and embrace God's love for us.

God's affectionate love will go to the farthest reaches to show you that he loves you. If you ever doubt his love, just look again at Jesus' agonizing death on the cross—for you. God's love always desires the best for you. God doesn't just love the world; he loves *you*. You are loved when you feel like you are loved and when you don't feel it. You can never be more loved than you are right now.

Encouragement and Prayer by John-Paul and Matt: Point your phone's camera at the QR code and follow the link or go to youtube.com /@FindingFreedomInJesusBook.

Reflective Exercises for
Personal or Group Discussion to Embrace That You Are Loved

1. Practice breathing exercises for three or four minutes each day. Breathe in: "perfectly loved"; breathe out: "now and forever." If you're in a small group, someone can set a timer, and the group can do the breathing together.

2. Go to YouTube, find a worship song with the theme of "loved," and listen to it several times each day. If you're in a small group, sing the song together.

3. Looking back at the chapter, what did you learn that you didn't know previously?

4. When you hear the word *love*, what definition comes to your mind? Take some time to ponder the biblical definition of *loved*: To be loved means that God loves you with an unconditional, unending care, compelling you to love God and neighbor in response. What part of the definition really speaks to you? How does this definition change your own definition of love?

5. *Living out love*:

    a) Are you caught in a cycle of sin? God loves you. He hasn't given up on you. He called you and loved you when you were still a sinner, and he continues to call you and wait for your return. It's never too late to return to God's love. Do you feel that God loves you today?

    b) As a result of being loved by God, you are empowered by his Spirit to love others with the same sacrificial love we see Jesus show on the cross. What specific ways can you reach out in love today to your "neighbor"? Here are several simple examples: a phone call, a visit, a listening ear, a donation, a prayer for those who irritate you, homemade cookies for a neighbor, or a free night of babysitting for young parents. Tell your family and friends, "I love you." Let others know in both words and actions that you love them.

6. Take time to meditate on and pray through Nehemiah 9:17; Hosea 2:13–14; Luke 10:27; John 3:16; Romans 8:39; and Ephesians 2:4–6. Allow the Lord to open your heart to the truth that you are loved in Jesus. You may want to choose one of these passages to memorize.

7. Have you checked out our social media posts where friends who are reading the book are posting testimonies of and praises for what God is doing in their lives as they find freedom in Jesus? Maybe you can share your story. #findingfreedominjesusbook

CHAPTER 3

Known

I am the good shepherd; I know my sheep and my sheep know me.

JOHN 10:14

I (Matt) remember sitting by myself in a crowded cafeteria as a freshman in high school. It was embarrassing, depressing, and just not cool. The room was full of laughter and joking around, but I was alone. God created us for relationships: "It is not good for the man to be alone" (Genesis 2:18). We find joy and contentment when we are known by friends and family, enjoying laughter together and having common interests.

Despite this need to be known and despite instant access to family and friends through social media, a 2019 survey commissioned by Edelman and Cigna showed that 52 percent of Americans feel lonely—52 percent![1] Loneliness is especially prevalent among young people, mothers of young children, and the elderly. While Los Angeles is home to 3.8 million people, countless thousands of people are still unknown. They connect on social media all day long, but how well are they known?

Who am I? I am known in Christ. I can be transformed when I embrace that truth.

Testimony: Point your phone's camera at the QR code for a video testimony from Eunji or go to youtube.com /@FindingFreedomInJesusBook.

I was born in South Korea, but I grew up in Tajikistan and Turkey. I experienced racism every day. I wanted to be seen and known, but not in this way . . .

Known in Our Culture

Our culture places a high value on being known. We have a psychological need to be seen and known. Attachment theory in psychology says that being known is foundational for self-identity and self-confidence. Studies show that those who are truly known within strong friendships have a reduced risk of depression and high blood pressure.[2]

Although we deeply desire to be known, loved, and respected, out of fear we tend to hide the messy parts of ourselves from others. This fear prompts us to hide our weaknesses, leaving us feeling unknown by and disconnected from others.

God's desire is that we realize we are fully known *and* fully loved by him. When we experience this kind of love, we can be ourselves. We can share with God the most vulnerable and private thoughts, fears, and experiences because he truly knows us, with all our baggage, and still accepts and cherishes us. We rarely know or are known this way in our culture.

What Does the Bible Say About Being Known?

Known in the Old Testament

Known at creation. In the Garden of Eden, Adam and Eve were fully known by God. Their relationship was secure, with open communication between them and God. After Adam and Eve sinned, however, they hid from God because they were afraid. We were created to be known, but with the introduction of sin came shame and the desire to hide.

Israel is known. Despite sin, God still wanted to know and be known by humans. He chose and knew the nation of Israel as his special people: "You only have I known among all the families of the earth" (Amos 3:2 NASB). Because God knew Israel, he lovingly cared for her well-being, including rescuing her from Egypt (Exodus 3:7). As you read the Old Testament, you will see explicit statements that God knew Abraham, Moses, David, and Jeremiah (Genesis 18:19; Deuteronomy 34:10; 2 Samuel 7:20; Jeremiah 1:5). Although the term *known* may not always be used in your particular English translation, it is implied that God knew and lovingly cared for many, including Hagar and Leah.

HAGAR IS KNOWN. Abraham's wife, Sarah, could not have children, so she told Abraham to have children through her maidservant, Hagar. When Hagar became pregnant, Sarah became jealous. Hagar fled. But Hagar was seen and known by God, who sent an angel to her with a message. After the angel of the Lord spoke to Hagar, she said, "You are the God who sees me" (Genesis 16:13). God saw Hagar, knew exactly where she was, and came to rescue her. She was intimately known and cared for by God.

LEAH IS KNOWN. Jacob had more than one wife. He loved Rachel but was tricked by her father into marrying Leah, the older sister. As a result, Leah felt unloved by Jacob, but God saw her struggles: "When the LORD saw that Leah was not loved, he enabled her to conceive" (Genesis

29:31). The names of her sons confirm that she was known by God. Reuben was first. A text note in the New International Version reads, "*Reuben* sounds like the Hebrew for *he has seen my misery*" (Genesis 29:32). Simeon was next. His name means *one who hears* (Genesis 29:33, text note). Leah knew that God had seen and heard her, which eventually led her to praise God as she named her fourth son Judah, whose name sounds like the Hebrew word for *praise* (Genesis 29:35, text note). Leah was known by God.

God fully knows everyone. God knows the hearts of *every* man and woman (2 Chronicles 6:30). Psalm 139 shows how fully God knows us: "You have searched me, LORD, and you know me. You know when I sit and when I rise; you perceive my thoughts from afar. You discern my going out and my lying down; you are familiar with all my ways" (Psalm 139:1–3). God doesn't just know a few things about us; he intimately knows everything about us.

Our sin is known. Because we are fully known by God, he also knows our sin and guilt (Psalm 69:5). It is impossible to hide anything from God, although we try. Because God fully knows and fully loves us, he keeps reaching out his hand to us, even in the midst of our sin, hoping we will repent and return to him. God does not give up on his people.

Known in the New Testament

Fully known by Jesus. Just as God saw and fully knew people in the Old Testament, Jesus knew "all things," "knew all people," and knew "what was in each person" (John 16:30; 2:24–25). Jesus said this about the relationship he had with all of his followers: "I am the good shepherd; I know my sheep and my sheep know me" (John 10:14). Jesus often knew when something was unspoken: "Jesus knew what they were thinking and asked, 'Why are you thinking these things in your hearts?'" (Luke 5:22). He knew the good and the bad: "I know you. I know that you do not have the love of God in your hearts" (John 5:42). Each of the letters written to the seven churches in Revelation 2–3 contains the words *I know*. Jesus knew the afflictions, deeds, love, and faith of the early churches. Because they were intimately and personally known, Jesus could give them personalized encouragements and challenges.

There is not one single detail about us that Jesus does not know. We can't hide anything from him, nor should we want to. For example, Jesus knew that the Samaritan woman had been divorced five times and was living with another man (John 4). Initially, the Samaritan woman didn't know who Jesus was, but Jesus knew who she was and intentionally interacted with her. Jesus' intimate knowledge of her sin led her to repentance, belief, and a relationship with Jesus.

God isn't afraid to interact with our messy lives. He knows our sin. God's ultimate desire is to have a relationship with us. Jesus opened the way and no longer holds our sins against us. The shame of Adam and Eve has been reversed, and hiding is no longer necessary.

Living Known Today

We've counseled many people who were in trouble, afraid, or trapped in sin. We have never heard them say, "Running away from God is the best decision I have ever made." I (John-Paul) remember one young man who grew up in the church but spent most weekends partying and hooking up with women. Finally, instead of running away, he ran toward God, got a mentor, and cleaned up his life. If only you could see his smile now! The Lord has completely transformed him.

When Jesus instructed us how to pray, being known by God was the foundation of prayer: "Your Father knows what you need before you ask him" (Matthew 6:8; see also Luke 12:30). How comforting it is to rest in the fact that God not only knows us, but also knows what we need even before we ask.

Our response. Those who are known by Jesus respond by following him and obeying his words: "My sheep listen to my voice; I know them, and they follow me" (John 10:27). Jesus said, "Whoever has my commands and keeps them is the one who loves me. The one who loves me will be loved by my Father, and I too will love them and show myself to them" (14:21). Do you see the cycle? We are known by God; we love him; we follow his commands; and Jesus reveals himself more and more to us, so that we know him with an ever-deepening knowledge and a closer and closer relationship with him. Because we are known by Jesus, we naturally want to know him more deeply. As Paul said, "I want to know Christ" (Philippians 3:10).

Heavenly hope. God has revealed himself and made himself knowable to the extent that we are "without excuse" (Romans 1:18–20). Although we can know God, we don't yet know him fully. We can grow in our knowledge here on earth, but we will fully know God in heaven: "Now we see only a reflection as in a mirror; then we shall see face to face. Now I know in part; then I shall know fully, even as I am fully known" (1 Corinthians 13:12). When we arrive at heaven's shores, we Christians will be welcomed in as old friends—fully known and fully knowing. It can be frustrating to worship a God who is spirit and unseen. I can't wait to see Jesus face-to-face and spend an eternity with him, fully knowing and enjoying my Savior forever.

Final Biblical Thoughts on Known

God is omniscient, which means he knows everything. He does not, though, just know insignificant details like the number of hairs on our head (Matthew 10:30); he knows us fully and personally. This knowledge leads him to guide, protect, and rescue us. The Bible shows over and over again that God knows his people, as seen in the lives of Moses, Jeremiah, David, Hagar, Leah, the Samaritan woman, and the members of the seven churches in Revelation. These individuals, along with Israel and now the church, are known and chosen to follow God and extend his name to the ends of the earth so that others might also know him.

We are known and chosen for a mission on earth, and when we get to heaven, we will see Jesus face-to-face and will fully know him, even as we are fully known.

In one sentence, to be known in Christ means that Jesus has a full, intimate, and loving knowledge of us, which results in a personal relationship with him.

Finding Freedom in Jesus

I (Matt) remember meeting with two students just before they tried to end their lives. It was an awful week. From their social media posts, I would have assumed their lives were going great. They were hiding and unknown. It is so easy to pretend that people know us on social media or to show only a portion of our true self to our family and friends. Does anyone really know you? Are you free to be your true self?

Many of us are terrified of being fully known. We hide because we think others won't accept us if they really knew us, warts and all. Thankfully, this isn't true with God. He knows everything about us— our struggles, sins, hopes, successes, and failures. He knows our past, present, and future. He knows the good, the bad, and the ugly parts of us.

An all-knowing but unloving God would be frightening. In such a case, it would make sense to hide. But our all-knowing God is also lovingly compassionate. We are not only fully known but also fully loved and fully forgiven. Being fully known by God allows us to approach him with confidence rather than with fear: "Let us draw near to God with a sincere heart and with the full assurance that faith brings, having our hearts sprinkled to cleanse us from a guilty conscience and having our bodies washed with pure water" (Hebrews 10:22). Because God fully knows us, there is no point in trying to hide from him. And because he loves us, we can be vulnerable in sharing our true selves with him. Do you pray to the Lord in confidence, knowing that he fully and personally knows and loves you?

God's full, intimate, and loving knowledge of you is an invitation into a beautiful, vulnerable, mutual, and personal relationship. God is with you; he is for you; he never abandons you; he always remembers you; he loves and cares for you when you are in trouble or distress. Because he is a loving Father and Good Shepherd, he has deep compassion for you. He knows every sin and all the shame you carry, but he does not turn away.

Encouragement and Prayer by John-Paul and Matt: Point your phone's camera at the QR code and follow the linkor go to youtube.com /@FindingFreedomInJesusBook.

Reflective Exercises for
Personal or Group Discussion to
Embrace That You Are Known

1. Practice breathing exercises for three or four minutes each day. Breathe in: "fully known"; breathe out: "fully loved." If you are in a small group, do the breathing together.

2. Go to YouTube, find a worship song with the theme of "known," and listen to it several times each day. If you're in a small group, sing the song together.

3. Looking back at the chapter, what did you learn that you didn't know previously?

4. Take some time to ponder the biblical definition of *known*: To be known in Christ means that Jesus has a full, intimate, and loving knowledge of you, which results in a personal relationship with him. What part of the definition really speaks to you?

5. *Living out known*: Take some time to pray and to write down in a journal all the different ways God knows you. What does it feel like to be fully known by God? Does it lead you to fear and hiding, or to comfort and confidence? Why do you feel that way? Meditate on this truth: You are known by God, fully and intimately, but also cared for and loved by God. Are you still hiding from God? Rest in the fact that he knows and cares for you, and run to your Good Shepherd. Confess to him your sin and let him cleanse you.

6. Take time to meditate on and pray through Genesis 16:13–14; Psalm 139:1–3; Amos 3:2; Matthew 6:8; John 10:14; and 1 Corinthians 13:12. Allow the Lord to open your heart to the truth that you are known in Christ. You may want to choose one of these passages to memorize.

CHAPTER 4

Beautiful

Your beauty should not come from outward
adornment, such as elaborate hairstyles and the
wearing of gold jewelry or fine clothes. Rather, it
should be that of your inner self, the unfading beauty
of a gentle and quiet spirit, which is of great worth in
God's sight.

1 PETER 3:3-4

When you look in the mirror, how do you feel? Are you happy
with what you see? Do you think you are beautiful? If you don't
feel beautiful, you're not alone. A British survey indicated that only
2 percent of women and 9 percent of men believe they are beautiful or
handsome.[1] I (Matt) once talked with a woman who was so disgusted
with her reflection as she looked in the mirror that she fell on the floor
crying. She did not think she was beautiful. As we will see, though,

followers of Jesus *are* beautiful. It is a statement of fact—100 percent true. Repeat this with me: "In Christ I am beautiful." For most of us, it is hard to believe. In order to believe that we are beautiful in Christ, we must embrace a biblical understanding of beauty, one that differs from our society's definition. What is biblical beauty?

Who am I? I am beautiful in Christ. I can be transformed when I embrace that truth.

Testimony: Point your phone's camera at the QR code for a video testimony from Brynne or go to youtube.com /@FindingFreedomInJesusBook.

On the outside, I was a bubbly, confident girl who loved Jesus. On the inside, though, I was slowly dying from an eating disorder . . .

Beautiful in Our Culture

Our culture's definition of beauty negatively impacts us. A recent Treadmill Reviews poll declared that the ideal man is 6 feet tall, 187 pounds, brunette, blue-eyed, and medium skin toned. The ideal woman is 5 feet 5 inches tall, 128 pounds, brunette, blue-eyed, and fair skin toned.[2] The ideal man and woman would have very different characteristics if the poll consisted entirely of African Americans, or Asian Americans, or Hispanics or Latinos, or if undertaken in a different culture. Although beauty is defined differently in different cultures, people in *all* cultures struggle with seeing themselves as beautiful. We are all negatively impacted by our culture.

Social media exercises a massive influence on how we view ourselves. Worldwide, the average person spends two and a half hours each day on social media. Through the use of photo filters, imperfections are effortlessly erased. Think about that: Two and a half hours per day of nearly perfect images inundate us. These "perfect" images manipulate us. When we look in the mirror, though, perfection isn't reflected back. We see wrinkles, acne, hair loss, and flabby muscles. Reality can't compete with fake social media posts. Researchers are finding that the selfie generation feels less attractive and less confident *after* posting their images.[3] Even when they use filters to improve their looks, they are still concentrating on the negative aspects of their appearance. Body image concerns have always existed, but social media has made these concerns worse.

We are unhappy with our appearance and conclude that we are not beautiful. This displeasure often leads to low self-esteem, body dissatisfaction, disordered eating, and seeking validation in all the wrong places. More than $450 billion is spent on beauty products per year globally—about $90 billion in the United States alone—to cover and hide our imperfections.[4] Just as we filter our social media photos, we alter our actual appearance through cosmetic surgery or the use of products to cover blemishes, stretch marks, and cellulite. In what way do you struggle with beauty? How have society and social media impacted you?

The definition of beautiful should *not* be tied to cultural norms. We need to redefine it from a biblical point of view and understand that we are beautiful in God's eyes. The biblical definition of beauty teaches us to focus less on external appearance and more on internal character.

What Does the Bible Say About Being Beautiful?

Beautiful in the Old Testament

External beauty. The men of Israel often chose beautiful wives based on external appearance rather than inward character or spiritual maturity: Abraham's wife Sarah, Isaac's wife Rebekah, and Jacob's wife Rachel were all beautiful women (Genesis 12:11; 26:7; 29:17). Later, when

Israel conquered the promised land, they chose beautiful women to marry from among the captives (Deuteronomy 21:11).

The kings of Israel were also captivated by external beauty. King David "had a fine appearance and handsome features" (1 Samuel 16:12). David was tempted by the "very beautiful" Bathsheba (2 Samuel 11:2), and when David became old, they searched for a "beautiful young woman" to keep him warm (1 Kings 1:1–3). David's son Solomon wrote the entire book of Song of Songs as a celebration of beauty: "You are altogether beautiful, my darling; there is no flaw in you" (4:7). It highlighted external beauty such as eyes, teeth, hair, neck, and bust. Solomon described his bride as "black and beautiful" (1:5 NASB) and called her the "most beautiful of women" (1:8). Esther rose to power and influence partly because she "had a lovely figure and was beautiful" (Esther 2:7).

Warnings about external beauty. There were occasional warnings against being captivated by external beauty: "Do not lust in your heart after her beauty or let her captivate you with her eyes," and "Like a gold ring in a pig's snout is a beautiful woman who shows no discretion" (Proverbs 6:25; 11:22).

Inner beauty. In order to correctly understand the deeper and full meaning of *beautiful*, we must recognize that God is beautiful: "One thing I ask from the LORD . . . to gaze on the beauty of the LORD and to seek him in his temple" (Psalm 27:4). The context of Psalm 27 shows that God's beauty has nothing to do with external appearance, but rather the beautiful actions he carries out on behalf of his people, such as keeping his people safe in the day of trouble (v. 5). Proverbs 31:30 defined internal beauty: "Charm is deceptive, and beauty is fleeting; but a woman who fears the LORD is to be praised." True and lasting beauty had nothing to do with external appearance, but rather with spiritual maturity, as the New Testament will show.

Beautiful in the New Testament

Jesus is beautiful. Just as the Old Testament says that God the Father is beautiful, the New Testament says that Jesus is beautiful—but it has nothing to do with his outward appearance. In fact, Jesus lacks external beauty (Isaiah 53:2). Jesus has a beautiful character that perfectly reflects God's beautiful character (Colossians 1:19). Jesus is the Good Shepherd. The Greek word for *good* can also be translated as "beautiful." Jesus' goodness, or "beauty," is seen in his beautiful actions: "The good shepherd lays down his life for the sheep" (John 10:11). Jesus' entire life was about beautifully serving others: "The Son of Man did not come to be served, but to serve, and to give his life as a ransom for many" (Mark 10:45).

Anointing. Jesus declared that the woman who anointed his head with expensive perfume "has done a *beautiful* thing to me" (Matthew 26:10, emphasis added). This text can also be translated, "She has done a *good* deed for me." Jesus praised her inner character, demonstrated by her loving deeds rather than her outward appearance. She was reflecting God's goodness by her good or beautiful action. For Jesus, *beautiful* meant doing good deeds, not having an attractive external appearance.

Inner beauty. The apostle Peter wrote one of the most important biblical passages about beauty: "Your beauty should not come from outward adornment, such as elaborate hairstyles and the wearing of gold jewelry or fine clothes. Rather, it should be that of your inner self, the unfading beauty of a gentle and quiet spirit, which is of great worth in God's sight" (1 Peter 3:3–4). Peter minimized the importance of outward beauty—jewelry, makeup, and hair—and stressed the importance of the inner beauty of character.

In Peter's culture, women dyed their hair and put on layers of makeup and wore fancy jewelry. They adorned their appearance to appear more beautiful. Since women did not have many rights in that culture, their external appearance was profoundly important to them. Peter, though, highlighted the definition of true beauty, which is found in one's inner character—purity, reverence, and a gentle, quiet spirit.

Lasting beauty. If we are influenced by cultural standards, even the most externally beautiful person ages and becomes less attractive. The outer person fades away, wrinkles increase, hair turns gray or falls out, and muscles weaken. If one focuses on outward appearance, disappointment will reign. True and lasting beauty is found in those who are kind, gentle, have honorable character, and do the right thing (1 Peter 3:5–6). They reflect God's beautiful character to all those around them. This inner beauty never fades away.

Living Beautiful Today

In my (Matt's) church, there was a seventy-year-old woman who few would say was externally beautiful at her age, but internally she was one of the most beautiful women I knew. She prayed for people and sacrificially served. When my wife's father passed away, she brought homemade cinnamon rolls to the house for breakfast. She must have gotten up at 5:00 a.m. to bake them, and they were delicious. She was beautiful because she reflected God's beautiful character through her kindness.

Beautiful feet. People who preach the good news to others are also called beautiful: "How beautiful on the mountains are the feet of those who bring good news, who proclaim peace, who bring good tidings, who proclaim salvation" (Isaiah 52:7). We all know that feet are *not* physically beautiful. This text focuses on the inner beauty of one who preaches to others. Those who share the gospel reflect the beautiful inner character of God (Romans 10:15).

Final Biblical Thoughts on Beautiful

Even though the Bible often uses the term *beautiful* to refer to external appearance, it also emphasizes the inner beauty found in one's good character. In this biblical view of beauty, one's outward appearance is not the most important part of what it means to be beautiful. Beautiful people are not those who were a certain height, had a certain eye color, or wore expensive jewelry. Rather, beautiful people are those who put their hope in God. That's it—if you put your hope in God, you *are* beautiful. Stop for a moment; did you catch that? If you put your hope in God, you are beautiful!

But this inner beauty does not stop there. Beautiful people express their hope in God and reflect God's beautiful and good character by serving others and reflecting the fruit of the Spirit in their lives: love, joy, peace, forbearance, kindness, goodness, faithfulness, gentleness, and self-control (Galatians 5:22–23). True and lasting beauty is *internal* and is *expressed externally* through kind actions toward others. True beauty never fades away with time.

In one sentence, beautiful people are those who hope in God and actively reflect his good character.

Finding Freedom in Jesus

At the beginning of this chapter, we said that only 2 percent of women and 9 percent of men believe they are beautiful or handsome. The Bible says that 100 percent of those who follow Jesus—100 percent—are beautiful.

Are you beautiful? Yes! If you've put your hope in Jesus, you are beautiful. It doesn't matter what society tells you. God looks at you and says, "You are beautiful, my child." Your external appearance does not matter. Of course, there is nothing wrong with external beauty. God created beauty. And we recognize it. But as Proverbs 31:30 declares, external beauty is fleeting and should not be our focus.

The world will try to defeat us with its filtered and photoshopped images. Bombarded with these phony photos, we are tempted to compare our outward appearance with others. Satan will use this weakness against us to weaken our self-image. To resist these negative influences, we must reduce our use of social media and meditate on biblical truth about beauty. Those who follow Jesus are beautiful. Period! Jesus' opinion about you is the only opinion that matters. His definition of beauty will transform your life.

Because of the influence of our culture and social media, it won't be easy to fully embrace the truth that "in Christ I am beautiful." It will take consistent and concentrated effort to resist and undo culture's influence, but you can rewire your self-talk and your perception of your own beauty. You can change your thinking, but it will take some work. Please be sure to do the reflective exercises to gain a more biblical view of who you are in Christ—*I am beautiful.*

Encouragement and Prayer by John-Paul and Matt: Point your phone's camera at the QR code and follow the link or go to youtube.com /@FindingFreedomInJesusBook.

Reflective Exercises for
Personal or Group Discussion to Embrace That You Are Beautiful

1. Practice breathing exercises for three or four minutes each day. Breathe in: "unfading beauty"; breathe out: "internally." If you're in a small group, do the breathing together.

2. Go to YouTube, find a worship song with the theme of

"beautiful," and listen to it several times each day. If you're in a small group, sing the song together.

3. Looking back at the chapter, what did you learn that you didn't know previously?

4. When you hear the word *beautiful*, how would you define it? Take some time to ponder the biblical definition of *beautiful*: To be beautiful is to be a person who hopes in God and actively reflects his good character. What part of the definition really speaks to you?

5. *Living out beautiful*:
   a) Stand in front of a mirror. Take a few moments to reflect on what you see externally. Then in your mind's eye imagine Jesus standing next to you. What would he say about your beauty? Would he emphasize your outward appearance, or would he look at your inner character? If this exercise is too difficult for you, ask someone you trust to reflect God's perspective about your inner character of beauty.
   b) Practice a regular social media fast by turning off your phone or limiting the amount of time you're on your phone each day. Work hard at not scrolling through images. To achieve this, you may need an accountability partner.
   c) Given that your beauty is found in your inner character expressing itself in external actions of kindness, do these exercises to increase your kindness to those around you: The next time you see

someone of the opposite gender, instead of focusing on their outward appearance, think about their traits that the Bible says are beautiful—gentleness, kindness, joy, and so forth. With practice, you can train yourself to focus on inner beauty instead of external appearance. Try to compliment the *inner* beauty of at least one person every day.

6. Take time to meditate on and pray through Matthew 26:10 and 1 Peter 3:3–4. Allow the Lord to open your heart to the truth that you are beautiful in Christ. You may want to choose one of these passages to memorize.

CHAPTER 5

Image Bearer

So God created mankind in his own image,
in the image of God he created them;
male and female he created them.

GENESIS 1:27

I am created in the image of God. In fact, every single human being in the history of the world has been created in God's image. I have infinite value and significance because I reflect my Creator. Did you know that? *You* are of *infinite value*. Many people don't understand this concept today because they don't believe that God exists or that he created us in his image. As a result, we not only see social sins like racism, sexism, and ageism; we also see a devaluing of human life in every kind of abuse, human trafficking, and wars. In order to fully understand our value as humans, we must embrace the biblical understanding of what it means to be an image bearer. When we realize that every person we encounter each day is an image bearer—a person of infinite value—it changes every interaction.

Who am I? I am an image bearer in Jesus. I can be transformed when I embrace that truth.

Testimony: Point your phone's camera at the QR code for a video testimony from Pastor Jeremy Treat or go to youtube .com/@FindingFreedomInJesusBook.

I've spent so much of my life trying to find my identity in my accomplishments, my career, my performance, and yet, as a Christian . . .

Image Bearer in Our Culture

Our society has no concept of the image of God; therefore it's no surprise that hatred, abuse, prejudice, and racism reign. We fail to treat those who don't look like us or act like us with love. We still struggle with racial issues within White, Black, Latino, Jewish, Palestinian, and Asian communities, and end up valuing one life or race over another.

Even within communities, insignificant issues influence how we value each other. Why is your skin so dark? Why is your skin so light? Why are you so heavy? Why are you so skinny? Why is your hair curly? Why is your hair straight? These issues obviously don't change who we are as image bearers. Furthermore, our culture has consistently devalued women, even though they are image bearers. Clearly, women do not have less value in the eyes of God. What does God's Word say about who I am as an image bearer? Without following the Bible's guidance, we can devalue ourselves and others.

What Does the Bible Say About Being an Image Bearer?

Image Bearer in the Old Testament

The Bible clearly teaches that humans are created in the image of God. Two different Hebrew words emphasize this truth. *Tselem* refers to an image that can represent God, and *demut* denotes a likeness between two things: "Then God said, 'Let us make mankind in our image [*tselem*], in our likeness [*demut*]'" (Genesis 1:26). Both males and females were made in God's image and likeness (v. 27).

In antiquity, kings would place statues (images) of themselves throughout their kingdoms as a sign of their ownership and rule. The statue itself was not the king, but it represented him. Likewise, human beings are not God, but we represent him throughout the world as image bearers. No created idol or image can convey what God is like. Only humanity can image the likeness of the one true God because we are created in his image.

Imago Dei. As image bearers, human beings were created to represent God and reflect his holy and just character on earth. Being made in God's image doesn't mean we are identical to God or that we possess God's divine attributes. Instead, we represent God. We reflect his moral, relational, and spiritual nature. The Latin phrase for "image of God" is *imago Dei*—the concept that humans are created in God's image, like a mirror or a reflection. Dignity is innate. All humans, regardless of gender, race, or ethnicity, are born with intrinsic value and worth because they are created in the image of God.

Sin's influence. However, we struggle to believe we are really made in God's image and likeness, don't we? We struggle with self-image and self-worth. Are you surprised? The devil's first temptation made Eve question her worth by stating that if she were to eat of the fruit from the garden, she would "be like God" (Genesis 3:5). Satanic lies! God delighted to create Eve in his likeness. She was already *imago Dei*; she did not have to do anything to earn that. The devil's temptation led to sin, which distorted the image of God in humans. But sin can never take it away. We still reflect God's image and likeness, though imperfectly.

False image bearers. Humans were created to reflect God's image, but unfortunately, throughout the Old Testament, we see that they made false "images" of the true God, as well as images and idols of false gods. For example, look at Moses on Mount Sinai, where he received the Ten Commandments. The people were upset that he was gone for so long. They asked Aaron to make them a god to show them the way they should go. "He took what they handed him and made it into an idol cast in the shape of a calf, fashioning it with a tool. Then they said, 'These are your gods, Israel, who brought you up out of Egypt'" (Exodus 32:4). Can you believe that? These are the people whom God miraculously delivered from Egypt just three months before. How quickly they forgot who the true God was and made an idolatrous image of a golden calf!

Metal images were created for idolatrous purposes, even though they were forbidden by God (Leviticus 19:4; 2 Kings 17:16 NASB). Due to influences from Canaanite culture, the Jewish people also worshiped stones and pillars, which was also forbidden (Exodus 23:24; 1 Kings 14:23). These images even served as household idols inside their Jewish homes (Judges 17:5). For Israel to experience spiritual renewal, they were commanded to destroy the false idols. How utterly sinful was their idolatry! They were looking for an image of God when all along *they themselves* were the image bearers, representing a holy God to the nations.

Image Bearer in the New Testament

Although the Old Testament may lead us to think there's no hope of being an image bearer, God had a plan to restore this lost image. The good news of the gospel is that the distortion of humanity due to sin can be redeemed in Christ progressively, allowing us to recover more and more of God's image.

Jesus the image bearer. Our sin prevents us from accurately reflecting God's image, as we see in the Old Testament stories of murder, war, idolatry, lies, racism, adultery, and abuse—all of which is the result of living in a depraved world due to the fall. Humanity's inability to reflect his image angered God (Romans 1:18–25). That was not his plan. Thankfully, God sent his Son, Jesus, "who is the image of God" (2 Corinthians 4:4). To know what God is like or how an image bearer should live, we just need to look at Jesus. His life and ministry remind us of what all image bearers should look like and how they should act. He is the model of true image-bearing humanity.

The restoration of humans as image bearers. As a result of Jesus' ministry, death, and resurrection, Christians have the hope of being perfectly transformed into the likeness of Christ upon their death and entrance into heaven. In the meantime, as we live here on earth, we have the promise and hope that we can be renewed: "Those God foreknew he also predestined to be conformed to the image of his Son" (Romans 8:29). All is not lost. There is hope for us to change since Christians "have put on the new self, which is being renewed in knowledge in the image of its Creator" (Colossians 3:10). Little by little, we "are being transformed into his image with ever-increasing glory, which comes from the Lord, who is the Spirit" (2 Corinthians 3:18).

God's plan is to restore the image of God in humanity. Upon belief in Jesus, the old self with its evil practices is laid aside: "Therefore, if anyone is in Christ, the new creation has come: The old has gone, the new is here!" (2 Corinthians 5:17). "Our old self was crucified with him so that the body ruled by sin might be done away with, that we should no longer be slaves to sin" (Romans 6:6). God progressively redeems the image of God in our lives. This does not mean we are instantly spiritually mature or perfectly able to reflect God to the world as image bearers. The battle against the flesh continues throughout this life. The new self is complete and yet has the capacity for growth, just as a baby is born complete but is able to grow and mature.

Image bearers in action. We are not image bearers because of something we do, but because God delighted to create us as image bearers. We *are* image bearers. Our actions, though, should reflect this truth.

Just as a mirror reflects the image of whatever is in front of it, we should reflect a likeness to God's character. Since Jesus is the "image of the invisible God" (Colossians 1:15), we should imitate and reflect Jesus' example of a life filled with justice, righteousness, humility, joy, kindness, and love.

Just like Jesus, we should treat others with dignity and respect because *every* human being with whom we interact has intrinsic and infinite value as an image bearer. James 3:9 points out the inconsistency of mistreating fellow humans: "With the tongue we praise our Lord and Father, and with it we curse human beings, who have been made in God's likeness."

False image bearers. The New Testament shows us that not everyone reflects God's image correctly. Those in Paul's day also made false idols. Sinful humanity "exchanged the glory of the immortal God for images made to look like a mortal human being and birds and animals and reptiles" (Romans 1:23). The book of Revelation describes a beast, an instrument of evil, whose sole purpose will be to fight against and lead God's people astray (Revelation 13:1–8). Humans will make an image of the beast and worship that image (vv. 14–15). Obviously, worshiping the beast and his image is sinful. We should worship God alone.

The New Testament explains that we are not mere products of evolution, stuck in our cycles of sin, hatred, and abuse. Jesus came to set us free by restoring and renewing God's image in us.

Final Biblical Thoughts on Image Bearer

Every single human being is made in the image and likeness of God. Throughout history, though, humans have struggled to believe this truth. We have sinned by creating and worshiping false idols and by mistreating other image-bearing humans. We lord it over others, wage war, ignore, and abuse—forgetting that we all are made in the image of God with infinite value. No human should view themselves as better than another. We are all equals in the sight of God—*imago Dei*.

But what does it mean to be made in the image and likeness of God? While the Bible doesn't give a clear explanation, it certainly means we were created to represent God and to reflect his holy and just character to the world around us. We are called to take on the characteristics of God and Jesus in our own lives. Like God himself, we are able to distinguish right from wrong and to create, not only children, but amazing art, buildings, poetry, hairstyles, and even rocket ships that fly to the moon.

The best example of what it means to be made in the image of God is to look at Jesus, who was the perfect "image of the invisible God" (Colossians 1:15). How did Jesus live? How did he treat others? What were his priorities? Being made in the image of God means we are called to become more and more like Jesus, reflecting his image to the world as a witness to his glory.

In one sentence, to be an image bearer means that you are made in the image and likeness of God, have infinite value, and reflect and represent his character as seen in your love for others.

Finding Freedom in Jesus

Our world is filled with hate speech that assaults and abuses others simply because they are a different race, color, creed, or religion—Black/White/Asian/Native American; Jewish/Palestinian; Russian/Ukrainian; Democrat/Republican; LGBTQ/straight; undocumented immigrant / citizen; Christian/Muslim/atheist. Acts of protesting against and canceling the other side are increasingly common, oftentimes resulting in violent clashes between opposing sides.

That person at work or school or in your neighborhood who irritates you—they are made in God's image and have value. That person you are tempted to look down on or ignore—they are made in the image of God and have value. That person who looks or acts differently than you do—they are made in the image of God and have value. That person who votes a different ticket than you do—they are made in the image of God and have value.

We are image bearers not because of what we do, but because God has created us as image bearers. When we fully understand that each person on the "other side" is an image bearer, the church as a whole and believers individually are able to see others as having infinite value and dignity. When you look at people, do you see them as image bearers who have value? What about when you get angry at someone? Do you still see them as possessing the *imago Dei*?

Our actions should reflect that we are image bearers. We should reflect a likeness to our Creator God and a likeness to Jesus' way of life as expressed in justice, righteousness, humility, kindness, love, and so forth. Christians should have a high view of humanity. Therefore, any racism, abuse, pride, pornography, self-harm, human trafficking, unforgiveness, favoritism, bullying, or slander is wrong and sinful simply because these acts and attitudes devalue other humans. Jesus ministered to Jews, Gentiles, and Samaritans (no racism; see Matthew 15:21–28), revealed himself to men and women (no gender discrimination; see John 4:4–26), forgave even those who placed him on the cross (no hatred; see Luke 23:34), and perfectly and righteously reflected God to the world (sinless; see Hebrews 4:15).

You can't earn the image of God, but you can live it out as you love others, forgive others, fight injustice, and preach the gospel, thereby reflecting God's image to our needy, broken, and hurting world that has forgotten that they, too, are made in the image of God.

Do you struggle with the idea of image bearer? On the one hand, do you see *yourself* as having infinite value since you were made in the image of the Creator God of the universe? Do you believe that Psalm 8:5–6 is true of you? "You have made them a little lower than the angels and crowned them with glory and honor. You made them rulers over the works of your hands; you put everything under their feet." On the other hand, do you struggle to see *others* as having infinite value as image bearers? Are there people you view as "less than"? Are there people you mistreat? Do you struggle with pride, racism, or slander?

The power of the Holy Spirit empowers us to believe that we are of infinite value and to treat others with dignity and respect because we "are being transformed into his image with ever-increasing glory, which comes from the Lord, who is the Spirit" (2 Corinthians 3:18). Since we were created by God as image bearers, we will only find our true joy, happiness, and fulfillment as we live our lives seeking to reflect his glory.

Encouragement and Prayer by John-Paul and Matt: Point your phone's camera at the QR code and follow the link or go to youtube.com /@FindingFreedomInJesusBook.

Reflective Exercises for
Personal or Group Discussion to Embrace That You Are an Image Bearer

1. Practice breathing exercises for three or four minutes each day. Breathe in: "in your likeness"; breathe out: "I glorify you." If you're in a small group, do the breathing together.

2. Go to YouTube, find a worship song with the theme of "image bearer," and listen to it several times each day. If you're in a small group, sing the song together.

3. Looking back at the chapter, what did you learn that you didn't know previously?

4. Take some time to ponder the biblical definition of *image bearer.* To be an image bearer means that you are made in the image and likeness of God, have infinite value, and reflect and represent his character as seen in your love for others. What part of the definition really speaks to you?

5. *Living out image bearer.*

    a) What lie or lies keep you from believing that *you* bear God's image? Do you struggle with feelings of unworthiness? Or do you see yourself as the climax of creation and struggle with pride? Spend time praying, thanking God for creating you as an image bearer.

    b) Do you struggle with pride or with insensitivity toward other image bearers? In what ways do anger, abuse, pornography, unforgiveness, and racism devalue *other people's* self-worth and fail to appreciate *their imago Dei*? Repent of any sins that demean another human being's worth.

    c) What can you do to help our world have a higher view of humanity, such as fighting against racism, abuse, pornography, or human trafficking?

6. Take time to meditate on and pray through Genesis 1:26–27; Romans 8:29; 2 Corinthians 3:18; and Colossians 1:15. Allow the Lord to open your heart to the truth that you are an image bearer in Christ. You may want to choose one of these passages to memorize.

CHAPTER 6

Free

It is for freedom that Christ has set us free.

GALATIANS 5:1

Going to the beach in Southern California is one of our favorite things to do—so much so that I (John-Paul) proposed to my wife at the beach. (She said, "Yes!" by the way. It was a great day.) People go to the beach for various reasons—some to surf, some to build sandcastles, some to swim or snorkel, and some to have a great time with family or friends. If you're lucky, you might see whales, sharks, or dolphins.

Imagine being at the beach one day and seeing a dolphin washed ashore, lying on the sand. Would your first reaction be panic? Don't dolphins need to be in water to live? Imagine, though, that when you approached the dolphin, the dolphin said to you (yeah, dolphins can talk in California!), "I don't want to go back into the ocean. I'm tired of swimming. I want to be free from the constraints of the ocean. I want to live on dry land." How crazy would this be? God created and designed dolphins to live and swim in the water. They can only thrive in the ocean.

In the same way dolphins cannot thrive on land, we were created to live and experience freedom the way God designed us to live.

Of all the terms we discuss in this book, *free* might be the most misunderstood. The world's twisted definition has negatively impacted us. When we hear the word *free*, we often think it means doing whatever we want. That is the world's definition. The Bible says we are free only in Jesus, which does not mean doing whatever we want. Without a biblical understanding of freedom, we risk heading down a path of destruction. We will find ourselves trapped by greed, lust, pride, lying, unfaithfulness, anger, and selfishness—the very opposite of the fruit of the Spirit, which is "love, joy, peace, forbearance, kindness, goodness, faithfulness, gentleness and self-control" (Galatians 5:22–23).

Who am I? I am free in Jesus. I can be transformed when I embrace that truth.

Testimony: Point your phone's camera at the QR code for a video testimony from Emily or go to youtube.com /@FindingFreedomInJesusBook.

When I was sexually assaulted, I was suicidal and felt shameful, used, dirty, and hopeless. I thought my life was over . . .

Free in Our Culture

If you ask non-Christians to describe what it means to be free, they might say, "You are free to do whatever you want." Gerard Pique, the famous Barcelona soccer player, once said, "The day I die, I will look back and hope that I have always done what I wanted." We live in America, the "land of the free," and we are free to do "whatever we want." Have you considered whether this incorrect definition contributes to high crime rates, increasing divorce rates, and inflammatory social media behavior? People justify harmful and hurtful actions under the guise of "freedom," falsely thinking they can do whatever they want, not realizing that by acting in these ways, they may be heading toward destruction. For example, I am free to "drink all I want" can lead to alcoholism, free to "have sex with whomever I want" can lead to sexual addiction and emotional damage, and free to "make all the money I want and use it only for myself" can lead to greed.

These cultural influences have penetrated the church, and so it is vitally important to biblically define the word *free*. Maybe a lack of clarity around the biblical definition of *free* is part of the reason that selfishness, greed, divorce, and lust are found at high levels even inside the church. We have been influenced by our society's definition of *free*. We are living out our "freedom" while damaging ourselves, our churches, and our witness to the Lord's name.

To truly understand and live out our freedom in Christ, we must turn to the Bible's definition of *free*.

What Does the Bible Say About Being Free?

Free in the Old Testament

Created free. God created human beings and designed them to be free. Freedom is part of who we are as people made in the image of God. When God created the man and the woman, he blessed them and placed them in the Garden of Eden with the ability to enjoy his beautiful creation. They had freedom to rule over the other animals and to eat of any tree—well, almost any tree: "You are *free* to eat from any tree in the garden; but you must not eat from the tree of the knowledge of good and evil, for when you eat from it you will certainly die" (Genesis 2:16–17, emphasis added).

Freedom lost. From the very beginning, *free* did not mean that Adam and Eve could do whatever they wanted, right? There was one tree they could *not* eat from. Why did God place that restriction on them? God told them not to eat from the tree of the knowledge of good and evil because it was not beneficial for Adam and Eve. They were free—free to live as God designed them so that they could thrive and flourish. Free to live their best life in the garden. They were free to eat from nearly every tree, but true God-ordained freedom included the command to avoid one tree, just one tree, for them to truly thrive. We all know that they ate the fruit from that tree, and sin entered human history and true freedom was lost.

Freedom has boundaries. From the very beginning of creation, to be free included restrictions that God put in place so human beings could live the best possible life, so they could flourish. Not everything is good for us. For example, money in and of itself isn't a bad thing. The Bible doesn't say money is evil, but that "the love of money is a root of all kinds of evil" (1 Timothy 6:10). God knew that our excessive pursuit of money could lead to some bad places, so he graciously put warnings in place about money. Some, though, don't follow God's ways and thus fall into the trap of greed.

Living Free Today

A friend of mine (John-Paul) became trapped in greed. He thought he could make a quick buck through many different means, including gambling, but his plans backfired. I watched him lose everything he had worked for, and his family suffered because of his greed. Succumbing to the enemy's temptations and falling into his traps can cost us everything. God designed us to thrive when we live according to his ways. His restrictions exist for our good.

The biblical definition of *free* includes obeying God: "I will walk about in freedom, for I have sought out your precepts" (Psalm 119:45). Freedom is defined as living God's way. To those who have a worldly perspective, this definition sounds like bondage. But true biblical freedom is living the way we were designed—walking with God, which includes listening to and obeying his desire for our lives. Dolphins must live in the ocean; human beings must obey God in order to thrive. That's how he created us.

Israel's lack of freedom. Because of the Israelites' sins, they often found themselves in bondage instead of freedom. The Israelites were enslaved in Egypt for hundreds of years until God came and set them free (Exodus 6:6). Israel fought against and eventually was overthrown by foreign nations. The people were carried off to foreign lands. Why did this happen? Just as in the Garden of Eden, "All this happened because you people sinned against the LORD and did not obey him" (Jeremiah 40:3). True freedom includes following God's commands.

Spiritual freedom. The Old Testament description of freedom includes spiritual freedom. Humans were not only physically enslaved, but they were also in bondage to sin. God despised that condition and wanted to free them from their anguish, burdens, and chains (Psalms 25:17; 73:5; 116:16). God promised that a coming Messiah would "proclaim freedom for the captives and release from darkness for the prisoners" (Isaiah 61:1). People needed physical freedom, but even more importantly, they needed spiritual freedom. These texts foreshadowed what will happen in the New Testament, when Jesus came to restore our true freedom.

Free in the New Testament

Free in Jesus. At the beginning of the Gospel of Luke, Jesus announced the focus of his ministry: "The Spirit of the Lord is on me, because he has anointed me to proclaim good news to the poor. He has sent me to proclaim freedom for the prisoners and recovery of sight for the blind, to set the oppressed free" (Luke 4:18, quoting Isaiah 61:1). Jesus came on a rescue mission to bring true freedom to people in bondage to sin. However, his intentions were not entirely clear to his original audience. Many Jews in the first century hoped for political freedom for Israel. They longed for a political messiah to come and free them from the foreign oppressor, Rome. The freedom Jesus brought came in a very unexpected way.

Free from. Jesus lived true, biblical freedom, and restored to humanity the true freedom that was lost in the Garden of Eden. Jesus "loves us and has freed us from our sins by his blood" (Revelation 1:5). Those who respond to Jesus' love, who know the truth (John 8:32) and live in his grace (Romans 3:24), are set free spiritually and physically.

SPIRITUALLY FREE. Sin has a stranglehold on humans; it traps and enslaves. Through his death on the cross, Jesus freed believers *from* sin, Satan, demons, and death (Luke 13:16; Acts 13:39; Romans 8:2). We receive this freedom when we respond in faith to the gospel. Jesus' love and sacrifice on the cross transformed our ability to resist sin and Satan's temptations and follow Jesus in biblical freedom.

PHYSICALLY FREE. Jesus also set people free from physical ailments, such as a bleeding disorder and from being crippled (Mark 5:29; Luke 13:12). While all can be set free spiritually from sin, only some are set free physically here on earth.

Free to. We are not free to do whatever we want. We are not free to continue sinning, because sin leads to bondage. Jesus set us free *from* sin and death, but he also freed us *to* live according to the way God designed us to live. The Spirit empowers us to experience true freedom and to live according to God's design (2 Corinthians 3:17). In our freedom, we are called to serve others humbly in love, love our neighbors as ourselves, and walk by the Spirit (Galatians 5:13–16). Paul used his freedom to become like a servant or slave: "Though I am free and belong to no one, I have made myself a slave to everyone, to win as many as possible" (1 Corinthians 9:19). Paul became a servant to others so they could come to know Jesus.

True biblical freedom empowers us to act the way God designed us to act. Our Creator God designed dolphins to thrive in the ocean and designed human beings to thrive only when they follow Jesus and his commands. Jesus' commands were called "the law that gives freedom" (James 2:12). Isn't that ironic? Jesus' law is not burdensome or oppressive. It doesn't lead to bondage, but rather to freedom. Obedience to God's way leads to a more fulfilling and abundant life. We Christians are free *from* sin and free *to* follow Jesus.

Heavenly hope. The struggle against sin is real. But don't get discouraged. We will experience times of freedom here on earth as we walk with Jesus and overcome sinful habits, but we won't experience full freedom or sinlessness until we reach heaven (Galatians 4:26). And so we are instructed to keep on fighting the good fight, standing firm and refusing to let ourselves be burdened by a yoke of slavery (Galatians 5:1). It will be a battle to live out our freedom, but it's a battle in which we are empowered by the Spirit. Don't give up. We have the assurance that the battle has already been won by Jesus. Only in Jesus do we find true freedom and abundant life.

Final Biblical Thoughts on Free

Although Adam and Eve were created free, they didn't listen to God. They ate from the forbidden tree and sinned. What happened? Their freedom turned into fear, shame, and the tendency to distort the concept of freedom. The Old Testament is the story of God freeing people held in bondage, only for them to return to bondage again and again. Freedom never meant we could do whatever we wanted, because God knows that doing whatever we want leads to misery and trouble. Our heavenly Father knows what is best for us because he designed us and knows the way we must live to thrive and find true joy and satisfaction.

In one sentence, to be free means we are set free *from* sin and death and are now free *to* live as we were created and designed to live—walking with Jesus and serving others, loving God and loving our neighbors.

Finding Freedom in Jesus

Although sin seems tempting and inviting, it brings bondage and captivity. Sin is like a trap door that leads to a dreary dungeon. The life of reckless sinfulness may lead to momentary satisfaction, but eventually it can only result in long-term emptiness.

Our (John-Paul's) church is located in the city of Inglewood, not far from south central Los Angeles, which is known for gang violence, drugs, and all kinds of inner-city issues. It's a rough place, but it's also the setting for a great opportunity to see God powerfully work. We have seen hundreds of families overcome the turmoil of the neighborhood, leave their addictions, and find true freedom in Jesus. Addictions may thrill for a moment, but God's freedom leads to an abundant life (John 10:10) filled with joy, peace, and purpose. Don't fall for fake freedom; look for the real thing that can only be found in Jesus.

Here's a quick example. One Sunday, I preached about the destruction of addictions. During my message, the Holy Spirit prompted me to say, "If you continue down this road of addiction, it's going to kill you." Right after the service, a woman came to me in tears, "Pastor, you were talking to me in that sermon." She shared that she was drinking heavily. Her doctor told her it was going to kill her, but she hadn't stopped. She said, "Thank you for letting God use you." She was transformed that very day. Every year on the anniversary of her sobriety, she comes to the front of the church after the service and shows me her sobriety coin, which she receives for making it another year without drinking any alcohol. It's been about six years now. I can't tell you how proud I am of her. She has found true freedom, just like Jesus said: "If the Son sets you free, you will be free indeed" (John 8:36).

Spirit-empowered. Thankfully, we are not on our own in this adventure of following Jesus in freedom. We are empowered by the Holy Spirit to live for God and for others. As we follow Jesus, empowered by the Spirit, we are transformed from greed to contentment, lust to love, selfishness to servanthood, and pride to humility. We are free to become more and more like Jesus.

Serving. True freedom is only found when we obey God, who commands us to have a heart for service. God created us to experience joy and happiness in service, not in selfishness. Research from Emory University found that when a person acts kindly or does an act of service, the pleasure centers of the brain light up.[1] God's way actually does lead to true satisfaction and happiness. Our heavenly Father wants us to thrive, and we only thrive when we follow him and put away our selfish desires. Are you finding joy and contentment in serving others? Who could you serve today, knowing that part of your mission is to cooperate with God to bring freedom to those who are enslaved to sin (Luke 4:18)?

Jesus' sermon in Luke 4 proves that he came to free the imprisoned. After that sermon, he drove out demons, freed the prisoners, healed the sick, and preached the good news of the gospel. His entire ministry brought freedom. What about you? Are you ready to bring all of your chains, addictions, and struggles to Jesus? Share your struggles with the One who sets people free, asking him to release you once again.

Encouragement and Prayer by John-Paul and Matt: Point your phone's camera at the QR code and follow the link or go to youtube.com /@FindingFreedomInJesusBook.

Reflective Exercises for
Personal or Group Discussion to Embrace That You Are Free

1. Practice breathing exercises for three or four minutes each day. Breathe in: "you have freed me"; breathe out: "I live for you." If you're in a small group, do the breathing together.

2. Go to YouTube, find a worship song with the theme of "free" (such as "I'm Free" by Percy Bady), and listen to it several times each day. If you're in a small group, sing the song together.

3. Looking back at the chapter, what did you learn that you didn't know previously?

4. When you hear the word *free*, how would you define it? Take time to ponder the biblical definition of *free*: To be free means you are set free *from* sin and death and are now free *to* live as you were created and designed to live—walking with Jesus and serving others, loving God and loving your neighbor. What part of the definition really speaks to you?

5. *Living out free*:
   a) Do you have sin patterns that have prevented you from experiencing full freedom? Try this practice each morning before starting your day: Kneel alongside your bed, thank the Lord that you have

been set free, and offer to him those parts of your life that are still in bondage.

b) If freedom means we humbly serve others in love (Galatians 5:13), in what way are you serving others? Think of specific ways you can serve those around you and then put the ideas into practice. For example, a single mom may need a babysitter or an older couple may need someone to mow their lawn.

c) John 8 says that the truth will set us free. Are you spending time in the Word of God to learn the truth? If not, how can you build the habit of spending time in the Word? Does your church have a Bible study group you could join?

6. Take time to meditate on and pray through Genesis 2:16–17; Psalm 119:45; Luke 4:18; John 8:36; Galatians 5:1; and 1 Peter 2:16. Allow the Lord to open your heart to the truth that you are free in Jesus. You may want to choose one of these passages to memorize.

CHAPTER 7

Shame-Free

Those who look to him are radiant;
their faces are never covered with shame.

PSALM 34:5

In the previous chapter, we focused on our freedom in Jesus. This chapter will deal with the topic of being shame-free and will focus on the feelings of guilt that many of us still have, even after experiencing freedom from sin. As we wrote in the introduction, when our students pay attention to their self-talk, they say some deeply negative things to themselves: "I'm no good. I'm not enough. I wish I were different. I'm a failure." These are the words of shame.

As parents, we do our best to walk our kids through negative self-talk, but the reality is that adults struggle with shame too. In fact, successful men and women struggle with shame, even some of our most admired CEOs, artists, entertainers, and athletes. The truth is we all struggle on some level with shame and negative self-talk. We speak harshly to others and are critical on social media, but the words we say to ourselves can be even more damaging. What about you? Do you say negative or harsh things to yourself?

Shame is a powerful emotion because we often inflict it on ourselves. Yes, we have sinned and are guilty before our holy God, but there is a solution to that, right? That's why Jesus came. Through faith, we can be forgiven of our sins. Why do we then continue to carry shame and talk to ourselves so negatively? Jesus doesn't talk to us that way.

Who am I? I am shame-free in Jesus. I can be transformed when I embrace that truth.

Testimony: Point your phone's camera at the QR code for a video testimony from Biani or go to youtube.com /@FindingFreedomInJesusBook.

Pornography filled my life with shame, especially when my mom found out . . .

Shame in Our Culture

Shame is a popular topic in our culture. Brené Brown is a bestselling author, researcher, renowned TED Talk speaker, and podcast host who has spent two decades studying courage, vulnerability, shame, and empathy. She defines shame as "believing that we are flawed and therefore unworthy of love and belonging."[1] The success of her TED Talks, blogs, and books shows us that the feeling of shame is widespread in our society. Many cultural factors perpetuate shame, such as societal expectations, unrealistic standards of perfection, and the influence of social media. We are inundated with crippling shame, aren't we?

What is the solution? Brené Brown says it can be found in

empathy—telling our story to others and allowing them to empathize with our struggles.[2] In other words, all of us are messed up, and because of our common experience of shame, we can stop the negative self-talk and be kind to ourselves.

We can learn a lot from Brené Brown. Sharing our shame in community is helpful, but even sharing our stories doesn't always help us eliminate our negative self-talk and overcome shame. We need a Higher Power to help us overcome. That's the premise of this entire book. It is only when we embrace our true identity through the power of the Holy Spirit and God's grace that we are truly transformed. We need a God who believes in us, empowers us, and pronounces us shame-free; and this kind of God is exactly what the Bible shows us.

What Does the Bible Say About Being Shame-Free?

Shame-Free in the Old Testament

Shame-free at creation. God created humans shame-free: "Adam and his wife were both naked, and they felt no shame" (Genesis 2:25). No sin. No hiding. No guilt. No shame. Just as we saw in the previous chapter, the true biblical meaning of *shame-free* can be discovered in the Garden of Eden account. Adam and Eve were created in the image of God to be free and shame-free. In fact, they were created with honor, which is the opposite of shame (Psalm 8:4–5).

Sin and shame. After sinning, shame gripped Adam and Eve, causing them to hide from God in fear (Genesis 3:8–10). As a result of sin, the experience of shame continued throughout the Old Testament. Israel worshiped false idols and disobeyed God's law. When they sinned, shame was a natural and unfortunate consequence: "Lord, you are righteous, but this day we are covered with shame . . . because of our unfaithfulness to you" (Daniel 9:7).

Shame is not the end of the story. God pursued Adam and Eve after their initial sin, and continually pursued the Israelites despite their numerous sins. Seeing how God continually pursued, forgave, and removed shame from sinners gives us hope.

Overcoming shame. God provided the only way for the people of Israel to overcome shame—to repent and take refuge in God (Psalm 25:3, 20; Jeremiah 31:19). The psalmist declared, "Those who look to him are radiant; their faces are *never* covered with shame" (Psalm 34:5, emphasis added). Trusting in God to remove shame also included following his law to avoid further shame: "May I wholeheartedly follow your decrees, that I may not be put to shame" (119:80). Genuine repentance involved turning away from sin and turning toward God, resulting in Israel's forgiveness and restoration. It removed their shame and brought them honor.

Messianic hope. Israel was stuck in the sin-shame-hide-repent cycle. Isaiah prophesied that a coming Messiah would stop the cycle and eliminate shame: "Instead of your shame . . . you will rejoice in your inheritance . . . and everlasting joy will be yours" (Isaiah 61:7). That was the promise. To be shame-free was the hope of every Jewish person as they waited for the expected Messiah: "At that time I will deal with all who oppressed you. I will rescue the lame; I will gather the exiles. I will give them praise and honor in every land where they have suffered shame" (Zephaniah 3:19). Honor would replace shame.

Shame-Free in the New Testament

The New Testament also reveals that when one chooses the world's way instead of God's way, shame is a consequence (Philippians 3:19). Since "all have sinned and fall short" (Romans 3:23), we desperately need help. Thankfully, Jesus came to eliminate shame and return us to the shame-free state in which God created human beings in the Garden of Eden.

Shame-free in John 2. Although the term *shame* isn't used by John, when we understand the cultural background of shame and honor in Jesus' time, we can see crippling shame released when Jesus miraculously changed water into wine. In that culture, weddings were huge community and social events in which families went into debt to throw the best party. One of the families in Cana ran out of wine, which would have brought crippling disgrace and shame to the family. My (Matt's) students from honor-shame cultures tell me, "You never run out of food or drink at a wedding because it's shameful, and that shame will last forever." When Jesus miraculously provided wine, he saved the family from long-lasting shame. Moreover, Jesus gave the family honor because he provided the best wine (John 2:10). They went from being the shamed family to the honored family. That's the Jesus way!

Shame-free in John 4. In John 4, Jesus encountered a Samaritan woman at the well. She had three strikes against her. First, she was a Samaritan—foreigners or outsiders in the eyes of Jews. Second, she was a woman, who were typically seen as second-class citizens in that culture. Men weren't even allowed to talk to women in public. What's more, Jewish people called Samaritan girls "menstruating women from the time they lie in their cradle" (Mishnah Niddah 4:1). A menstruating woman in Jewish culture was believed to be spiritually unclean and therefore unwelcome in public places or at worship services because anything she touched would become spiritually unclean. Third, she would have been acknowledged as a sinner because she was divorced five times and was now living with a sixth man (John 4:18). In that culture, when a woman committed any sexual offense, their honor was lost forever. She was in continual shame, with no hope. The three shameful strikes against her should have called her "out."

When Jesus offered her living water (John 4:10), he invited her to become clean, pure, and forgiven. Can you imagine? This woman lived every day with the stigma of being unclean and shamed, but Jesus spiritually restored her. He returned her to the status of shame-free and honored. The Samaritan woman instantly changed from being "that sinful, shameful woman" on the outskirts of society to "that honored woman." Why was she honored? Because she introduced her entire town to the "Savior of the world" (John 4:42)! The people of that region met Jesus through her testimony. Some call her the first missionary in the New Testament. Three strikes, but she wasn't out; she was starting over. Jesus knew her sin, but instead of bearing debilitating shame, she found honor in Jesus. Jesus didn't care about her past; he cared about her future. From shame to honor—that's the Jesus way.

Caution. Please do not misunderstand. The Samaritan woman's life was sinful and hurtful to the Lord. We don't want to make light of sin. In the midst of her sin and shame, though, instead of experiencing rejection and judgment, what she really needed was to return to the Lord in repentance to receive forgiveness and the removal of shame. Believing in Jesus is the only way to remove shame: "The one who believes in him will never be put to shame" (Romans 9:33). We can't remove shame ourselves, and it is destructive and exhausting to continue to carry it. Do you have shame in your life? Aren't you getting tired of carrying it?

How did Jesus abolish shame? Jesus abolished shame on the cross—a cruel instrument of death that brought shame on the one who was hung on it (Deuteronomy 21:22–23). It's important to remember that prior to his crucifixion, Jesus had never experienced shame because he was sinless (Hebrews 4:14–15). Jesus willingly allowed himself to be hanged on a wooden cross, cursed, and filled with our shame. The shame-free One became shamed in our place. Why would Jesus do that? "For the joy set before him he endured the cross, scorning its shame, and sat down at the right hand of the throne of God" (Hebrews 12:2). Jesus willingly and joyfully carried the burden that was too heavy for us to carry. The cursed cross turned into total triumph over the enemies of sin, Satan, shame, and death (Colossians 2:13–15). Our sin and shame have been removed.

The parable of the prodigal son. In Luke 15, the prodigal son asked for his inheritance *before* his father died and then he squandered it all on wild, sinful living in a foreign land. How shameful! In that culture, the entire community would reject him if he tried to return home. But when the father saw his son in the distance, he ran to him, lifting up his tunic and exposing his bare legs. While it doesn't sound like a big deal to us, for a man to display his bare leg in that culture was shameful. And so to avoid shame, men wouldn't run. Why did this father run? Because he was willing to bear the shame so that the son would be spared the shame of rejection of the community. The father ran to get to his son before the community could get to him.

The father also gave his robe to the son, put shoes on his feet, and held a feast in his honor. All of these actions eliminated the son's shame and brought him honor in the community. It's as if the father were saying, "I know what you did. You know what you did. But you have repented. I forgive you. I take away your shame. You are now safe at home, my child." The father in the parable represents God. God, through his Son, takes on our shame by becoming shame in our place. God always provides a way home.

Final Biblical Thoughts on Shame-Free

God created human beings to be shame-free. Our sin, though, separates us from him and brings shame. Throughout the Old Testament, the Israelites were stuck in a sin-shame-hide cycle, sinning and hiding from God rather than seeking his forgiveness. And yet God continually called them back to himself, forgiving them and taking away their shame.

The New Testament tells us that Jesus lovingly and joyfully went to the cruel cross, absorbing its shame. He doesn't want us to carry shame, so he took our curse and bore our shame. Unfortunately, in our bondage to sin, guilt and shame enter our lives. Instead of returning immediately to God in repentance, we're prone to run and hide from the One who desires to forgive and restore us to being shame-free.

In the parable of the prodigal son, the miracle of changing water to wine, and the encounter with the Samaritan woman at the well, Jesus' goal was to forgive and to remove shame. The prodigal son did horrible things, wishing his father dead, taking his inheritance, and losing it all. The wedding family did a shameful thing in that culture when they ran out of wine at a wedding. The Samaritan woman had three shameful strikes against her. She should have been "out." Yet Jesus took the shame away from all of them.

The Bible tells the story of human sin and shame, followed by God's attempt to restore them to the created state of forgiven, free, and shame-free. When we refuse to return to God and allow him to take our shame, it's as though we are saying to God, "No. Your plan isn't good. My plan is better. I will carry the weight of my sin and shame myself." Nope. His plan is best. We should run to our loving Father because only there can we be shame- free. From shame to honor—that is the Jesus way.

In one sentence, shame-free means Jesus has forgiven our sins, but also taken away the burden and weight of our guilt and shame, replacing shame with honor.

Finding Freedom in Jesus

Not only do we sin, but to make it worse, we beat ourselves up for sinning, piling more shame on our lives through negative self-talk: "I'm a loser. I'm not worthy. God could never forgive me." Of course, Satan plays a role in this shame cycle by continually accusing us. Are you still carrying shame? Jesus says to all of us, "I don't care about your yesterday. I care about your tomorrow." Nobody, including Satan, can hold your past over you, making you feel dirty or shameful. You can respond, "Yes, I did fail, but my sins have been completely forgiven through the blood of Jesus. Jesus took on himself my sin and shame on the cross. I am shame-free in Jesus." When Satan accuses you, tell him to talk to Jesus about your sin and shame, because Jesus now carries it.

Run to Jesus. Today is a good day to start afresh, unburdened by shame's influence. If the shame-free life can only be found when we run *to* Jesus, why do we usually run *away from* Jesus and hide, like Adam and Eve did? Hiding our wounds from God always makes our problems worse, right? Perhaps this is why Satan is always associated with darkness, with hiding, whereas God is associated with light, with bringing things into the open.

Guilt and shame are powerfully destructive feelings. We are praying that all of us will "draw near to God . . . having our hearts sprinkled to cleanse us from a guilty conscience" (Hebrews 10:22). We should not fall into the sin-shame-hide cycle that Israel experienced. We will sin, but when we do, we can immediately run to Jesus. Don't be afraid. Our loving and gracious God waits for us to come to him: "Let us then approach God's throne of grace with confidence, so that we may receive mercy and find grace to help us in our time of need" (Hebrews 4:16). Rather than hide, are you ready to reveal your shame and hidden sin to God and perhaps to a trusted friend, pastor, or counselor as well? Hidden shame kills; exposed shame dies: "Then I acknowledged my sin to you and did not cover up my iniquity. I said, 'I will confess my transgressions to the LORD.' And you forgave the guilt of my sin" (Psalm 32:5).

How do we begin this movement toward confession? The approach looks different for every person, but the removal of sin and shame starts with the cross. Imagine yourself at the foot of the cross on which Jesus died to remove your shame. Now envision yourself at the throne of God in heaven. There sitting on the throne is Jesus, the crucified and resurrected Lamb of God. In prayer, empowered by the Holy Spirit, give him all the sin you have ever committed. Hold nothing back. He already knows every time you've sinned. Be slow and methodical in this exercise. Don't rush.

Then ask him to reveal the shame and guilt you carry and then to remove it and carry it for you. It may help if you can visualize piling up sin and shame in front of you and asking Jesus to remove it all. Spend time in prayer, asking Jesus to forgive all your sins and remove all your shame. Perhaps you could write down the sin and shame and cross it off as a symbol that you are forgiven and freed from shame. Are you ready to release your shame to Jesus?

One of my (Matt's) former students prayed through her shame. She had been content in her marriage and happily serving in youth ministry—until it all fell apart due to another person's sin. And then shame entered her self-talk: "I'm a divorcee. I'm a sinner. I'm a loser. There's no hope for me." After going to several counseling sessions, she decided to run *to* Jesus instead of *away from* him. She met him in prayer but continued to feel unworthy.

As she prayed one day, she began to visualize all of her sins in her mind's eye. She could "see" her sins surrounding her and distancing her from Jesus. She kept telling Jesus, "This is who I am. All these sins around me—that's *me*. If I'm too far gone for you, I understand." Then she "saw" the following in her mind's eye (stated in her own words): "Jesus started pushing away the sinful things surrounding me. One by one, he pushed away each sin until he was standing right in front of me. Finally, I said, 'I'm so, so sorry.' And he put his hands on my shoulders and said, 'I love you.'" This prayer time transformed her life.

Shame-free in Jesus. The stories of the Samaritan woman and my former student show us that Jesus' goal was to restore us to a shame-free state. Jesus knows our sins, but instead of hiding, we can come to Jesus to process our sin and shame and allow him to transform us. Jesus sees our shame, but instead of turning away in disgust, he extends his loving, nail-pierced hands, showing us the scars to remind us that he took our shame on the cross so we wouldn't have to carry it. This is the testimony that Biani shared in the video at the beginning of this chapter. When she finally brought her sin of pornography and its shame to the Lord, he took it all and set her free.

God has crowned us with honor (Psalm 8:4–5). When we come to Jesus in faith, not only does he lovingly remove our shame; he also gives us honor. From shame to honor—that's the way of Jesus. We encourage you to do the exercise below, which will help you offer *your* shame to Jesus for him to carry.

Encouragement and Prayer by John-Paul and Matt: Point your phone's camera at the QR code and follow the link or go to youtube.com /@FindingFreedomInJesusBook.

Reflective Exercises for
Personal or Group Discussion to
Embrace That You Are Shame-Free

1. Practice breathing exercises for three or four minutes each day. Breathe in: "shame removed"; breathe out: "honor given." If you're in a small group, do the breathing together.

2. Go to YouTube, find a worship song with the theme of "shame-free," and listen to it several times each day. If you're in a small group, sing the song together.

3. Looking back at the chapter, what did you learn that you didn't know previously?

4. Take some time to ponder the biblical definition of *shame-free*: To be shame-free means that Jesus has forgiven your sins and has taken away the burden and weight of your guilt and shame, replacing shame with honor. What part of the definition really speaks to you?

5. *Living out shame-free*:
   a) Are you hiding from the Lord because of your shame? Perhaps you're covering up your shame through perfectionism, overwork, busyness, or addictions. Are there influences or abuse from your past you still carry? Sometimes shame comes to us, not because of the sin we ourselves committed, but because of the sins of others, such as cruelty or mistreatment. Make a list of any sin or shame that comes to mind.

b) Listen to (or read) John 4:1–26 (listen on biblegateway.com or on a Bible app). As you listen to the passage, in your mind's eye "watch" Jesus' interaction with the Samaritan woman. When the passage ends, create a mental picture of yourself at the well and pray to Jesus. Tell him about *your* sin and shame. Ask him to forgive you and take your shame and replace it with honor. Don't be in a hurry as you pray—take time to sit with Jesus at the well. See the "*How do we begin this movement toward confession?*" section on pages 91–92 for further ideas.

6. Take time to meditate on and pray through Genesis 2:25; Psalms 32:5; 34:5; John 4:10; Romans 9:33; and Hebrews 12:2. Allow the Lord to open your heart to the truth that you are shame-free in Jesus. You may want to choose one of these passages to memorize.

restored by Christ

Faith in Jesus restores us to our true selves, to the way God created us to be—sin-free and in perfect communion with him. Keep remembering that this book's overall goal is to embrace our true identity and find freedom in Jesus.

In Jesus, I am...

8. Rescued
9. Forgiven
10. Righteous
11. Redeemed
12. Reconciled
13. Saved
14. Holy

Please don't forget to do the breathing and reflective exercises. There is no transformation without dedication, empowered by the Holy Spirit.

CHAPTER 8

Rescued

He has rescued us from the dominion of darkness and brought us into the kingdom of the Son he loves.

COLOSSIANS 1:13

In 2020, when the whole world shut down during the COVID-19 pandemic, most of us expected we would be shut down for only a couple weeks to flatten the curve, but it felt like a lifetime. During that time, I (John-Paul) needed to be rescued. I lost my younger brother in 2017, and in 2020, I lost my older brother to COVID-19. If this wasn't bad enough, I was doing my best to lead the church through a pandemic hot spot in Los Angeles, finish the final year of my doctoral program in theology, and, with my wife, raise two kids under ten years old. Being under so much pressure, I cried out to God. If he wouldn't show up, everything was going to fall apart. I needed to be rescued.

Have you been there? Persecuted? Trials? Sickness? Friends, family, or foes harassing you or abandoning you? Like me, you need a rescuer. Perhaps you try to fix things yourself. Or maybe you just throw your hands in the air and give up. We need some good news, and we have it: God is our rescuer, and he sent his Son, Jesus, to rescue us from our troubles and bring us into his heavenly kingdom.

Who am I? I am rescued in Jesus. I can be transformed when I embrace that truth.

Testimony: Point your phone's camera at the QR code for a video testimony from Dr. Matt Williams or go to youtube .com/@FindingFreedomInJesusBook.

I was surrounded by people who drank a lot of alcohol and did drugs. My brother quit drugs, started going to church, and invited me to go . . .

Rescued in Our Culture

The term *rescue* in our culture means much the same as it did in the Bible: to save from a dangerous or distressing situation. As a former lifeguard, I (Matt) knew the importance of always being on guard and ready to jump in to rescue a floundering swimmer. My eyes always scanned the water for signs of distress. In the same way, I believe that God's eyes are scanning the world for those who need rescue.

I (John-Paul) remember when Hurricane Katrina hit New Orleans in 2005. An estimated sixty thousand people climbed onto their rooftops to escape the rising waters. Rescue boats eventually appeared to take them to safety. The struggling people didn't just need to get to dry land; they needed a *wholistic* rescue—food, water, and rebuilt homes. Around that time, I went on a road trip from California to Florida and drove through some of the devastated areas. As I witnessed firsthand the destruction, I was led to encourage my church to provide food, supplies, and housing for the needy.

As we think about the city, state, country, and world in which we live, we see the enormous need for wholistic rescue—physical needs (for the unhoused, poor, and sick), emotional needs (rampant anxiety and depression), relational needs (broken relationships and loneliness), and spiritual needs.

What Does the Bible Say About Being Rescued?

Rescued in the Old Testament

God rescues. God persistently and powerfully rescued his people in the Old Testament. The biggest rescue mission was from captivity in Egypt (Exodus 18:10), but God also rescued Israel from other foreign nations, including Midian, Philistia, and Ammon. God rescued Daniel from the lions' den (Daniel 6:27) and rescued others from persecution, the sword, death, fears, and sin (Psalms 7:1; 22:20; 33:19; 34:4; 39:8). God was always present and ready to rescue: "The angel of the LORD encamps around those who fear Him, and rescues them" (Psalm 34:7 NASB).

Living Rescued Today

A woman approached me (John-Paul) after church. "I'm in trouble. Pastor, I'm not gonna lie. I'm part of a prominent gang in Los Angeles, and I'm lost. If I keep heading in this direction, I'm either going to go to jail or die. I need you to pray for me that God would help me and my babies." I knew she needed to be rescued. She and I prayed, and our church helped her in many ways. Today she is a disciple of Jesus Christ and committed to the church. She and her family are thriving because she acknowledged God and allowed him to rescue her.

Why does God rescue? God rescues because of his compassion and love (Nehemiah 9:27; Psalm 44:26). He "rescued me because he delighted in me" (2 Samuel 22:20). God loves to rescue because his people are precious to him. I forget that sometimes; don't you? God rescues because he is like a shepherd who watches over and cares for the sheep: "As a shepherd looks after his scattered flock when he is with them, so will I look after my sheep. I will rescue them from all the places where they were scattered on a day of clouds and darkness" (Ezekiel 34:12).

A messianic rescuer. The Old Testament looked forward to a future rescue: "At that time I will deal with all who oppressed you. I will rescue the lame; I will gather the exiles. I will give them praise and honor in every land where they have suffered shame" (Zephaniah 3:19). The most miraculous of all rescue plans was the New Testament's fulfillment of these prophecies when Jesus appeared on the scene.

Rescued in the New Testament

Jesus the rescuer. Israel was awaiting God's *military* rescue by the Messiah against the foreign enemy, Rome. They thought they needed a warrior-king, but Jesus had a bigger and better rescue plan. Even before Jesus' birth, John the Baptist's father prophesied that Jesus would "rescue us from the hand of our enemies" (Luke 1:72–74). Jesus fulfilled God's Old Testament promises by rescuing and blessing his people (Romans 11:26; in fulfillment of Isiah 59:20).

Rescued from. Although Jesus rescued people physically in his ministry through healing and by providing bread and fish, his greatest rescue was a spiritual rescue that resulted from his death on the cross and resurrection from the dead. Jesus rescued us from a number of spiritual issues, including sin, Satan, and wrath:

SIN. We are rescued from sin's influences and its lingering guilt and shame: "Grace and peace to you from God our Father and the Lord Jesus Christ, who gave himself for our sins to rescue us from the present evil age" (Galatians 1:3–4). We now have the ability to resist sin and live for Jesus.

SATAN. Before being rescued by Jesus, we lived in the darkness, captive to sin, and under the influence of Satan, "the ruler of this world" (John 12:31 NASB). Now, though, we are God's rescued children, citizens of the kingdom of God: "He has rescued us from the dominion of darkness and brought us into the kingdom of the Son he loves" (Colossians 1:13). Jesus has rescued us by enabling us and empowering us to fight against Satan and his demonic minions. Their influence can be overcome.

WRATH. Rescue isn't just about the present; it's also about the future when we will arrive at the heavenly shores for the final—and eternal—rescue. Instead of facing the wrath of God, we will be warmly welcomed into heaven through "Jesus, who rescues us from the coming wrath" (1 Thessalonians 1:10). Not only are we rescued from the sinful influences of this world, but we can confidently hope in Jesus' eternal rescue.

Rescued to. We were rescued *from* darkness and rescued *to* live in a new way. Rescued people live differently; they follow Jesus' way of life as "children of light" (Ephesians 5:8). We live according to Jesus' example out of gratitude for the rescue that we have already experienced. We don't live to earn rescue.

Jesus was rescued. On the cross, the soldiers taunted Jesus: "He trusts in God. Let God rescue him now if he wants him, for he said, 'I am the Son of God'" (Matthew 27:43; quoting Psalm 22:8). Jesus cited this same psalm as he hung on the cross: "My God, my God, why have you forsaken me?" (Psalm 22:1). This psalm was also fulfilled when Jesus' hands and feet were pierced (v. 16). Was Jesus rescued? It didn't seem like he was rescued, but look at the rest of the psalm: "He [God] has not despised or scorned the suffering of the afflicted one; he has not hidden his face from him but has listened to his cry for help" (v. 24). God listened and didn't hide his face from Jesus, even while he was being afflicted.

Did God rescue Jesus? Psalm 22 goes on to say, "All the ends of the earth will remember and turn to the LORD" (v. 27). Something happened on the cross; something happened in the suffering and death of Jesus that led to all the ends of the earth turning to the Lord. How was this a rescue when Jesus was killed on the cross?

When Jesus died on the cross, it seemed there would be no rescue story . . . until the resurrection happened. Yes, he died, but then he was resurrected from the dead. Bingo! *That* was Jesus' rescue. The resurrection proved that God can turn suffering and death into something good, right? The resurrection proved that God rescued Jesus. In the cross there was a deeper rescue than what we initially thought.

In Jesus' death, we see God's decisive and final rescue plan. Through his death on the cross, Jesus triumphed over sin, death, and Satan so that we can experience forgiveness and removal of shame. I know it's absurd to think that anything good could come from death, but it's true. Paul wrote, "He forgave us all our sins, having canceled the charge of our legal indebtedness, which stood against us and condemned us; he has taken it away, nailing it to the cross. And having disarmed the powers and authorities, he made a public spectacle of them, triumphing over them *by the cross*" (Colossians 2:13–15, emphasis added).

Surprisingly, Jesus' death was a rescue plan. The cross was triumph. This truth changes our interpretation of suffering. God doesn't cause suffering, but he can use suffering for good: "We know that God causes all things to work together for good to those who love God" (Romans 8:28 NASB).

Paul was rescued. Paul was rescued from a myriad of suffering: "You, however, know all about my . . . persecutions, sufferings—what kinds of things happened to me in Antioch, Iconium and Lystra, the persecutions I endured. Yet the Lord rescued me from *all* of them" (2 Timothy 3:10–11, emphasis added). How could he say that God rescued him from *all* suffering? Look at his list of persecutions: prison, floggings, lashes, beatings, stonings, shipwrecks, bandits, hunger, thirst, cold, and lack of clothing (2 Corinthians 11:23–29).

Paul suffered, and yet even in his suffering, Paul did not lose hope in God's rescue plan. He embraced Christ's promise: "'My grace is sufficient for you, for my power is made perfect in weakness.' . . . That is why, for Christ's sake, I delight in weaknesses, in insults, in hardships, in persecutions, in difficulties. For when I am weak, then I am strong"

(2 Corinthians 12:9–10). Was Paul rescued? The Bible says yes. Maybe part of the biblical definition of *rescue* includes the ability to withstand difficult times. Paul said that God gave him strength to stand up to suffering (2 Timothy 4:17).

Rescue doesn't always mean we are rescued *from* all suffering, but that we are rescued *within* our suffering and given strength to withstand it. After all, maturity and growth often come through hardship. Pure gold is only found after it goes through the fire: "In all this you greatly rejoice, though now for a little while you may have had to suffer grief in all kinds of trials. These have come so that the proven genuineness of your faith—of greater worth than gold, which perishes even though refined by fire—may result in praise, glory and honor when Jesus Christ is revealed" (1 Peter 1:6–7). Have you found this to be true in your life?

Rescued and suffering. What did rescue mean for Paul and for Jesus? It did *not* mean the absence of all trials and suffering. Jesus suffered. Paul suffered. God rescues, but not always in the way or at the time we desire. Despite trials in this life, we can *rest* in these truths:

- Jesus himself experienced suffering. When I go through trials, this truth helps me. It's comforting to know that I don't experience any type of temptation or suffering that Jesus himself did not experience. He understands my struggles.
- Jesus is always with us in the midst of our suffering. Not only does Jesus understand our struggles, but he is present with us when we suffer. Family and friends may abandon us, but God will be with us every step of the way: "The Lord stood at my side and gave me strength" (2 Timothy 4:17). We are not alone when we struggle.
- Our final rescue is yet to come. In the future, God will rescue us by bringing us into his heavenly kingdom: "The Lord will rescue me from every evil attack and will bring me safely to his heavenly kingdom. To him be glory for ever and ever" (2 Timothy 4:18). We may suffer now, but our suffering will end when we enter an eternity free from all struggle and suffering.

Heavenly hope. Remember what happened when Jesus prayed in Gethsemane? "His sweat was like drops of blood falling to the ground" (Luke 22:44). The act of sweating blood is called hematohidrosis, and it is caused by extreme distress. Suffering was not easy for Jesus, nor is it easy for us. Therefore, Jesus taught us in the Lord's Prayer to ask God to "rescue us from the evil one" (Matthew 6:13 NLT). We need daily rescue, but even more, we need eternal rescue. We pray for God to rescue us from our present trials as we await our final rescue in heaven: "Our light and momentary troubles are achieving for us an eternal glory that far outweighs them all" (2 Corinthians 4:17).

Final Biblical Thoughts on Rescued

Just as God rescued the Israelites, Daniel, Jesus, Paul, and so many others, God rescues you and me from this dark world and brings us into his kingdom as his children. He does not always take away our struggles, but he provides the hope and strength we need as we wait for our eternal rescue when we will be ushered into the Lord's presence forever.

Rescue means that Jesus is with us; therefore we don't give up, nor do we lose hope. Just as Jesus was resurrected from the dead, we will be resurrected and will live eternally in glory with God our rescuer, who "will wipe every tear from their eyes. There will be no more death or mourning or crying or pain" (Revelation 21:4).

In one sentence, rescued means that God delivers you from trials in this evil world and will bring you into his eternal kingdom.

Finding Freedom in Jesus

Maybe you're in the middle of a huge trial, and you see no way out of it—a broken relationship, cancer, joblessness, anxiety, depression. Do you trust that God is your rescuer? Do you pray for him to rescue you from trials here on earth, even though there are no guarantees of a carefree life? Jesus suffered and died a cruel death on the cross and yet kept his faith, entrusting his life to God all the way to his final breath: "Father, into your hands I commit my spirit" (Luke 23:46). Looking to Jesus helps us to find the example, the faith, and the strength, even in our difficulties. Are you ready to be rescued?

God is our rescuer. God will rescue us all the way to heaven. But what about our present circumstances when we don't feel like we are being rescued—when we experience physical, mental, or relational suffering? Like Paul and Jesus, we need to trust that sometimes there's a deeper plan or purpose we can't see. Have you ever had a friend with cancer tell you, "I've grown so much through this pain"? Now, we are *not* saying that cancer or suffering is good; it's undeniably *not* good! But we are saying that God can use hard times to mold us and bring beauty out of pain as we await our eternal rescue. God can work good out of evil, as we see on the cross: "We know that in all things God works for the good of those who love him" (Romans 8:28). Do you believe that? May our prayer be the same as Jesus' prayer in Gethsemane before going to the cross: "My Father, if it is possible, may this cup be taken from me. Yet not as I will, but as you will" (Matthew 26:39).

We are rescuers. After we are rescued, we become rescuers. The rescued rescue through the power of the Holy Spirit. Physical, emotional, relational, and spiritual needs are all around us. Do you see yourself as a rescuer? God wants to use you to help and rescue those around you. The poor, widow, orphan, anxious, depressed, abused, sick—they need you. Are you ready to rescue others?

Encouragement and Prayer by John-Paul and Matt: Point your phone's camera at the QR code and follow the link or go to youtube.com /@FindingFreedomInJesusBook.

Reflective Exercises for
Personal or Group Discussion to Embrace That You Are Rescued

1. Practice breathing exercises for three or four minutes each day. Breathe in: "I am rescued"; breathe out: "now I rescue." If you are experiencing some tough trials right now, try this: Breathe in: "I am rescued"; breathe out: "someday eternally rescued"—asking for faith to believe in God's ultimate rescue plan for you. If you're in a small group, do the breathing together.

2. Go to YouTube, find a worship song with the theme of "rescued," and listen to it several times each day. If you're in a small group, sing the song together.

3. Looking back at the chapter, what did you learn that you didn't know previously?

4. Take time to ponder the biblical definition of *rescued*: To be rescued means that God delivers you from trials in this evil world and will bring you into his eternal kingdom. What part of the definition really speaks to you?

5. *Living out rescued*:
   a) From what have you been rescued? Spend time thanking God. From what are you still seeking God's rescue? What's holding you back from asking God to rescue you? Spend time praying about the current

difficulties in your life, asking God to rescue you from your struggles. Reach your hand out to him and ask him to take you into his "rescue boat."

b) If you're in the midst of trials, pray that you can experience the Lord's presence and peace despite the trials. My (Matt's) best friend had cancer and still feels negative effects from chemotherapy. It has now been nearly five years since chemotherapy ended, but he still struggles with nausea and exhaustion. It has been a battle! And yet his faith continues to be strong. When you struggle, pray for continued faith and for a vision of how God can use your trials to mature you as you await your final rescue when you will walk the golden streets in heaven hand in hand with Jesus.

c) The *rescued* become Holy Spirit-empowered *rescuers*. Think about specific people and the actions you can take to rescue them. Think about your immediate neighborhood, but also think bigger. Remember that you can start with small steps, such as a kind word or brief phone call, and these steps can gradually get bigger. Just get started.

6. Take time to meditate on and pray through Exodus 18:10; 2 Samuel 22:20; Psalm 34:7 NASB; Ezekiel 34:12; Colossians 1:13; 2 Timothy 4:18; and Revelation 21:4. Allow the Lord to open your heart to the truth that you are rescued in Jesus. You may want to choose one of these passages to memorize.

CHAPTER 9

Forgiven

If we confess our sins, he is faithful and just and will forgive us our sins and purify us from all unrighteousness.

1 JOHN 1:9

You don't know what I've done. I'm a bad person. I can never be for-given!" Countless people have told us that. Do you ever feel that way? You think you're too far gone? Well, what about Adam and Eve, who broke the *one* commandment God gave them? What about David, who committed adultery with Bathsheba and had her husband mur-dered? What about Samson, who slept with a prostitute? What about Peter, who denied knowing Jesus three times? What about the apostle Paul, who persecuted Christians before coming to faith?

Do you really think you're too far gone for God's forgiveness? The

Bible contains pages upon pages of stories of forgiven sinners. It's never too late. There is always a way back.

Who am I? I am forgiven in Jesus. I can be transformed when I embrace that truth.

Testimony: Point your phone's camera at the QR code for a video testimony from Jacob or go to youtube.com /@FindingFreedomInJesusBook.

I was in the middle of a broken dating relationship. I was a sinner. In prayer, I pictured myself in this huge white room, but I was chained up. Jesus walked over to me . . .

Forgiven in Our Culture

Our culture can easily define forgiveness as "stop feeling anger with or resentment toward someone." The problem isn't the definition; it's the application. Forgiveness experts tell us that the hardest person to forgive is ourselves. We struggle mightily with accepting forgiveness. We also struggle to forgive others. We live in a "cancel culture." When someone hurts or offends us or disagrees with our point of view, we cancel them. We ignore them, avoid them, stop talking to them. It's so rare these days for someone to sincerely apologize—to say the words "I'm sorry. Will you please forgive me?" Our culture struggles with offering and accepting forgiveness.

What Does the Bible Say About Being Forgiven?

Forgiven in the Old Testament

Human sin. Adam and Eve disobeyed the one command God gave them (Genesis 2:16–17), but God provided a way to forgiveness by providing garments of skin to cover their nakedness and remove their shame.

Depending on how you look at it—as depressing or encouraging—the ongoing story of the Old Testament is that of human beings breaking God's commands, and God providing pathways to forgiveness. We learn through the story of Israel's exodus and wilderness journey that God is perfectly sinless and holy. It isn't possible for him to be in the presence of the unholy; whenever the two mix, bad things happen. We need forgiveness because sin ruins our relationship with our holy God and with each other.

A way for forgiveness. God loves humanity so intensely that he provided a pathway to forgiveness to cleanse us from our sins. The Law of Moses instructed the Israelites how to obtain forgiveness. For example, when they sinned, they were to sacrifice a bull, sprinkle its blood in certain locations, and burn it so "they will be forgiven" (Leviticus 4:13–20). Human sin was symbolically placed on the animal; and the human guilt was removed once the animal was sacrificed. One of the key themes in forgiveness is "washing" or "cleansing." The people were commanded to wash after a sacrifice or after a sin, and the washing with water symbolized sin being washed away (16:26).

Did God always forgive his people? God forgave because he "is compassionate and gracious, slow to anger, abounding in love" (Psalm 103:8). Our holy God desired a close relationship with sinful humans, and forgiveness was the pathway to restoring that relationship. God was always willing to forgive, but only if there was repentance and a desire to stop sinning: "If my people, who are called by my name, will humble themselves and pray and seek my face and turn from their wicked ways, then I will hear from heaven, and I will forgive their sin and will heal their land" (2 Chronicles 7:14).

In the time of the prophet Jeremiah, God asked, "Why should I forgive you? Your children have forsaken me and sworn by gods that are not gods. I supplied all their needs, yet they committed adultery and thronged to the houses of prostitutes" (Jeremiah 5:7). If there was no repentance, no change of heart and lifestyle, and no real desire to follow God, there could be no forgiveness. They must "turn from their wicked ways; then I will forgive their wickedness and their sin" (36:3). Forgiveness was always available, but it was conditional upon true repentance.

King David repents. Most scholars believe that Psalm 51 was David's confession of his sin of adultery and murder: "Have mercy on me, O God, according to your unfailing love; according to your great compassion blot out my transgressions. Wash away all my iniquity and cleanse me from my sin" (Psalm 51:1–2). David confessed, repented, and was forgiven, although he still suffered the consequences of his sin—the son who was conceived as a result of his adultery died (2 Samuel 12:13–14). The truth is that we can be forgiven by God and still experience the consequences of our actions.

Human response to forgiveness. When we receive forgiveness, our response must be praise and worship: "Praise the LORD, my soul, and forget not all his benefits—who forgives all your sins" (Psalm 103:2–3). Forgiveness should never be taken for granted. God is so good to forgive us undeserving humans.

Hope for the future. The Israelites' ongoing sin problem showed that they needed a better way for their future. Isaiah prophesied that the iniquities of the people would be placed on a coming Messiah, a Suffering Servant, who would be "pierced for our transgressions" as he "bore the sin of many" (Isaiah 53:5, 12). The Messiah would provide a solution to the sin problem: "'In those days, at that time,' declares the LORD, 'search will be made for Israel's guilt, but there will be none, and for the sins of Judah, but none will be found, for I will forgive the remnant I spare'" (Jeremiah 50:20). To learn how the Messiah accomplished this, we turn to the New Testament.

Forgiven in the New Testament

Jesus brings forgiveness. In fulfillment of the Old Testament prophecies, Jesus came to earth and brought a new way of forgiveness. The Law of Moses required an animal's blood to be sacrificed for forgiveness (Hebrews 9:22). Now, though, instead of animals, Jesus—the Messiah, the Suffering Servant—went to the cross as the perfect and final sacrifice. John the Baptist called Jesus "the Lamb of God, who takes away the sin of the world" (John 1:29). Jesus was the final and perfect sacrificial Lamb.

At the Last Supper, Jesus used wine to represent his blood: "This is my blood of the covenant, which is poured out for many for the forgiveness of sins" (Matthew 26:28). Jesus, the sinless one, took away our sins through his sacrifice on the cross: "God made him who had no sin to be sin for us" (2 Corinthians 5:21).

Jesus forgives. Jesus didn't just bring a new pathway to forgiveness; he personally forgave individuals. Among the many whom Jesus forgave was a paralyzed man: "Son, your sins are forgiven." The Jewish leaders knew that only God can forgive sins, so they questioned Jesus, "Why does this fellow talk like that? He's blaspheming! Who can forgive sins but God alone?" Jesus' answer made it clear that Jesus is God: "I want you to know that the Son of Man has authority on earth to forgive sins" (Mark 2:5–10).

Jesus also forgave a sinful woman who anointed his feet with expensive perfume: "Jesus said to her, 'Your sins are forgiven'" (Luke 7:48). It's true that only God can forgive sins, but it's also true that Jesus is God! Therefore, Jesus can forgive sins.

How do we find forgiveness? Forgiveness comes through repentance, confession, and belief in Jesus. To repent means to "turn away" from our sin. It is a 180-degree turn. We stop sinning, or at least we try to stop sinning. An important aspect of repentance is confession, where we agree with God that we have sinned: "If we confess our sins, he is faithful and just and will forgive us our sins and purify us from all unrighteousness" (1 John 1:9). We turn *away from* sin, and we turn *to* Jesus in faith: "Everyone who believes in him receives forgiveness of sins through his name" (Acts 10:43). Many times, while wrestling with sin, we rationalize or justify our sin, which causes us to continue living in our sin, instead of repenting and being forgiven.

What does forgiveness mean? God's forgiveness takes away our sin and guilt, restoring our relationship with him. The dirty stain that sin causes is spiritually cleansed: "Let us draw near to God . . . having our hearts sprinkled to cleanse us from a guilty conscience and having our bodies washed with pure water" (Hebrews 10:22). Because of our faith in Jesus, God is "not counting people's sins against them" (2 Corinthians 5:19). It's like an Etch A Sketch. When we make a mistake in our sketch, a simple shake erases it all. God, through our faith in Jesus, "shakes" the list of our sins and removes them from us "as far as the east is from the west" (Psalm 103:12). Past sins are not written in permanent ink and will not be held against us. We can be washed and cleansed through repentance and faith in Jesus.

The prodigal son. The parable of the prodigal son is a great example of forgiveness. Jewish leaders complained that Jesus "welcomes sinners and eats with them" (Luke 15:2). Jesus told the parable of the prodigal son, who asked for the money he would have inherited from his father upon his death. His father gave him the money, and he left. He lost his inheritance in sinful living and decided to return home to his father for help, not knowing whether his father would receive him. Yet when he returned home, he found only forgiveness.

Jesus taught that "there is rejoicing in the presence of the angels of God over one sinner who repents" (15:10). The parable of the prodigal son reveals that the father forgave and accepted the son, but it also shows that the father reinstated him with full rights into the household. Forgiveness was not just washing away the dirt, but also restoring the relationship. This amazing story teaches that it's never too late to seek forgiveness.

Why does God forgive? When the prodigal son decided to return home, "his father saw him and was filled with compassion for him; he ran to his son, threw his arms around him and kissed him" (Luke 15:20). In that culture, the son brought shame to the family and should have been disowned for demanding his inheritance before his father's death. Also, fathers never ran in that culture because running brought them shame. The father in the parable represents our compassionate and loving God, who is willing to run to the repentant sinner and take on the shame, in order to forgive. God compassionately forgives because of his grace (Ephesians 1:7).

Transformed by forgiveness. Forgiveness expert Everett Worthington reminds us that forgiveness transforms every part of our being—physical, emotional, relational, and spiritual.[1] Physically, forgiveness decreases heart attacks and blood pressure. Emotionally, forgiveness decreases fear, anger, sadness, and shame. Relationally, forgiveness eliminates the distance between us and God and between feuding human beings. Spiritually, we find salvation, joy, and peace. Forgiveness brings complete transformation to our lives. God designed our bodies to thrive when we experience and extend forgiveness.

Living Forgiven Today

One Sunday, I (John-Paul) preached a sermon about forgiveness and spoke of the negative spiritual, psychological, and physical impacts that unforgiveness has on us. After church, a member approached me to share her story. She had struggled with abdominal pain and ulcers for a long time, but after she finally forgave someone, her abdominal pain and ulcers completely went away. Our bodies are designed to thrive when we accept and experience God's forgiveness, as well as when we extend it to others.

Those who are forgiven forgive. In fact, our experience of God's forgiveness transforms our lives so dramatically that if we don't forgive, we must question if we've truly experienced God's forgiveness. Jesus said it this way: "Forgive us our sins, for we also forgive everyone who sins against us" (Luke 11:4). We are not *earning* our forgiveness through forgiving others. No, it is clear that we are forgiven solely by grace through faith (Ephesians 2:8). But once we are forgiven, we will forgive those who have hurt us as a response to the grace and forgiveness God has shown us. As we have been forgiven multiple times for our sins, we are called to forgive others just as much: "'Lord, how many times shall I forgive my brother or sister who sins against me? Up to seven times?' Jesus answered, 'I tell you, not seven times, but seventy-seven times'" (Matthew 18:21–22). Forgiveness transforms us from vengeful, bitter, angry people into loving and compassionate people.

Living Forgiven Today

One of my (Matt's) students who struggled with anger, bitterness, and unforgiveness decided to forgive her mom for all the cruel things she had done. Over many prayer sessions, this student brought each painful memory to the Lord in prayer, visualizing Jesus with her in that memory, and asking Jesus to heal her pain and empower her to forgive her mom. Through this long process, she became a transformed woman, and her relationship with her mom was transformed as well. Extending forgiveness to others is evidence that Jesus has forgiven us.

Final Biblical Thoughts on Forgiven

Although God is sinless, we humans are not. Therefore, in the Law of Moses, God provided a way for forgiveness so that the Israelites could be cleansed and forgiven and their relationship with God restored. God did this because he is loving and compassionate.

The Old Testament's expectation of a coming Suffering Servant who would take on the sins of the people was fulfilled in Jesus. Jesus was the sinless Lamb of God who willingly chose the cross to provide a way for forgiveness. Those who repent of their sins and believe in Jesus find forgiveness. All of the dirty sin and guilt are washed away. God runs to the repentant sinner and welcomes them back home with hugs.

Jesus modeled forgiveness while he was on earth and calls us to forgive those who have hurt us, just as the Lord has forgiven us.

In one sentence, to be forgiven means that God, through confession and faith in Jesus, washes away the dirt and guilt of your sin.

Finding Freedom in Jesus

Accepting forgiveness. Can we admit we have sinned? I have sinned. You have sinned. Because of our sin, God the Father sent his Son, Jesus, to endure the pain of the cross in order to forgive us. Jesus chose to pay the price of our sin so we could be washed clean. As Jesus told the disciples, "You are already clean because of the word I have spoken to you" (John 15:3). The disciples lacked faith and often messed up, and yet Jesus declared them clean.

In Jesus, sin no longer defines who we are. We are forgiven. Cleansed. Washed. Without stain. Paul said we are "without stain or wrinkle or any other blemish, but holy and blameless" (Ephesians 5:27). God said to Jerusalem, "Though your sins are like scarlet, they shall be as white as snow" (Isaiah 1:18).

Is something keeping you from believing that Jesus forgives you? Haven't you carried the sin and guilt long enough? Are you ready to let Jesus carry your sin all the way to the cross? Dr. Karl Menninger, a noted twentieth-century psychiatrist, reportedly said that if patients in psychiatric hospitals could be convinced that their sins were forgiven, 75 percent of them could walk out the next day.

Forgiving others. Perhaps your struggle is not with accepting God's forgiveness for yourself but with extending forgiveness to those who have hurt you. While Satan may tempt us to seek revenge, the apostle Paul urged us to forgive: "Bear with each other and forgive one another if any of you has a grievance against someone. Forgive as the Lord forgave you" (Colossians 3:13). We should forgive because Jesus forgave us, but also because unforgiveness has a negative impact on us physically, emotionally, relationally, and spiritually. Hurts and sins that are not dealt with leave lasting wounds, anger, and bitterness. Such feelings run deep and won't magically disappear.

Is forgiving others easy? We know that forgiving others can feel almost impossible. And yet not to forgive is dangerous because it is the number one open door that allows Satan access to us. Forgiving others is spiritual warfare; it's a battle. The Bible says that when we don't forgive, we become vulnerable to demonic attacks: "I have forgiven in the sight of Christ for your sake, in order that Satan might not outwit us. For we are not unaware of his schemes" (2 Corinthians 2:10–11). I don't want that! Being angry with others also opens up a door to Satan's influence: "'In your anger do not sin': Do not let the sun go down while you are still angry, and do not give the devil a foothold" (Ephesians 4:26–27).

Even though the act of forgiving others is not easy, with the help of the Holy Spirit we are empowered to forgive. We have prayed with people to help them forgive serious hurts, including abuse, rape, slander, lies, and abandonment, among many other hurts.

I (Matt) was praying with a young woman who was trying to forgive an abusive ex-boyfriend. As she was praying, all of a sudden, we thought an earthquake had hit (we live in Southern California, where earthquakes are common). She said, "It seems like the whole room is moving back and forth." We both felt it. Praying for forgiveness toward someone who has hurt you is a big deal in the spiritual world. I think that's why it felt like an earthquake as we prayed. Satan was trying to scare us so we'd quit praying. It didn't work. She forgave her ex-boyfriend and was released from her unforgiveness, anger, and bitterness that very day. This act of forgiving wasn't easy, but it sure was a good day when she was able to forgive and release him to Jesus.

Think about the broken relationships in your church that have resulted from ongoing anger and unforgiveness. Imagine what your church would be like if every person who had been forgiven sought to forgive those who had hurt them and become reconciled. Our churches would be transformed, and their testimony in the world would reflect God's character and Jesus' prayer for unity in the church (John 17:23). We urge you to follow the model explained in the exercises on forgiving others.

Our prayer is that we will fully experience God's forgiveness in our lives and then extend forgiveness to those who have wronged us. Who am I? I am forgiven—washed clean, white as snow!

Encouragement and Prayer by John-Paul and Matt: Point your phone's camera at the QR code and follow the link or go to youtube.com /@FindingFreedomInJesusBook.

Reflective Exercises for
Personal or Group Discussion to Embrace That You Are Forgiven

1. Practice breathing exercises for three or four minutes each day. Breathe in: "washed clean"; breathe out: "white as snow." If you're in a small group, do the breathing together.

2. Go to YouTube, find a worship song with the theme of "forgiven," and listen to it several times each day. If you're in a small group, sing the song together.

3. Looking back at the chapter, what did you learn that you didn't know previously?

4. Take some time to ponder the biblical definition of *forgiven*: To be forgiven means that God, through confession and faith in Jesus, washes away the dirt and guilt of your sin. What part of the definition really speaks to you?

5. *Living out forgiven*: Using the model of Colossians 3:13—"Forgive as the Lord forgave you"—we can receive God's forgiveness and extend forgiveness to others:

   a) **As the Lord forgave you.** Take some time to sit before the Lord and confess and ask for forgiveness for any sin that the Holy Spirit brings to mind. Feel free to visualize yourself talking directly to Jesus, asking him to cleanse you of every sinful stain. This gives us perspective that we ourselves are sinners who have hurt God. First John 1:9 assures us that God forgives every sin that we confess.

   b) **Forgive.**
   - Ask the Spirit to bring to mind someone you need to forgive. If you are comfortable doing so, visualize that person in your mind's eye.
   - Remember the offense and the pain under the Holy Spirit's protection.
   - Remember the cross of Jesus, which makes forgiveness possible.
   - Visualize Jesus in the painful event with you. Ask him to heal your pain and then to help you forgive the person and remove any desire for revenge. When you are ready, announce that you forgive the person.

- If you are visualizing, ask Jesus to take the person away from you in your mind's eye. Forgiveness does not let them off the hook; it removes them from *your* hook and places them on God's hook. We trust Jesus to offer grace and mercy to the person if they repent or bring them to justice if they do not repent.
- Ask Jesus to remove all bitterness and anger from your heart and to heal any pain from that experience.

6. Take time to meditate on and pray through 2 Chronicles 7:14; Psalm 103:2–5; Jeremiah 5:7; Mark 2:10; Colossians 3:13; and 1 John 1:9. Allow the Lord to open your heart to the truth that you are forgiven in Jesus. You may want to choose one of the passages to memorize.

CHAPTER 10

Righteous

God made him who had no sin to be sin for us, so that
in him we might become the righteousness of God.

2 CORINTHIANS 5:21

When I (Matt) was six years old, I stole some matches from my parents, went to a nearby park, and started a fire underneath a pine tree. Not smart! The police caught me and took me to the police station. Six years old and already in the slammer! The officer called my parents to pick me up. I didn't have to sit in front of a judge in a court of law, but if I had, what could I say to a judge? I was guilty.

My brother-in-law was a judge. Just being in the courtroom with him was nerve-racking. He demanded respect as a judge. Can you imagine standing before God—the perfect and holy Judge—pleading your case before him in his courtroom? "I'm not that bad"; "I deserve to go to heaven." Yeah, right! There's no way. You're a sinner; you're guilty.

Want to hear the good news? Through faith in Jesus, we are righteous; we are declared not guilty. It's hard to accept this truth. Too many kids have been told by teachers, parents, or authority figures, "You're a bad kid." How can God call us righteous?

Who am I? I am righteous in Jesus. I can be transformed when I embrace that truth.

Testimony: Point your phone's camera at the QR code for a video testimony from Daniela or go to youtube.com /@FindingFreedomInJesusBook.

I believed the gospel at age fourteen, but my church was not healthy. I became very legalistic, thinking that my good works could earn me righteousness before God . . .

Righteous in Our Culture

Though the term *righteous* is a religious word, it's an idea found in our culture. But instead of using the term *righteous*, we often use words such as *virtuous*, *honorable*, *ethical*, or *honest*. Someone who thinks they are always right or morally superior is often called *self-righteous*. Let's turn to the Bible and do a deep dive in order to fully understand this term, which some believe is the most important salvation concept.

What Does the Bible Say About Being Righteous?

Righteous in the Old Testament

God is righteous. God is fully righteous (Ezra 9:15), which means he always does the right thing and acts according to his own standard of right and wrong. The Hebrew word for righteous in the Bible refers to something that conforms to a standard—for example, a road that is flat and straight, like it's supposed to be. The word was used in religious contexts to refer to one who lived in accordance with God's moral standard.

Humanity's call to righteousness. God's people were called to be righteous, to live in step with God's standards of right and wrong. Noah was the first person in the Bible to be called righteous: "Noah was a righteous man, blameless among the people of his time, and he walked faithfully with God" (Genesis 6:9). Noah showed his righteousness in building the ark.

Abraham was righteous through faith, or belief, in God: "Abram [later changed to Abraham] believed the LORD, and he credited it to him as righteousness" (Genesis 15:6). Abraham was declared righteous before any act of obedience—solely on the basis of faith. He went on to live out his faith in righteous obedience (Genesis 17:11; 22:2).

Eventually, God gave the Israelites the Law of Moses to help them understand how to lead righteous lives and emulate God's righteousness. Although the law was good (Psalm 19:7–9), human beings could never attain righteousness by obeying the law or doing good works (Ecclesiastes 7:20). Righteousness was through faith and was demonstrated through righteous and faithful living. As Habakkuk 2:4 says, "The righteous person will live by his faithfulness." Righteous people were those who obeyed God.

Living justly. Not only did righteous people in the Old Testament live righteously, but they were also called to promote righteousness and justice in the world because God cares about those in need: "The LORD works righteousness and justice for all the oppressed" (Psalm 103:6). Because justice is important to God, it is important that Christians stand in the gap and advocate for the oppressed and pursue justice for the weak, the poor, and victims of human trafficking, racism, or abuse of power. We sometimes use the term *social justice* to describe administering justice in the world, but we need to be careful to define social justice *biblically* and not culturally. Social justice is displayed when power and authority are exercised in conformity with God's righteous standards.

Living Righteous Today

When the COVID-19 pandemic hit, the schools in Los Angeles sent their children home to study and learn online. We quickly noticed that many families didn't have enough computers to do school from home. As a church, we stood in the gap by partnering with community groups to provide laptops for those in need. Here's an important point when seeking justice in our neighborhoods: We have to be aware of the issues. Are you involved enough in your community to know the needs?

Hope for the unrighteous. Sadly, the Israelites disobeyed God again and again. Was there any hope for them? The prophets knew that God's people were not imitating God's righteousness, but they were hopeful that God would restore righteousness in the future through a Righteous Savior: "'The days are coming,' declares the LORD, 'when I will raise up for David a righteous Branch, a King who will reign wisely and do what is just and right in the land. In his days Judah will be saved and Israel will live in safety. This is the name by which he will be called: The LORD Our Righteous Savior'" (Jeremiah 23:5–6).

A righteous Messiah. Some Old Testament passages refer to a future Savior or Messiah as a warrior-king like David, but other passages speak of how the Messiah will suffer and become a sacrificial offering to bring righteousness: "After he has suffered, he will see the light of life and be satisfied; by his knowledge my righteous servant will justify many, and he will bear their iniquities" (Isaiah 53:11). Notice the phrase "my righteous servant will justify many." The words *righteous* and *justify* are derived from the same Hebrew word. We could translate it this way: "My righteous servant will bring righteousness to many."

How will the Messiah bring righteousness? Unexpectedly, the Old Testament prophesies that he will bring it through his own suffering: "He was pierced for our transgressions, he was crushed for our iniquities; the punishment that brought us peace was on him, and by his wounds we are healed" (Isaiah 53:5). We will be healed of our sins and spiritual troubles and brought to righteousness through the Messiah's suffering on our behalf. The Messiah will bring a spiritual victory so that his people can share in his righteousness. Let's turn to the New Testament to see how Jesus transforms us into righteous men and women in him.

Righteous in the New Testament

Jesus fulfilled the Old Testament expectation that the Suffering Messiah would sacrifice himself in order to bring righteousness and justice for his people. Although he was perfectly righteous and sinless (Acts 3:14; Hebrews 4:15), "'he himself bore our sins' in his body on the cross, so that we might die to sins and live for righteousness; 'by his wounds you have been healed'" (1 Peter 2:24, citing Isaiah 53:5). Jesus took all of our sin and guilt through his painful suffering on the cross so that we might be righteous before God.

Declared righteous. What does it mean to say we are "righteous" in Jesus? It means we are declared righteous despite our guilt. The term *righteous* comes from the courts of law. Even though we are guilty sinners, God sees us through the lens of Jesus' sacrifice. As the Righteous Judge, God declares us not guilty because of our faith in Jesus.

Imputed righteousness. It gets even better. Not only are we *declared* righteous, but we actually *receive* Jesus' perfect righteousness through our faith in him: "God made him who had no sin to be sin for us, so that in him we might become the righteousness of God" (2 Corinthians 5:21). Biblical scholars call this "imputed righteousness," which means that God's righteousness gets credited, given, or placed into our account. By putting faith in Jesus, his righteousness *becomes* ours. This means that

God looks at us as if we were actually righteous or guiltless, as if we had perfectly obeyed his commands—all because of Jesus.

We are cleared of all charges against us. Although our sin makes us guilty, God declares the verdict of "not guilty," *and* we receive Jesus' righteousness. That's what it means to be righteous in Jesus. Amazing!

Forgiven and righteous. There is overlap between the terms *forgiven* and *righteous* because salvation is beautifully multifaceted. Forgiveness means that our sin and guilt are washed away. We are now white as snow. The term *righteous* adds another facet. Not only are our sins washed away (= forgiven), but the holiness, perfection, and righteousness of Jesus are given to us (= righteous) as well. Jesus' own righteousness is credited to our account. Forgiveness takes away sin; righteousness gives us Jesus' righteous and sinless nature. Sin is like being dressed in dirty rags, and forgiveness takes off the dirty rags. Righteousness clothes us with Jesus' clean, white robe. Take a moment to think about that image in your own life.

Let's use another analogy. God is the Righteous Judge, and he is perfectly sinless and righteous. When we stand before him in the heavenly courtroom, we are sinners—unrighteous, guilty, and deserving of death. When we look over at God the Judge, though, we see our Savior Jesus. Jesus extends his nail-pierced hands to his Father and pleads our case. God looks at our sin and guilt through the lens of our faith in Jesus' sacrifice on the cross. When God sees Jesus' sacrifice, he takes our sin, cancels all the charges against us, and gives us Jesus' righteousness. What a glorious exchange! In an actual court of law, all that the judge can do is declare someone righteous. God, though, both *declares* us righteous and *gives* us Jesus' righteousness.

Living Righteous Today

One Sunday, after I (John-Paul) preached on the parable of the prodigal son, a man said to me, "Pastor, will God really forgive me for anything I've done?" I quoted 1 John 1:9 and said, "Of course he will." He said, "Pastor, I've done a lot of bad things. I might die today, and all I want to know is if God forgives me, can I really spend eternity with him in heaven?" I said, "According to the Word of God, you can. Do you want to receive Jesus as your Lord and Savior?" He said, "Yes." In that moment, Jesus' righteousness was credited to him. He had a lot of work ahead of him to live a transformed life, but in an instant, he was transformed from sinner to righteous through faith in Jesus.

By faith alone. One point of caution: Human beings can never do anything to earn this righteousness. It is given to us by grace through faith alone. God's righteous character is given to us through our faith in Jesus (Romans 3:22).

Living righteously. Although we are righteous in Jesus through faith and not by works, we are asked to live a righteous life. Good works rise out of a response to God's righteousness and grace. We cannot earn righteousness, but we are called to "hunger and thirst for righteousness" (Matthew 5:6). When we "seek first his kingdom and his righteousness" (Matthew 6:33), we "offer [ourselves] as slaves to righteousness leading to holiness" (Romans 6:19). We are righteous in Jesus, but we are daily called to live morally pure and righteous lives in conformity to Jesus' character.

Living justly. Paul was thankful when the Corinthians had a "readiness to see justice done" (2 Corinthians 7:11). Those who are righteous are called to act justly and administer justice in our world. It is imperative to remember the oppressed and marginalized, just as God does. Living justly or righteously is not a reason to gloat or be prideful; we have a high calling to humbly serve others.

Evangelism and social justice. Should we emphasize saving souls *or* express the heart of God against hatred, prejudice, and racism? Should we share the gospel with words *or* do good works to help the poor and oppressed to live better lives by helping the unhoused find homes, giving meals to the hungry, or supporting single parents? We can do *both*! We can save souls *and* help the needy. We can preach salvation to save souls for all of eternity *and* help the oppressed to live better lives here on earth. The righteous live righteously *and* seek justice. That's the biblical way.

Help me! Living a righteous life and helping the needy are difficult to do on our own. In fact, we can't possibly do this without the help and empowerment of the Holy Spirit and the guidance of the Bible. We read, study, meditate, and live out the Scriptures as we hold to this truth: "All Scripture is God-breathed and is useful for teaching, rebuking, correcting and training in righteousness" (2 Timothy 3:16). While our commitment to Scripture takes effort and discipline, we say yes to God's transformation of our character through our study of the Bible. There's no transformation without dedication through the Spirit's power, but the dedication is worth it as we find true freedom, peace, love, and hope in Jesus and bring hope and justice to our communities.

Heavenly hope. Although we are righteous now, there is a future hope that we have more awaiting us after death: "Now there is in store for me the crown of righteousness, which the Lord, the righteous Judge, will award to me on that day—and not only to me, but also to all who have longed for his appearing" (2 Timothy 4:8).

Final Biblical Thoughts on Righteous

Jesus is the only righteous one, but he wants humans to share in his righteousness. Because of sin, though, we fail to live up to God's righteous standards. The term *righteous* comes from the legal world. If a court rules in favor of a defendant, the defendant is declared "righteous," which means acquitted, or cleared, of all charges. Through faith, we are cleared of all charges against us, declared free from guilt.

Case dismissed! We are not just declared righteous; we *are* righteous in Christ. We are transformed from guilty sinners to guiltless. The full payment has been made for our sins on the cross, and "there is now no condemnation for those who are in Christ Jesus" (Romans 8:1).

After we receive the gift of righteousness, we are asked to imitate God's righteousness by living morally pure, or righteous, lives out of gratitude for God's gift of salvation. We can't earn righteousness through good works, as Daniela shared in her video testimony. Rather, living righteously is a natural overflow from our gratefulness for what God has done for us. We follow Jesus' teachings, with a special emphasis not only on evangelism but also social justice, helping the oppressed to experience better lives here on earth.

In one sentence, to be righteous means that God clears you of all charges, declares you not guilty, *and* allows you to receive Jesus' righteousness as your own through faith in Jesus.

Finding Freedom in Jesus

When you think about your life, are you disappointed? When you pay attention to your self-talk, is it mostly negative? Guess what? You *are* a sinful person. But guess what? That's why Jesus came! When God looks at you through the lens of your faith in Jesus, he does not see all of your sin and guilt; he sees Jesus' sacrifice paid on your behalf. It's okay to admit we are sinners, but it is *not* okay to stay there with debilitating self-talk. It is too easy to live in the past and drown in our mistakes and guilt. We pray that you are able to see yourself the way God sees you—innocent, guiltless, pure, and stainless. God looks at you as if you had never sinned, because Jesus' righteousness is yours by grace though faith. We need to embrace our true identity in Jesus. Try saying this out loud: I am righteous in Jesus.

Resist Satan. Not only are we prone to negative self-talk, but Satan accuses us and piles on guilt trips. When this happens, remind Satan that Jesus has forgiven you of all of your sins and given his righteousness to you. Jesus defends you day and night. Rest in Jesus and resist the devil (James 4:7).

Faith alone. Our righteousness rests on our faith in Jesus. There is no work you can do that will make you more righteous or make God happier with you. Self-justification or boasting in your works is abolished. You can't earn your righteousness through good works. You don't have to weigh your "good" and "bad" deeds to see if God is happy with you today. We can simply say, "Thank you, God." That's so freeing, isn't it?

Good works. If you had to stand before the righteous God today and plead your case based on your works, you're in trouble. You would be declared guilty. But what if Jesus were to stand up to defend you? What if Jesus said, "I'll take their sin and guilt"? What if Jesus were to meet the righteous standards of God on your behalf? Are you guilty? Yes! Have you sinned? Yes! But through Jesus, are you now declared righteous? Yes! Are all charges against you dropped? Yes! Jesus stepped down from glory to take your guilt. May you rest in the truth of your identity in Christ: You are righteous.

Encouragement and Prayer by John-Paul and Matt: Point your phone's camera at the QR code and follow the link or go to youtube.com /@FindingFreedomInJesusBook.

Reflective Exercises for
Personal or Group Discussion to Embrace That You Are Righteous

1. Practice breathing exercises for three or four minutes each day. Breathe in: "his righteousness"; breathe out: "now mine." If you're in a small group, do the breathing together.

2. Go to YouTube, find a worship song with the theme of "righteous," and listen to it several times each day. If you're in a small group, sing the song together.

3. Looking back at the chapter, what did you learn that you didn't know previously?

4. Take some time to ponder the biblical definition of *righteous*: To be righteous means that God clears you of all charges, declares you not guilty, *and* allows you to receive Jesus' righteousness as your own through faith in Jesus. What part of the definition really speaks to you?

5. *Living out righteous*:
   a) Do you feel like you need to prove yourself to God, trying to earn your righteousness? As children, we are told that if we want anything in life, we have to work for it. Here's the good news: God sees Jesus' sacrifice on the cross instead of your sin. There is nothing you can add to the cross. We joyfully do good works out of gratitude. This week, concentrate on this: When you pray, read your Bible, go to church,

do evangelism, or do acts of social justice, you are doing them out of gratitude for the completed work of Jesus, *not* to earn anything from God.

b) Thinking about what we learned in this chapter about justice, name three specific ways to help the needy in your community and then try to put those into practice.

6. Take time to meditate on and pray through Genesis 15:6; Psalm 11:7; 2 Corinthians 5:21; and 1 Peter 2:24. Allow the Lord to open your heart to the truth that you are righteous in Jesus. You may want to choose one of these passages to memorize.

CHAPTER 11

Redeemed

*In him we have redemption through his blood, the
forgiveness of sins, in accordance with the riches of
God's grace.*

EPHESIANS 1:7

After Adam and Eve sinned, God asked them a simple but profound
question: "Where are you?" (Genesis 3:9). Our all-knowing God was
not asking because he didn't know the answer. He knew they had disobeyed him. He knew they were hiding because they were wrestling with
guilt and shame. Nevertheless, God pursued them. He didn't destroy
them; he didn't give up on them. He still loved, still cared, still pursued.

God's desire is always to redeem his wayward creation, to pay the
price to free us from our captivity to sin and death, even when we try
to hide from him. We are loved beyond measure. "Where are you?" is a

question God still asks each of us when we sin, hide, or wander away from him. Are you ready to be found and redeemed by your Creator?

Who am I? I am redeemed in Jesus. I can be transformed when I embrace that truth.

Testimony: Point your phone's camera at the QR code for a video testimony from Mia or go to youtube.com /@FindingFreedomInJesusBook.

I was so far gone and deep in a pit. There is no peace in the enemy's camp, and his goal is to drive you into your own demise. It was in my bedroom, bent over on the floor in the room next to my daughter playing in her room, that the enemy had gotten me almost to where he wanted me—dead. But God . . .

Redeemed in Our Culture

Maybe your understanding of redemption comes from shopping and coupons or from the expression "redeem the time." Another use of the term *redeemed* came just after the Civil War ended. Redemption, by definition, is the act of setting free, which is what happened in the South when former Black slaves were incorporated back into society as free men and women. At the same time, though, there were some White Southerners who sought to bring back White supremacy and reverse the freedoms that former slaves had experienced. This group ironically called their effort "the redemption movement," which is the opposite meaning of the term *redemption*. What a sad use of the term!

Although the Emancipation Proclamation in 1863 legally freed, or redeemed, slaves, the law could not be implemented in places still under Confederate control. As a result, slavery continued in some places. The end of slavery in the United States is commemorated as June 19, 1865, when Major General Gordon Granger brought news to about 250,000 slaves in Galveston Bay, Texas, that all enslaved people were now free, or redeemed. As of 2021, June 19 is celebrated as a national holiday known as Juneteenth, also known as Freedom Day or Jubilee Day.

In biblical times, slavery was deeply ingrained in ancient Greek and Roman cultures. Slaves were acquired through wars or as punishment for crimes, but others sold themselves into slavery to pay off debts. Some suggest that 30 percent of people were enslaved during the time of Jesus, which means fifteen million people were slaves. It's hard to grasp a number that enormous—representing a larger population than that of New York, Chicago, and Los Angeles combined! Although slavery in those cultures was not based on race, slaves were considered property rather than individuals with rights.

This background is essential for us to fully understand the meaning of the word *redeem* in Scripture because the Bible borrowed the term from the slave market to explain what God has done for us through Jesus' death.

What Does the Bible Say About Being Redeemed?

Redeemed in the Old Testament

When people experienced economic struggles during Old Testament times, they could sell their land, their possessions, or even themselves to others in order to pay their debts. When the indebted person obtained enough money, they could pay off the debts and buy back their land, property, or freedom. This buying back was referred to as "redeeming": "If one of your fellow Israelites becomes poor and sells some of their property, their nearest relative is to come and redeem what they have sold" (Leviticus 25:25). To redeem meant to pay the debt and set a person free. If someone did not redeem them, they were stuck in slavery. Slavery was not God's intention. He commanded the people to free any slave in the seventh year, the Year of Jubilee (Exodus 21:2). Human enslavement was not meant to be a permanent state.

God is the Redeemer. Although humans could redeem other humans or their property, God was the ultimate Redeemer: "They remembered that God was their Rock, that God Most High was their Redeemer" (Psalm 78:35). When his people found themselves in unfortunate circumstances, our all-powerful God acted as a redeemer. He heard, saw, and acted. As God's people, we are never left alone. We don't have to live in hopelessness. Rather, we should call out to and trust God, our Redeemer!

God's first act of redemption occurred after Adam and Eve sinned in the Garden of Eden. His solution is found in Genesis 3:21: "God made garments of skin for Adam and his wife and clothed them." We usually think that the garments resolved the problem of their nakedness, which it does, but what had to take place for God to make garments of skin? A sacrifice. An animal's blood was spilled. A price was paid for the sin of the first human beings, which foreshadowed Jesus' own blood, poured out to redeem humanity.

When Israel was enslaved and oppressed by Egypt, God redeemed, or freed, them from captivity. God saw and cared for their plight (Exodus 6:6). This story of redemption was retold over and over again throughout the Old Testament as a reminder that God was a Redeemer. Throughout the Old Testament, God redeemed his people from oppression, all kinds of distress, sin, and even death (Psalms 107; 119:134; 130:8; Hosea 13:14).

Why does God redeem? God redeemed because of his compassionate love for his people: "I have indeed seen the misery of my people in Egypt. I have heard them crying out because of their slave drivers, and I am concerned about their suffering. So I have come down to rescue them from the hand of the Egyptians and to bring them up out of that land into a good and spacious land" (Exodus 3:7–8). God always reached out to redeem—even when his people sinned against him. Why? Because he loved them. His love *compelled* him to act, as we see in John 3:16: "God so loved the world that he gave his one and only Son."

Redeemed for a purpose. After being redeemed by God, Israel was called to tell the wondrous story, obey his commands, and sing joyfully (Psalms 107:2; 119:134; Isaiah 24:14). God's redemptive actions were the basis for treating the oppressed, the foreigner, the orphan, and the widow with dignity and care (Deuteronomy 24:17). We respond to redemption with grace toward others so they may also experience God's redemption. The redeemed redeem.

Redeemed in the New Testament

Jesus the Redeemer. Even before Jesus' birth, John the Baptist's father prophesied that Jesus would redeem Israel (Luke 1:68–69). Although Israel expected the Messiah to physically redeem them from the political oppression of Rome, Jesus redeemed them from much more—not just physically but also spiritually. His redemption reached the Jewish people as well as surrounding nations and cultures: "With your blood you purchased for God persons from every tribe and language and people and nation" (Revelation 5:9). Jesus "gave himself as a ransom for all people" (1 Timothy 2:6). Jew and non-Jew alike could all be redeemed in Jesus.

Spiritually redeemed. Though we may not be physically enslaved and in need of redemption from physical slavery, we are all spiritually enslaved and in need of redemption from spiritual slavery: "All have sinned and fall short of the glory of God," and "The wages of sin is death" (Romans 3:23; 6:23). Disobedience to the Law of Moses meant that humans are guilty of sin and deserving of death. We need a Redeemer.

The payment. Jesus was willing to make the payment for us: "Christ redeemed us from the curse of the law by becoming a curse for us, for it is written: 'Cursed is everyone who is hung on a pole'" (Galatians 3:13). What payment did Jesus make to redeem those who were spiritually enslaved? The Old Testament expectation was a perfect and blemish-free animal sacrifice for sins. But Jesus took the place of an animal sacrifice. Jesus offered *himself* as a *sacrifice* on the cross: "You were redeemed . . . with the precious blood of Christ, a lamb without blemish or defect" (1 Peter 1:18–19). This was not a cost-cutting measure. No way! It was an excruciating, torturous, and costly payment. Jesus loved us so much that he paid the ultimate price to set us free, to redeem us.

Redeemed from. Jesus redeems us from all wickedness and from an empty way of life (Titus 2:14; 1 Peter 1:18). Jesus took the curse on himself and redeemed us from spiritual slavery to sin along with its guilt, shame, and death. As sinners, we seem to be without hope. We need a redeemer. This is what makes one of the Bible's most popular verses so powerful: "God so loved the world that he gave his one and only Son, that whoever believes in him shall not perish but have eternal life" (John 3:16). Jesus paid the price on our behalf because he loves us: "Christ loved us and gave himself up for us as a fragrant offering and sacrifice to God" (Ephesians 5:2). Through Jesus, "we have redemption, the forgiveness of sins" (Colossians 1:14). We have been redeemed *from* so much!

Redeemed to. Jesus redeemed us *from* living according to the world's sinful ways, but he also set us free *to* live according to God's ways. Jesus came "to redeem those under the law, that we might receive adoption to sonship" (Galatians 4:5). We are redeemed *from* spiritual slavery *to* become God's children. As in every family, there is a family code of conduct. Those who are redeemed should live like redeemed people—not like those trying to earn their redemption. No, Jesus has already done the earning part.

In response to Jesus' sacrificial death, we are asked to live appropriately: "You were bought at a price. Therefore honor God with your bodies," and be "eager to do what is good" (1 Corinthians 6:20; Titus 2:14). We respond to our redemption with faithful living—following our Redeemer, Jesus. Redemption transforms the way we live, walk, and talk.

The redeemed of the Lord should also be working to set other people free, to redeem those held captive in any way. Christians should be at the forefront of solving the problems of human trafficking, homelessness, poverty, demonic oppression, and the persecuted church internationally.

People should also experience our transformed lives in the way we do business in professional settings. If we have been redeemed, we ought not act or behave like those in our society who often lie, cheat, and steal for personal gain. We should "conduct [ourselves] in a manner worthy of the gospel of Jesus Christ (Philippians 1:27). We are called to live as the redeemed of the Lord through the power of the Holy Spirit.

Living Redeemed Today

I (Matt) have a friend who owns a steel business. His business isn't just about money; it's about ministry and redeeming those who work with him. He has hired a chaplain to minister to his whole employee base. In the last fifteen years, he has seen twenty-two employees come to faith in Jesus at his business. Because the Lord has redeemed his life, he is transformed—and not just on Sunday. He lives as a Christian businessman throughout the week. The redeemed of the Lord live differently.

Heavenly hope. Even though our Redeemer has paid the price to rescue us and set us free from our captivity to sin and death, our struggles will continue as long as we live: "We ourselves, who have the firstfruits of the Spirit, groan inwardly as we wait eagerly for our adoption to sonship, the redemption of our bodies" (Romans 8:23). One day in the future, we will finally experience our full redemption (Ephesians 1:14). We eagerly await this complete transformation of our redeemed life, when we will be completely set free from sin, skipping down the golden streets of heaven. Until then, we continue to present our hurts, habits, and hang-ups to our Redeemer, asking him to free us from their burden. Though we experience our redemption in part now, we will soon experience it completely for all of eternity

(Hebrews 9:12). Isaiah 35:9 confidently assures us, "No lion will be there, nor any ravenous beast; they will not be found there. But only the redeemed will walk there." I'm really looking forward to my full redemption!

Final Biblical Thoughts on Redeemed

The history of the world is also the history of God redeeming people, beginning with Adam and Eve, continuing throughout the Old Testament, and on to today. Because of his love, God's plan was to redeem humanity through his Son, Jesus. Just as slaves in the market-place of Jesus' day were set free when someone paid the ransom price, we humans are spiritually enslaved to sin and death and in need of redemption. We can't pay the price ourselves. Thankfully, Jesus paid the ultimate price to redeem us, sacrificing his own perfect and sinless life on the cross as our sacrificial Lamb. Jesus, the sinless God-man, was offered up for sinful humanity. We are not just redeemed *from* something; we are also redeemed *to* something. God redeems us *from* sin, curses, and death and redeems us *to* freedom, joyful singing, and God-honoring lives. When we walk in the redemption of Jesus Christ, we are able to experience the purpose God has for us on earth, helping others be redeemed from whatever enslaves them.

In one sentence, to be redeemed means that Jesus paid the price to free you from slavery to sin and shame, allowing you to live a God-honoring life.

Finding Freedom in Jesus

Who are you? God's child who is meant to be free. The Garden of Eden demonstrated that. But when sin entered the world, you became captive to sin, judgment, and death. Since our Redeemer God is loving and com-passionate, he sent Jesus to redeem you, to pay the ransom price of his own blood on the cross. Your shackles have been removed. The devil has no hold on you anymore. You have been set free; you are redeemed in Jesus. Did you catch all of that? You many want to read that paragraph again. It's powerful!

You are now free to be God's through faith, free to live the way God desires you to live (see chapter 6 on "free"), and free from the wrath and guilt of sin (see chapter 7 on "shame-free"). This is such good news, but sometimes hard to fully accept. When the lies and the Liar come, and they will, flood them with these truths: "Jesus is my Redeemer, and I am redeemed. There is nothing I can do to earn my redemption. This is who God says I am. I've been set free."

We often struggle with our self-worth, but do we understand the implications of our redemption? If Jesus, the perfect, sinless son of God was sacrificed to secure your redemption, then what is your value? What is your worth? Jesus died to redeem *you*—from spiritual enslavement to adoption as son or daughter (Galatians 4:5). What a transformation! You are of infinite value, loved beyond measure.

We are God's—completely and wholly his! "This is what the LORD says—he who created you, Jacob, he who formed you, Israel: 'Do not fear, for I have redeemed you; I have summoned you by name; you are mine'" (Isaiah 43:1). Jesus has redeemed you by name!

Encouragement and Prayer by John-Paul and Matt: Point your phone's camera at the QR code and follow the link or go to youtube.com /@FindingFreedomInJesusBook.

Reflective Exercises for
Personal or Group Discussion to Embrace That You Are Redeemed

1. Practice breathing exercises for three or four minutes each day. Breathe in: "bought with a price"; breathe out: "set free for God." If you're in a small group, do the breathing together.

2. Go to YouTube, find a worship song with the theme of "redeemed" (perhaps the old song "I've Been Redeemed"), and listen to it several times each day. If you're in a small group, sing the song together.

3. Looking back at the chapter, what did you learn that you didn't know previously?

4. Take some time to ponder the biblical definition of *redeemed*: To be redeemed means that Jesus paid the price to free you from slavery to sin and shame, paving the way for you to live a God-honoring life. What part of the definition really speaks to you?

5. *Living out redeemed*: How does the concept of "redeemed" and the truth that Jesus died to pay the price to set *you* free to change your self-talk and help you understand your self-worth? Take some time to jot down your thoughts on each of these transformations.

6. Take time to meditate on and pray through Psalm 78:35; Romans 8:23; Ephesians 5:2; Colossians 1:14; and 1 Peter 1:18–19. Allow the Lord to open your heart to the truth that you are redeemed in Jesus. You may want to choose one of these passages to memorize.

CHAPTER 12

Reconciled

*While we were God's enemies, we were reconciled to
him through the death of his Son.*

ROMANS 5:10

Brothers and sisters hold grudges. Spouses no longer talk to each
other. Neighbors have ongoing feuds. Political parties refuse to
communicate with one another. Race problems continue. Countries
are at war. It seems that hatred, hostility, and broken relationships are
everywhere. As a society, have we made any progress toward living
together in peace?

Spiritual problems run as deep as ever too. The church's witness
has led some to deconstruct their faith and leave the church. They are
tired of hypocrisy. Children have been victims of abuse inside and outside the church and may never fully trust God as a good Father.

Does God care? What is his solution to these relationship problems?
The answer is found in the term *reconciled*.

Who am I? I am reconciled in Jesus. I can be transformed when I embrace that truth.

Testimony: Point your phone's camera at the QR code for a video testimony from Cindy or go to youtube.com /@FindingFreedomInJesusBook.

The sinful decisions of a close friend destroyed our relationship and crippled my relationship with the Lord. It shattered my world, but I buried my feelings . . .

Reconciled in Our Culture

Our world is filled with hostility and broken relationships, and so the term *reconciled* is used a lot. We can reconcile disputes, broken marriages and friendships, and race issues. Even though *reconciled* is frequently used, disputes aren't always settled, friends and family remain unreconciled, and racial tensions persist. Anger, bitterness, and unforgiveness are more common in our culture than true reconciliation.

We need God's power to restore broken relationships. Without his help, we are too stubborn, prideful, and selfish. Let's turn to God's Word for a better understanding of the possibilities for biblical reconciliation in the church.

What Does the Bible Say About Being Reconciled?

Reconciled in the Old Testament

Intimate relationship. God created human beings in his image with the ability to communicate with him: "So God created mankind in his own image, in the image of God he created them; male and female he created them. God blessed them *and said to them . . ."* (Genesis 1:27–28, emphasis added). Don't skip too quickly over the phrase "and God said to them." God's direct communication with Adam and Eve in the garden signals that their relationship was intimate and good.

Broken relationship. Sin changed everything: "The LORD God called to the man, 'Where are you?' He answered, 'I heard you in the garden, and I was afraid because I was naked; so I hid'" (Genesis 3:9–10). Sin brought distance and fear between God and humans. A sign that the relationship was broken was hiding from him and avoiding communication. *Reconciled* simply means to restore a broken relationship. And Adam and Eve needed to be reconciled.

Reconciled. Have you wondered why the term *reconciled* doesn't show up hundreds of times in the Old Testament? It may surprise you that there is no specific Hebrew word for the English term *reconciliation*. The idea of reconciliation, though, is found everywhere. As you read the Old Testament you'll see this cycle: The Israelites sin, God provides a sacrificial system to forgive sin, and the relationship is restored. The term *atone*, which is related to *reconcile*, appears about ninety times in Exodus, Leviticus, and Numbers. The sacrificial system in the Law of Moses atoned for human sin, so that the broken relationship between God and humans could be restored. God didn't abandon sinners; he didn't destroy them. He loved them enough to forgive them and to put a system in place to reconcile the broken relationship.

God's love. God loved humans so much that he desired a relationship with them. It wasn't because God was lonely. The one God exists in three persons—the Trinity. Father, Son, and Spirit were and are in perfect fellowship. God created human beings in order have a personal relationship with them. When they sinned and broke that relationship, God still desired a relationship and continued to call them to return: "Return, Israel, to the LORD your God. Your sins have been your downfall" (Hosea 14:1). Though the Israelites were sinful and undeserving, God provided a way of atonement and reconciliation.

To see a vivid picture of God's yearning to restore the broken relationship, read the book of Hosea. Hosea was a prophet who was told by God, "Go, marry a promiscuous woman and have children with her, for like an adulterous wife this land is guilty of unfaithfulness to the LORD" (Hosea 1:2). His wife, Gomer, eventually left him, but God told Hosea, "Go, show your love to your wife again, though she is loved by another man and is an adulteress. Love her as the LORD loves the Israelites, though they turn to other gods" (3:1). In this living metaphor, Hosea was called to continue to love his wife, who symbolized the nation of Israel. Israel was the adulteress who committed idolatry, but God did not disown or abandon her. He continued to reach out, calling her to repentance and seeking to reconcile the broken relationship.

Messianic hope. The Old Testament foreshadowed the great act of reconciliation when God would send his Son Jesus to restore mankind to himself and fix all broken relationships. God took the initiative in reconciling broken relationships when he prophesied: "Out of Egypt I called my son" (Hosea 11:1), a text fulfilled by Jesus in the New Testament (Matthew 2:14–15).

Reconciled in the New Testament

The New Testament used the word *reconciled* to emphasize that God desired to restore the broken relationship with humanity. He not only wanted to forgive sins and credit Jesus' righteousness to believers, but he also desperately desired an intimate relationship with humanity.

Problem solved. What problem did Jesus solve? Well, as a result of sin, we were enemies of God: "Once you were alienated from God and were enemies in your minds because of your evil behavior. But now he has reconciled you by Christ's physical body through death to present you holy in his sight, without blemish and free from accusation" (Colossians 1:21–22). While the Old Testament sacrificial system was sufficient to atone for sins and restore the relationship between God and his people, it was temporary and looked ahead to a greater sacrifice for sin. Jesus' death on the cross fulfilled the sacrificial system: "God was reconciling the world to himself in Christ. . . . Be reconciled to God" (2 Corinthians 5:19–20; see also Hebrews 9:11–14).

Do we earn or deserve reconciliation? Of course not. The most amazing aspect of reconciliation is that God desires to restore his relationship with us while we are still sinning: "While we were God's enemies, we were reconciled to him through the death of his Son." (Romans 5:10). God truly loves us.

Peace. Reconciliation also brings peace to our formerly hostile relationship with God: "Since we have been justified through faith, we have peace with God through our Lord Jesus Christ" (Romans 5:1). Reconciliation means we now have an intimate, close, and peace-filled relationship with God.

Living Reconciled Today

I (John-Paul) was at the barbershop when a man began to ask his barber questions about why bad things happen to good people. He was angry with God. He had experienced so much hardship that he found it hard to have a relationship with God, saying there was no way that God is good. He had lost multiple family members and was suffering from a physical illness. The conversation kept going back and forth, until finally the barber pointed to me and said to the man, "Why don't you ask him about it. He's a pastor." I told him what the Bible says about suffering and hardship among believers. Bad things can happen to good people. Christians are not exempt from hardship. Through our conversation, he went from a man who was angry with God to a man who reconciled his relationship with God and still attends our church. God loves humanity at its worst in order to bring us to our best, to restore his relationship with us.

Human relationships reconciled. God also cares about broken relationships among humans: "If you are offering your gift at the altar and there remember that your brother or sister has something against you, leave your gift there in front of the altar. First go and be reconciled to them; then come and offer your gift" (Matthew 5:23–24). Love motivates us to restore broken relationships. It may not always be possible to restore broken relationships, but "as far as it depends on you, live at peace with everyone" (Romans 12:18). We should reach out, forgive, and do all we can to bring harmony and restoration to any broken relationship we have.

The term *reconciled* reminds us that our identity in Jesus includes a community aspect. We are part of something bigger than just ourselves. God has reconciled us to himself as individuals, but his desire is to reconcile us to all those around us, creating a community of believers who love one another and experience peace and unity instead of conflict and disunity.

Living Reconciled Today

Years ago, I (Matt) worked at a ministry in which two people did not get along. In fact, they didn't even talk to each other. They thought it was a problem just between the two of them. The truth is that it affected the entire ministry team and those we ministered to. Jesus said we should be known as people who love one another and who are unified (John 17). Let's put the *unity* back in comm-unity!

Racial reconciliation. God also desires racial reconciliation. The Jew-Gentile tensions in the first century may sound like the divisions we are familiar with today. When the New Testament was written, Jewish people called Gentiles "sinners," "unclean," and "dogs." Intense hostility and hatred defined the relationship. God's goal was to restore peace between races: "[Jesus] himself is our peace, who has made the two groups one and has destroyed the barrier, the dividing wall of hostility, by setting aside in his flesh the law with its commands and regulations. His purpose was to create in himself one new humanity out of the two, thus making peace, and in one body to reconcile both of them to God through the cross, by which he put to death their hostility" (Ephesians 2:14–16). All human division and all racial division should end in the church because God is the God of reconciliation. We still have work to do in this area, don't we?

Living Reconciled Today

I (John-Paul) will never forget preaching a sermon on racism and division in the body of Christ. I asked everyone who is struggling with racism to come to the altar and lay it at the feet of Jesus and ask him for forgiveness and restoration of broken relationships. Immediately, a White man walked to the front of the church and fell to his knees weeping. In a matter of moments, a myriad of races and ethnicities was represented at the altar. We were no longer alienated or hostile toward one another. We became one in Jesus and reconciled to one another. It's an ongoing battle in our diverse community, but we have to begin with a first difficult step.

The ministry of reconciliation. After our relationship with God is reconciled, God calls us to the ministry of reconciliation: "We are therefore Christ's ambassadors, as though God were making his appeal through us. We implore you on Christ's behalf: Be reconciled to God" (2 Corinthians 5:20). The reconciled help others find reconciliation. We seek out the lost and broken, those who don't know God. We share the good news of the gospel, the message of reconciliation and peace with God, so their lives can be transformed and relationships restored.

God's goal in restoring relationships is peace and unity (John 17:23). The goal is not just lack of hostility, but truly walking hand in hand with cooperation and in sincere unity—a peaceful world where we genuinely like one another. Wouldn't that be amazing! When we Christians reach this goal, the world will take notice. Our restored relationships and unity will testify to the world of God's love that is able to break down all barriers.

Final Biblical Thoughts on Reconciled

From the beginning of creation, as soon as the first humans sinned in the Garden of Eden, God provided a way to restore that broken relationship. He later provided a system of sacrifices in the Law of Moses to overcome the hostilities caused by sin. Hosea's unconditional love and forgiveness toward his unfaithful wife was a symbol of God's grace and compassion for his unfaithful people. He did not give up on them. God wanted to reconcile the world to himself despite their sin.

God loved the world so much that he sent Jesus to die on the cross, fulfilling and replacing the sacrificial system. Now, through faith in Jesus' death, human relationships with God can be restored. The hostility is taken away, and we have peace, friendship, and an intimate relationship with God. We have been reconciled in Christ.

There can also be reconciliation in human relationships. Because we are reconciled in Christ, we are empowered to do all we can to restore our own broken relationships with family, friends, and others. This includes the goal of racial reconciliation, modeled in the restored relationship between Jew and Gentile in the New Testament.

We are also given the ministry of reconciliation. The joy that comes from living in an intimate, restored relationship with God motivates us to share this good news with others. God wants the whole world to be reconciled in Christ, and we get to play an active role in his plan.

In one sentence, to be reconciled means that God restores your broken relationship with him through Jesus' death on the cross, empowering you to reconcile with others.

Finding Freedom in Jesus

We are both fathers of two children. When Matt's oldest son was three years old, he decided he was tired of Dad. He walked out of the house and headed down the street. He was running away. Yep, three years old! Matt ran to him, hugged him, held him in his arms, and kissed him. We would do anything to restore relationships with our children. Isn't God the same way with us?

Reconciled with God. If you ever wonder if God loves you, look at the lengths to which God went to restore your relationship. God sent Jesus to die for you—even while you were still a sinner. You were at your worst, but God loved you so much that he reached out to restore an intimate relationship with you. God loved humanity at its worst to bring us to our best. He didn't wait until we deserved it; he made the first move. He provided a way for reconciliation. Have you responded to him?

Reconciled human relationships. Reconciled people seek reconciliation in their human relationships, mirroring the reconciliation received from God. Do you have broken relationships in your family, with your friends and neighbors, or in the church? Is it time for you to make the first move? We often wait for the other to take the initiative, but God modeled true reconciliation by making the first move toward us.

Before we move on, we need to note two things: First, in the case of abuse, while forgiveness is always important, restoring the relationship is not always advised. Seek protection and good counsel. Boundaries are important and necessary for protection. Second, we cannot be reconciled with everyone since reconciliation is a two-way street. Both parties need to desire and work for reconciliation, and some people just don't want to restore broken relationships. As the apostle Paul wrote, "As far as it depends on you, live at peace with everyone" (Romans 12:18). We should do all we can, but sometimes it won't be enough. If someone refuses to reconcile with us, it doesn't mean we don't continue to pray for God's best for them.

True reconciliation in our human relationships can only take place when the Holy Spirit empowers us. Without his help, we are too stubborn, prideful, and selfish. Broken relationships are harmful since they often leave us feeling frustrated, angry, and alone. Reconciled relationships can transform anger, bitterness, resentment, judgment, hostility, and unforgiveness—along with the resulting stress, anxiety, and high blood pressure—into peace, empathy, goodwill, and friendship. To reconcile a broken relationship is difficult but worth it for so many reasons.

Racial reconciliation. If God's desire was to reconcile the hatred between Jew and Gentile in the first century, it is certainly his desire to reconcile the races today. Imagine if we put this into practice. Imagine if the hostility we experience between races were to end. Christians should be at the forefront of the racial reconciliation movement. Jesus' death on the cross seeks full reconciliation—with God and with each other. We are called to participate in racial reconciliation, and it begins with small steps. What is your church doing in this area? What are you doing?

Evangelism and missions. Our reconciliation with God should also lead to evangelistic and missionary zeal, since we are ambassadors of reconciliation. We should care about those who still have a broken relationship with God. God's ultimate desire is that the hostility between every human being and God is reconciled, and we play an important role in that mission: "God was reconciling the world to himself in Christ, not counting people's sins against them. And he has committed to us the message of reconciliation" (2 Corinthians 5:19). This verse is not just for missionaries; it's for every one of us. Are you reaching your family, friends, and neighbors with the message of reconciliation? Are you supporting missionaries who are called to go to other cultures?

Reconciliation should lead us to extend empathy and forgiveness, to deepen relationships, and to engage with those with whom we disagree. In our deeply divided world, we need God's help and power to forgive, love, and seek reconciliation.

Encouragement and Prayer by John-Paul and Matt: Point your phone's camera at the QR code and follow the link or go to youtube.com /@FindingFreedomInJesusBook.

Reflective Exercises for
Personal or Group Discussion to Embrace That You Are Reconciled

1. Practice breathing exercises for three or four minutes each day. Breathe in: "relationship with God restored"; breathe out: "restoring relationships." If you're in a small group, do the breathing together.

2. Go to YouTube, find a worship song with the theme of "reconciled," and listen to it several times each day. If you're in a small group, sing the song together.

3. Looking back at the chapter, what did you learn that you didn't know previously?

4. Take some time to ponder the biblical definition of *reconciled*: To be reconciled means that God restores your

broken relationship with him through Jesus' death on the cross, empowering you to reconcile with others. What part of the definition really speaks to you?

5. *Living out reconciled*:
    a) God's love, grace, and compassion are clearly seen in his effort to restore the broken relationship with you. He paid the highest price in sending Jesus to die on the cross. The suffering and agony he experienced is a powerful invitation from God: "Be reconciled to God." He is inviting you to run to him to restore a peace-filled, intimate relationship. Take time to thank God for the gift of your reconciliation, for the gift of his friendship. Have you been reconciled to God? He awaits you.

    b) God is also inviting you to go to that person with whom you have a broken or damaged relationship in order to be reconciled to them through Jesus. Why do we expect others to be perfect when we ourselves are broken? God reached out to us while we were still sinners; shouldn't we do the same? Think of a specific damaged relationship you have. Just as God took the first step in our reconciliation, are you ready to take the first step toward reconciling with your brother or sister? Are you ready to put away anger, bitterness, hurt, and unforgiveness? What can you do this week to improve the chances of reconciliation? Do you need to send them a text, set up a coffee date, or ask for their forgiveness? Can you start with simply praying for them?

c) Racial reconciliation—so much still needs to be done here. One way to begin is to ask others about their stories and the challenges they've faced because of their race or culture. When we understand the different races and cultures better, it helps us love, forgive, and accept those who look different from us.

6. Take time to meditate on and pray through Hosea 3:1; Joel 2:12–13; Romans 5:10; and 2 Corinthians 5:19–20. Allow the Lord to open your heart to the truth that you are reconciled in Christ. You may want to choose one of these passages to memorize.

CHAPTER 13

Saved

Salvation is found in no one else, for there is no other name under heaven given to mankind by which we must be saved.

ACTS 4:12

Have you ever felt like you were drowning in your troubles: "Save me, O God, for the waters have come up to my neck" (Psalm 69:1)? As we write this chapter, John-Paul's mother-in-law is in the hospital with COVID-19. "Help, Lord!" There are times when only the Lord can save. Not only do we need the Lord to save those who are physically sick, but we also need him to save those who are spiritually sick. Both of us are active in evangelism and often pray, "Lord, please save this person."

Who am I? I am saved in Jesus. I can be transformed when I embrace that truth.

Growing up, church was all I knew, but I didn't have a relationship with God. When I was twenty-one, I was going to clubs and drinking a lot. My life was spiraling . . .

Saved in Our Culture

Saved means to keep safe or rescue from harm or danger. The term is used in many ways in our culture. One might save a person's life, save money, or save a friend from religious oppression. A savior could be a great political leader or an athlete who heroically wins a game in the last second. Since the word is so broadly used in our culture, we will head straight to the Bible.

What Does the Bible Say About Being Saved?

Saved in the Old Testament

God saves. God saved his people in the Old Testament. The clearest example was the exodus when God saved the Israelites out of captivity in Egypt and brought them to the promised land (Exodus 14:30). It was a miraculous salvation, as Moses showed God's true power to Pharaoh through ten plagues, culminating in Passover, when the first-born Hebrew children were saved.

God saved Israel from various physical and spiritual dangers: the hand of the enemy, natural disasters, evil people, sins, and death (1 Samuel 4:3; 10:19; Psalms 59:2; 39:8; 72:13). In the book of Judges, whenever a foreign nation oppressed God's people, God raised up a judge—a leader to save and rescue his people (2:18). Even though human judges saved the nation, it was really God who saved them (7:2).

God lovingly saves. God was known as the Savior who chose to save his people because of his love and faithfulness (Psalms 6:4; 57:3). Not only did God love enough to save, but he was also powerful enough to save: "The LORD your God is with you, the Mighty Warrior who saves. He will take great delight in you; in his love he will no longer rebuke you, but will rejoice over you with singing" (Zephaniah 3:17). Think about that: God is the Mighty Warrior who loves and delights in you so much that he saves you *and* sings over you!

Messianic salvation. While God was the Savior in the Old Testament, the prophets talked about a future messianic Savior: "Say to Daughter Zion, 'See, your Savior comes!'" (Isaiah 62:11). This messianic Savior would save not only Israel but also "everyone who calls on the name of the LORD" (Joel 2:32). God desires to save everyone in the world: "Turn to me and be saved, all you ends of the earth; for I am God, and there is no other" (Isaiah 45:22). This expectation leads us to examine the arrival of our messianic Savior, Jesus.

Saved in the New Testament

Jesus saves. In 1935, when Biola University was located in the center of Los Angeles and known as the Bible Institute of Los Angeles, a large red neon sign was installed in 1935 that vividly projected the message "Jesus Saves." The red sign was not by accident. Red signifies the blood of Jesus, and the words shone brightly as a beacon of hope pointing the city to salvation in Jesus. The 7-foot neon sign can still be seen today atop what is now the Ace Hotel in downtown Los Angeles.[1]

The terms *saved* and *salvation* are at the center of the gospel message. Prior to Jesus' birth, an angel revealed to Joseph in a dream that *saved* would be the central message of Jesus' ministry: "[Mary] will give birth to a son, and you are to give him the name Jesus, because he will *save* his people from their sins" (Matthew 1:21, emphasis added). The name Jesus in Hebrew means "God saves," or "Yahweh is salvation." At

Jesus' birth, an angel declared the salvation message to the shepherds: "Today in the town of David a *Savior* has been born to you; he is the Messiah, the Lord" (Luke 2:11, emphasis added).

Saved because. God saves us because he is a God of love, grace, and mercy (Ephesians 2:5; Titus 3:5). God sent Jesus because he wanted the world to be saved: "The Son of Man came to seek and to save the lost" (Luke 19:10). This message of salvation should be proclaimed to everyone because God desired "all people to be saved and to come to a knowledge of the truth" (1 Timothy 2:4). He is not just the Savior of Israel but the "Savior of the world" (John 4:42), all the way "to the ends of the earth" (Acts 13:47).

Saved from. God saved us from the guilt and wrath that results from sin (Romans 5:9). If not for God's saving action in Jesus, we would all experience eternal death because of sin. We are fallen beings, but God wants to save us from eternal separation from him. Not only are we saved to live eternally in heaven with Jesus, but our life here on earth is enhanced when we are saved (see chapter 16 on "alive"). We are saved from meaningless lives because Jesus came to bring us abundant and full life in the present—a life filled with joy, peace, purpose, and love (John 10:10). Our lives aren't perfect, but with Jesus, we can find joy even in the toughest circumstances.

The irony of salvation is that the only way to save one's life is to lose it: "Whoever wants to save their life will lose it, but whoever loses their life for me will find it" (Matthew 16:25). When Jesus saved me (John-Paul), it changed the entire trajectory of my life. I am saved for all of eternity, but in a real sense, Jesus saved me from myself here in this life—from a life filled with self-seeking desires to a life filled with purpose as I walk with Jesus and serve him. The amazing thing is that when we serve, we find true joy and happiness.

Saved by. How is a person saved? We are saved when we repent of our sins (2 Corinthians 7:10). To repent simply means to reverse the direction of one's life, to go from walking away from God to walking toward God, from living a sinful life to following after Jesus, from following the world's ways to following God's ways. We are saved by faith, which is the same Greek word that can also be translated "believe": "Believe in the Lord Jesus, and you will be saved" (Acts 16:31). When we believe in Jesus, we put our *full* trust in him. It's not just an intellectual agreement that Jesus is Lord, it is a commitment to following Jesus. We should never think we are saved through something we do ourselves, "for it is by grace you have been saved, through faith—and this is not from yourselves, it is the gift of God" (Ephesians 2:8). Works cannot save us.

Saved through. We live in a world that suggests there are many ways to heaven, but that is not the message of the Bible. We are saved only and exclusively through Jesus: "Salvation is found in no one else, for there is no other name under heaven given to mankind by which we must be saved" (Acts 4:12). This is not a popular message in our postmodern world, but it is truth. Jesus is the only way to God.

Living Saved Today

A man who goes to my (John-Paul's) church grew up without a father—a void that led him to the Nation of Islam in his search for identity and belonging. As a Muslim, he was familiar with Jesus as a man but not as a Savior or Messiah who forgives sins. His Christian friend gave him a Bible, and he began to read it. Psalm 68:5 spoke to him: God is "a father to the fatherless." He read more about Jesus and learned that he was more than a man. He was the way to gain access to a loving relationship with God the Father. He learned that Jesus died for his sins. In his words, "Jesus rescued me from fatherlessness and eternal separation from God the Father. Now, I'm living a life full of God's fatherly love with the confidence that I will spend eternity with my heavenly Father."

Saved for. Being saved is not the finish line, but rather the starting line. We will only find life, purpose, hope, and meaning when we completely commit our lives to following Jesus' way. We can't live in whatever way we want. Jesus "has saved us and called us to a holy life" (2 Timothy 1:9). We don't work *for* our salvation, since it is entirely by grace through faith (Ephesians 2:8–9), but we do work *out* our salvation (Philippians 2:12). We "make every effort to be found spotless, blameless and at peace with [God]" (2 Peter 3:14).

Faith always leads to faithfulness. Saved people live different lives because they are now in relationship with their Savior. The goal of the Christian's life is to become more and more like Jesus—more loving, more caring, more serving, more just, and more compassionate. Once we are saved, we are like the red neon sign at Biola University—we become ambassadors of the message of salvation: "Whoever turns a sinner from the error of their way will save them from death and cover over a multitude of sins" (James 5:20). What a wonderful mission God has given each one of us, helping others to be saved!

Saved or healed? Physical healing and spiritual salvation are related because salvation is wholistic and not just spiritual. In fact, the Greek term *sozo*, "to save," is sometimes translated "to heal." External physical healing may be a sign of inner spiritual saving. For example, Isaiah 35 says that God "will come to save you" (v. 4), and explains what *save* means by listing various healings: "Then will the eyes of the blind be opened and the ears of the deaf unstopped. Then will the lame leap like a deer, and the mute tongue shout for joy" (vv. 5–6).

Who eventually fulfilled these miraculous healings? Jesus. Jesus summarized his saving ministry: "The blind receive sight, the lame walk, those who have leprosy are cleansed, the deaf hear, the dead are raised, and the good news is proclaimed to the poor" (Matthew 11:5). Jesus healed both physically and spiritually.

Another example of healing came when a bleeding woman touched Jesus' cloak: "Jesus turned and saw her. 'Take heart, daughter,' he said, 'your faith has healed you.' And the woman was healed at that moment"

(Matthew 9:22). The term translated "healed" is from the Greek root word *sozo*, "to save." When Jesus heals her, he is not only saving her from *physical* disease but also *spiritually* saving her soul from sin. The disciples also at times physically healed people as a sign of an internal spiritual salvation (Acts 14:9). God continues to physically heal people today, although not all are healed physically in this life. We pray for healing and trust God's sovereignty, whether or not we experience physical healing, knowing that one day, all will be completely healed in heaven. Whether or not we are healed (or saved) physically here on earth, we can most certainly be healed (or saved) spiritually.

Saved from demons. Finally, the term *saved* is found when Jesus saves, or cures, those who are demonized or demon-possessed: "Those who had seen it told the people how the demon-possessed man had been cured" (Luke 8:36; the NIV translates the Greek term *sozo* as "cured"). Jesus saves this demonized man who lived among the tombs by driving out the demons. He saves him from both physical and spiritual danger.

In Matthew 12, Jesus taught a parable about driving out a demon ("impure spirit" in the NIV): "When an impure spirit comes out of a person, it goes through arid places seeking rest and does not find it. Then it says, 'I will return to the house I left.' When it arrives, it finds the house unoccupied, swept clean and put in order. Then it goes and takes with it seven other spirits more wicked than itself, and they go in and live there. And the final condition of that person is worse than the first" (vv. 43–45).

Pay attention to the importance of being spiritually healthy. When the demon left the man and couldn't find someone else to occupy, it returned to the person it had left, hoping he was unoccupied, or empty, so it could demonize him again. Because Jesus wasn't fully occupying the person's life, the demons returned, and it was worse the second time. One cannot partially follow Jesus—it's all or nothing.

Jesus is my Savior. It may sound cliché to say that Jesus is my Savior, but when you look at the biblical evidence, you see that Jesus has saved me from so much. I can only imagine what my life would be like if Jesus had not come to save me personally, and I'm thankful that he has used me to reach others so they can also be saved to an abundant life now and an eternal life in heaven. I am saved in Jesus, and he has completely transformed my life.

Final Biblical Thoughts on Saved

To be saved means that God delivers us from the bondage and penalty of sin's consequences. We are saved from sin, guilt, and death, and sometimes healed from physical diseases or released from demons. We are saved by grace through faith, but our faith always leads to faithful living. Jesus offers us salvation so that we can have a second chance at life, an opportunity to experience a spiritual rebirth into a full and abundant life lived in the power of the Holy Spirit. This new life will never end since we are saved to live eternally with Jesus in heaven.

In one sentence, to be saved means that you are delivered from sin, shame, and death by grace through faith, receiving all that the Savior has for you both now and eternally.

Finding Freedom in Jesus

Salvation is not just a doctrinal truth to understand but should be fully experienced in our lives. Life is sometimes difficult, isn't it? It helps me to remember that I'm not alone in these difficult times. The Lord is with me: "The LORD is close to the brokenhearted and saves those who are crushed in spirit" (Psalm 34:18). When tough times come, and they will, we must continually hope in our Savior: "Why, my soul, are you downcast? Why so disturbed within me? Put your hope in God, for I will yet praise him, my Savior and my God" (Psalm 42:5). Because Jesus saves, heals, and drives out demons, we can keep on hoping and believing.

What does it mean to believe in Jesus in order to be saved? Our churches sometimes reduce the meaning of salvation, with dire consequences. It is not enough to simply say, "I accept Jesus as my Savior."

Salvation begins with believing in Jesus as our Savior and repenting of our sins, but that's just the beginning of the process. It's not just head knowledge but also a commitment of the entire person. Some say, "When we believe in our hearts, we are saved." But this reduces the truth that belief is a 100 percent commitment to the ways of Jesus—with not just our hearts but also our minds, hands, eyes, tongues, and feet. The whole person is involved in belief. What our brains think, what our eyes look at, where our feet take us—in all these things we are called to follow Jesus with our whole lives.

Those who are saved turn away from living and thinking the way that comes naturally to us in this evil world and instead turn to living and thinking the way Jesus desires. We choose God's ways over the world's ways. Being saved affects how we talk, what movies we watch, what music we listen to, what people we hang out with—our lives are completely transformed.

As we saw in Jesus' parable about the demonized man in Matthew 12, it is important to fully believe in Jesus with our entire lives—to be fully occupied by Jesus. Without Jesus in our lives, we open ourselves up to all kinds of destructive evil. Have you believed in Jesus for salvation? Does your lifestyle match your belief?

Who am I? I am one in whom God, the Mighty Warrior, delights. He loves me so much that he sings over me and saves me (Zephaniah 3:17). Think about that: God delights in you so much that he sings over you!

Encouragement and Prayer by John-Paul and Matt: Point your phone's camera at the QR code and follow the link or go to youtube.com /@FindingFreedomInJesusBook.

Reflective Exercises for
Personal or Group Discussion to
Embrace That You Are Saved

1. Practice breathing exercises for three or four minutes each day. Breathe in: "saved by faith"; breathe out: "now and forever." If you're in a small group, do the breathing together.

2. Go to YouTube, find a worship song with the theme of "saved," and listen to it several times each day. If you're in a small group, sing the song together.

3. Looking back at the chapter, what did you learn that you didn't know previously?

4. Take some time to ponder the biblical definition of *saved*: To be saved means that you are delivered from sin, shame, and death by grace through faith, receiving all that the Savior has for you both now and eternally. What part of the definition really speaks to you?

5. *Living out saved*:
   a) Spend time on your knees in prayer, thanking God for your salvation. Where would you be now if it weren't for Jesus' saving touch on your life? Write down your testimony story of salvation *from* and *to*. With whom could you share your testimony?
   b) Are you tempted to take advantage of God's grace? We are saved by grace through faith, but we are saved to a life that faithfully follows our Savior. If

someone followed you all week, what evidence would they see that would convince them that you've been saved by Jesus?

c) To what did God save you? Besides holiness, part of our mission is to share the message of salvation with others. With whom could you share the message? "Whoever turns a sinner from the error of their way will save them from death and cover over a multitude of sins" (James 5:20). Think of two specific people and begin to pray for them and think of ways you can share with them in both words and actions.

6. Take time to meditate on and pray through Isaiah 45:22; Zephaniah 3:17; Matthew 1:21; 16:25; and Ephesians 2:8. Allow the Lord to open your heart to the truth that you are saved in Christ. You may want to choose one of these passages to memorize.

CHAPTER 14

Holy

We have been made holy through the sacrifice of the body of Jesus Christ once for all.

HEBREWS 10:10

"Holy, holy, holy is the Lord God Almighty" comes from Revelation 4:8. It is a song sung by—this may sound weird—four creatures in heaven, and they sing it continually for all of eternity. The picture is one where honor and praise is focused on God alone, who is like no other being. This unusual scene is fitting for God because he is holy.

What isn't fitting is the idea that *I* am holy in Jesus. What? Yes, that's what the Bible says: I am holy. I struggle to believe that *I* am holy. My experience with sin tells me the opposite. I'm a sinner. Once again, it's crucial to have a biblical understanding of our identity in Christ in order to embrace the truth of who we are in Jesus.

Who am I? I am holy in Jesus. I can be transformed when I embrace that truth.

Testimony: Point your phone's camera at the QR code for a video testimony from Patrick or go to youtube.com /@FindingFreedomInJesusBook.

I'm from South Carolina, where we practice cultural Christianity. I was a church kid. I was almost holy by default. Almost . . .

Holy in Our Culture

Our culture borrows many Christian concepts because of our history. Even though the term *holy* may not be used, the concept of "holy" is seen, for example, in events such as weddings and funerals. The term *holy* means set apart, and these events are set apart as special and dignified, even by those who are not religious. Let's turn to the Bible to understand the fuller meaning of the term.

What Does the Bible Say About Being Holy?

Holy in the Old Testament

God is holy. The word *holy* is used more than five hundred times in the Old Testament (NIV). God alone was truly holy: "Holy, holy, holy is the LORD Almighty; the whole earth is full of his glory" (Isaiah 6:3). God's holiness means that God is unique: "There is no one holy like the LORD" (1 Samuel 2:2). God is completely different than everything and everyone else in all of creation. His character is holy, and all his ways are holy (Psalm 77:13).

What does holy mean? The word *holy* means "set apart." God is completely sinless and morally pure, so he is set apart from sinful humans. Although only God is holy in character, anything that is devoted to or set apart for God—for his service or to worship him—is called holy in the Bible. The city of Jerusalem, the sanctuary, the temple, and the various instruments used for worshiping God were all called holy. They were set apart for God's purposes. We will focus our attention in this chapter on the identity of *people* as holy.

Humans become holy. God is perfectly holy, but humans are sinful. After Isaiah's vision of the holy throne room of God, he admitted that he was unholy: "'Woe to me!' I cried. 'I am ruined! For I am a man of unclean lips'" (Isaiah 6:5). Since God is sinless and humans are sinful, how can humans be called holy? God's people could become holy only because God chose them and made them holy: "I am the LORD, who made you holy" (Leviticus 22:32). Out of all the people in the world, God chose the children of Israel to be holy, or set apart, to serve and follow him. When God's people were called holy, it meant they were set apart from all the other nations and dedicated to serving and following only God.

Holy living. The Israelites were holy, but they were also commanded to respond by living holy lives: "Be holy, because I am holy" (Leviticus 11:44). God was the standard of holiness, and the Law of Moses and its commands showed the Israelites how to reflect God's holy character in their lives. When God's people obeyed his commands, they reflected his holy character.

Why was it important to live holy lives? Living a holy life was honoring to God and was a way to worship him: "Exalt the LORD our God and worship at his footstool; he is holy" (Psalm 99:5). Living a holy life also served as a witness to foreign nations so that they could also find and follow God: "Then the nations will know that I am the LORD, declares the Sovereign LORD, when I am proved holy *through you* before their eyes" (Ezekiel 36:23, emphasis added). Notice the phrase "through you." The people's holy living witnessed to the nations that God is the Holy One. They were to act differently from the nations around them by separating themselves from all that was unholy, sinful, and worldly and by following God's commands. When they did this, foreigners would be attracted to following God.

Israel's unholiness. Unfortunately, the children of Israel did not always honor God with holy living. They sinned by breaking the commands and committed idolatry by worshiping pagan gods. Instead of being set apart from foreigners, they intermingled and even married them (Ezra 9:2). That's the opposite of holy. Isaiah painted a bleak picture: "Woe to the sinful nation, a people whose guilt is great, a brood of evildoers, children given to corruption! They have forsaken the LORD; they have spurned the Holy One of Israel and turned their backs on him" (Isaiah 1:4). God's holiness demanded holiness from his people. When they did not live holy lives, God disciplined, or judged, them in order to bring them back to himself in repentance. God's goal was always restoration.

Future hope. Isaiah prophesied that Israel would experience a future restoration, a time when they would repent and return to God. When this happens, they "will be called the Holy People" (Isaiah 62:12), and "a highway will be there; it will be called the Way of Holiness; it will be for those who walk on that Way. The unclean will not journey on it; wicked fools will not go about on it" (35:8). God would empower his people to reflect his holiness to the world. Those prophecies were fulfilled in the New Testament, when a new way of holiness appeared through the internal guidance and empowerment of the Holy Spirit rather than by means of the external commands found in the Law of Moses.

Holy in the New Testament

Jesus is holy. The Old Testament revealed that God is holy, and the New Testament agreed and also added that Jesus is holy. The angels announced that a Holy One would be born to Mary, and the demons correctly understood that Jesus was "the Holy One of God" (Mark 1:24; Luke 1:35). Since Jesus is God, he is holy.

Christians are holy. Just as the people of Israel were chosen to be holy, Christians are now "a chosen people, a royal priesthood, a holy nation, God's special possession" (1 Peter 2:9). How were Christians made holy? "We have been made holy through the sacrifice of the body of Jesus Christ once for all" (Hebrews 10:10). Christians no longer needed to perform the sacrifices found in the Law of Moses because Jesus is the final and perfect sacrifice on the cross.

Believers in Jesus are holy. They are not holy because they are sinless, but rather because Jesus died for them: "Christ loved the church and gave himself up for her to make her holy, cleansing her by the washing with water through the word, and to present her to himself as a radiant church, without stain or wrinkle or any other blemish, but holy and blameless" (Ephesians 5:25–27). Let that sink in.

Who am I in Jesus? Holy. Radiant. Without stain. Without wrinkle. Without blemish. Blameless.

Jesus lived the sinless life we could not live and paid the price we could not pay, so that we may be holy. We are holy because of what Jesus did, not through our own effort, works, or achievements.

Holy transformation. When we think of what we used to be like and the transformation we experience through Jesus, it is a drastic change: "Neither the sexually immoral nor idolaters nor adulterers nor men who have sex with men nor thieves nor the greedy nor drunkards nor slanderers nor swindlers will inherit the kingdom of God. And that is what some of you were. But you were washed, you were sanctified, you were justified in the name of the Lord Jesus Christ and by the Spirit of our God" (1 Corinthians 6:9–11). We were stuck deep in the mud, but Jesus sanctified us, which is a theological word for "made us holy." The unholy are transformed to be holy in Christ.

Living Holy Today

God changes lives. Matt's classes and John-Paul's church contain people who used to be like those Paul described in 1 Corinthians 6:9–11. We have former drunkards, former gang bangers, former drug and alcohol addicts, former prisoners, former abusers, former atheists, former Buddhists—former everythings! Matt had a student who used to be in a gang in Los Angeles. He was a bad dude. He sold drugs and had killed a man. Now, though, through faith in Jesus, he is holy, set apart by God. What an amazing transformation!

Holy living. We are holy, but it doesn't mean we can make light of sin or exploit our identity as holy. We should reflect God's holy character in our daily lives: "Just as he who called you is holy, so be holy in all you do; for it is written: 'Be holy, because I am holy'" (1 Peter 1:15–16). Holy people are called to live holy lives: "God did not call us to be impure, but to live a holy life" (1 Thessalonians 4:7). Our identity in Christ is holy, but we are called to grow in holiness and strive to be more like Jesus every day. To use theological words, we are already sanctified—holy—and engaged in the process of sanctification—being made holy. We are holy, but being made holy. It may sound odd, but it is biblically true.

Set apart from sin. When we put into practice our identity as holy people, we are set apart *from* something and *to* something. Christians are set apart *from* evil. Though the Roman believers to whom Paul wrote used to live lives of sin, Paul urged them to change: "Just as you used to offer yourselves as slaves to impurity and to ever-increasing wickedness, so now offer yourselves as slaves to righteousness leading to holiness" (Romans 6:19). We change from an impure, sinful way of life to a holy, or pure, way of life, modeled after Jesus. It includes setting apart our bodies from every kind of sin: "There must not be even a hint of sexual immorality, or of any kind of impurity, or of greed, because these are improper for God's holy people" (Ephesians 5:3). We are set apart *from* evil.

Set apart to obedience. We are set apart *from* sin, but we are also set apart *to* obedience: "As God's chosen people, holy and dearly loved, clothe yourselves with compassion, kindness, humility, gentleness and patience. Bear with each other and forgive one another if any of you has a grievance against someone. Forgive as the Lord forgave you. And over all these virtues put on love" (Colossians 3:12–14). Holy people have holy character traits and do good works. We are forgiving and loving. We should stand out in this dark, evil, hate-filled world as "a holy temple in the Lord" (Ephesians 2:21). We are witnesses to God's holy character, and we honor God's name through holy living. Others should be able to tell by the way we live that we are Christians.

Living Holy Today

When my wife and I (Matt) were missionaries in Spain, a Swedish woman said, "There is something different about you. What is it?" She saw that we lived differently than those around us. We invited her to our home and talked with her for eight hours about Jesus. Jesus is the reason we are different. She was attracted to the light of Jesus shining through our lives. That is exactly how God desires to reach the world. We live for him and reflect his holy character, and as a result, the people we encounter are attracted to Jesus. In a world that thinks Christians are hypocrites and judgmental, our kindness and love for others ought to reflect the light and love of Jesus.

Help! Paul taught that holy living meant our lives shouldn't have even a hint of sexual immorality, and that we are called to be forgiving, loving, giving, and more. Wow, that sounds impossible, doesn't it? Yes, it is impossible! In fact, we *can't* overcome sin and live holy lives—on our own. We need help, and thankfully, we have help.

First, the Word of God, the Bible, helps us know what a holy life looks like: "Sanctify them by the truth; your word is truth" (John 17:17). As we read the Bible, and learn what holiness is, its truth teaches us how to live. A devotional life is not performed out of habit or to check off a box to show that we've completed it; it is performed to grow in knowledge of our Lord's character so that we might imitate his holiness.

Second, the Holy Spirit helps us live holy lives. We are "sanctified by the Holy Spirit" (Romans 15:16). There is no transformation without dedication—and the Spirit's help, of course.

Heavenly hope. Who am I? I am holy in Christ right now, and I am called to be transformed to live a holy life, set apart *from* sin and set apart *to* godly living. It will be a continual struggle to experience these truths because we continue to sin, don't we? Is there any hope? Yes, there is. In heaven, the living creatures will cry out day and night for ever and ever, "Holy, holy, holy is the Lord God Almighty" (Revelation 4:8), but guess who else will be there in the throne room? You and I! You will also be there, completely holy. "Let us rejoice and be glad and give him glory! For the wedding of the Lamb has come, and his bride has made herself ready. Fine linen, bright and clean, was given her to wear" (Revelation 19:7–8). You and I are the bride of Christ, and we will be clean and holy, 100 percent without sin. We are holy right now in Christ, but someday we will be completely holy. We will be dressed in white, without stain, without sin, worshiping the Holy One who died to make us holy, forever and ever.

Final Biblical Thoughts on Holy

Holiness is a divine attribute—God is set apart from all others. God is holy; human beings are not holy. Since God in all three persons (Father, Son, and Spirit) is holy and completely set apart from sin, he can't be in relationship with sinful humans. God solved that problem by giving his holiness to persons through faith. Israel was not holy because of their good works, but because God chose them to be holy by setting them apart from the other nations. Part of Israel's holiness was to live as a holy, or set apart, nation that followed God's holy law.

Jesus is the embodiment of God's holiness who makes unholy humans holy through his death on the cross. God couldn't just ignore human sin because his holiness demands holiness in his followers. By sending his Son to take sin's penalty, God made a way for his holy demands to be met in Jesus. At the moment of belief, Christians become holy in Christ; they are radiant, without stain, and blameless. There is nothing more we can do to make us more holy. I am holy in Christ through faith.

Just as the Israelites were called to holy living, Christians are called to a holy lifestyle. Being holy naturally leads to holy living. Christians are sanctified and yet growing in sanctification. A good tree must bear good fruit. We are set apart from the ways of the world. We stand out. We imitate Jesus through the power of the Holy Spirit, walking as he walked, avoiding temptation and sin, and living lives of service, love, and righteousness. Those who are holy are wholly devoted to God and his ways. We offer our lives in service and sacrifice to others in order to make God's name great in this dark, evil world.

In one sentence, to be holy in Jesus means that you are set apart *from* sin and *to* obedience to God.

Finding Freedom in Jesus

When we believe in Jesus, we are transformed from unholy to holy. We are set apart from this world and dedicated to God. There is nothing I can add to make me more holy—not works, not prayer, not church attendance, nothing. Are you able to accept that you are holy through faith in Jesus, or are you still trying to prove yourself to God? Be sure to take time daily to thank God for the gift of holiness.

We are holy, and yet growing in holiness. Yes, we will make mistakes and commit sin, but we keep trusting Jesus and the Spirit's power to transform us: "He who began a good work in you will carry it on to completion until the day of Christ Jesus" (Philippians 1:6). We forsake sin and the world and live a godly way of life, following the example Jesus set for us. Are you ever tempted to give up hope that you'll ever live a holy life? Be sure to see the reflections below for practical ways to keep growing in holiness.

We are holy, but we don't think of ourselves as better than others. We can stay humble because we know that our holiness is a gift from God and not the result of anything we've done. Christians are so often seen as prideful and judgmental, but these attitudes have no place in a Christian; they are sinful. The Lord has chosen to give us his holiness, despite our sins and brokenness. Holy people should be characterized by humility and thankfulness to God for calling them into relationship, recognizing that we have a long way to go in overcoming sin. How are you doing in the areas of being prideful and being judgmental?

Do you feel holy? Most likely, you don't feel holy, right? I mean, we still sin every single day. You might even be beating yourself up for the sin you committed yesterday, last month, or two years ago. Satan will continually accuse and condemn you, so it is crucial to embrace and be transformed by the truth of our identity in Christ: I am holy in Jesus.

Encouragement and Prayer by John-Paul and Matt: Point your phone's camera at the QR code and follow the link or go to youtube.com /@FindingFreedomInJesusBook.

Reflective Exercises for
Personal or Group Discussion to Embrace That You Are Holy

1. Practice breathing exercises for three or four minutes each day. Breathe in: "I am holy"; breathe out: "dedicated to God." If you're in a small group, do the breathing together.

2. Go to YouTube, find a worship song with the theme of "holy," and listen to it several times each day. If you're in a small group, sing the song together.

3. Looking back at the chapter, what did you learn that you didn't know previously?

4. Take some dedicated time to ponder the biblical definition of *holy*: To be holy in Jesus means that you are set apart *from* sin and *to* obedience to God. What part of the definition really speaks to you?

5. *Living out holy*:
   a) Most of us struggle to believe we are holy in Jesus. Try this prayer exercise. Sit at the foot of the cross in your mind's eye. See Jesus, hung on the cross because of his love for you. See yourself dressed in the filthiest of rags, which symbolizes your sin. Thank Jesus that you have been made holy through faith, set apart from sin—the dirty rags are taken away and replaced with a "robe of his righteousness" (Isaiah 61:10).

b) Everyone struggles with living holy lives day by day. If you do not have a trustworthy accountability partner to help hold you accountable in your weak areas, please seek one out. Sin easily entangles, and we must fight against it.

6. Take time to meditate on and pray through Isaiah 35:8; Ezekiel 36:23; Ephesians 5:25–27; Colossians 3:12–14; 1 Peter 2:9; and Revelation 4:8. Allow the Lord to open your heart to the truth that you are holy in Jesus. You may want to choose one of these passages to memorize.

Because Jesus has restored us, we can be confident that our lives are found in him. We can experience an abundant and full life here on earth through faith in Jesus and through the power of the Holy Spirit. Our experience on earth is only a part of the goodness of our salvation. It is not the end of the story. We can be assured that there is more in store for us in heaven. Keep remembering that the overall goal of this book is to embrace our true identity and find freedom in Jesus.

In Jesus, I am . . .

confident in Christ

15. Blessed
16. Alive
17. Empowered
18. Victorious
19. Adopted
20. Co-Heir
21. Hopeful

And please don't forget to do the breathing and reflective exercises. There is no transformation without dedication empowered by the Holy Spirit.

CHAPTER 15

Blessed

*Praise be to the God and Father of our Lord Jesus
Christ, who has blessed us in the heavenly realms
with every spiritual blessing in Christ.*

EPHESIANS 1:3

When was the last time you paused to thank God for your blessings? If we are honest, it's easier to focus on what we *don't* have than to be grateful for what we *do* have. Too often, we are filled with discontent. We want a promotion, a better grade in school, a bigger house, a partner to share life with, a new car, and the latest fashionable clothes. Why is it so difficult to be thankful for what we have?

Research from PositivePsychology.com has shown that those who practice gratitude are up to 40 percent happier.[1] To practice gratitude essentially means paying attention to the many ways we are blessed. Gratitude is being thankful for what we have and content with what God has already given us. Do you see how blessed you are?

Who am I? I am blessed in Jesus. I can be transformed when I embrace that truth.

Testimony: Point your phone's camera at the QR code for a video testimony from Joanna or go to youtube.com /@FindingFreedomInJesusBook.

Desperate to fill the void left by a distant father, I sought the romantic attention of men, but God's validation and blessings were all I ever needed . . .

Blessed in Our Culture

The word *blessed* is used in churches all the time, and it's used in our culture with multiple meanings, with little thought given to the God who blesses. *Blessed* is usually a synonym for *lucky*, such as, "You are so blessed to have a wonderful wife [husband]," or "I was blessed with this new car." Blessings are typically limited to descriptions of material achievements or possessions.

#Blessed is a trending topic on social media, with more than 150 million tags on Instagram and more than 100 million on Facebook as of the date of writing this book, but about 1 million tags are added every two weeks. The hashtag is used to indicate how great life is. One might feel #blessed about a new dress, a new house, a dog, or even a juicy hamburger at In-N-Out Burger. Obviously, none of these uses include the biblical meaning of blessed.

What Does the Bible Say About Being Blessed?

Blessed in the Old Testament

Adam and Eve blessed. God's first words to Adam and Eve were a blessing: "God blessed them and said to them, 'Be fruitful and increase in number; fill the earth and subdue it. Rule over the fish in the sea and the birds in the sky and over every living creature that moves on the ground'" (Genesis 1:28). Our Creator God blessed humans with the ability to procreate—"be fruitful"—and to reign with him—"rule over". God was completely sovereign and powerful and could do whatever he wanted. What did he do? He created human beings. What were his first words to them? A blessing. Wow, what an expression of God's loving and giving character! He blessed people and provided benefits so they could thrive and prosper.

Blessings for all. God's blessings didn't end with Adam and Eve. He blessed Noah after the flood (Genesis 9:1). Even after humanity's outrageous act of sinfulness at the Tower of Babel (11:1–9), God didn't stop blessing the people he created. He blessed Abraham with the promise that his family would become a powerful nation: "I will make you into a great nation, and I will bless you; I will make your name great, and you will be a blessing" (12:2). Human sin couldn't stop God's blessings and favor. God's blessings are not a response to our goodness; they flow out of the goodness of God.

God's blessings weren't limited to a few individuals or to the nation of Israel alone. Abraham's blessing was to be extended to all people: "All peoples on earth will be blessed through you" (Genesis 12:3). God's eye was on the entire world even back in the account we find in Genesis. The Old Testament shows God's love for the entire world: "I will send some of those who survive to the nations . . . and to the distant islands that have not heard of my fame or seen my glory. They will proclaim my glory among the nations" (Isaiah 66:19).

Material blessings. In the Old Testament, God's blessings were usually material, including children, wealth, livestock, victory in war, and land: "The LORD has blessed my master abundantly, and he has become wealthy. He has given him sheep and cattle, silver and gold, male and female servants, and camels and donkeys" (Genesis 24:35). The Israelites experienced these material blessings during their lifetime.

Blessings versus curses. The promise of God's blessing was not a magic formula that guaranteed a good life no matter how the Israelites lived. God's blessings came to those who lived faithfully: "When such a person hears the words of this oath and they invoke a blessing on themselves, thinking, 'I will be safe, even though I persist in going my own way,' they will bring disaster on the watered land as well as the dry" (Deuteronomy 29:19). It was expected that God's people would continue to follow and obey the One who blessed them: "All these blessings will come on you and accompany you if you obey the LORD your God" (28:2). If they did not follow God and meet the covenant obligations found in the Law of Moses, they would receive curses instead of blessings (28:15).

There may not have been a magical formula that guaranteed blessings, but there was a unique correlation between obedience to God and his blessings: "My son, do not forget my teaching, but keep my commands in your heart, for they will prolong your life many years and bring you peace and prosperity" (Proverbs 3:1–2).

Joshua: a blessed life. Just after Moses declared the promise of blessings for obedience, Joshua taught what it meant to live a blessed life. Joshua, who led the Israelites into the promised land after the death of Moses, was told, "Be careful to obey all the law my servant Moses gave you; do not turn from it to the right or to the left, that you may be successful wherever you go. Keep this Book of the Law always on your lips; meditate on it day and night, so that you may be careful to do everything written in it. Then you will be prosperous and successful" (Joshua 1:7–8).

God promised Joshua the blessing of success, his presence, and his protection on his journey as Israel's leader, but it was conditional on Joshua's obedience to the covenant laws. Was Joshua successful? Yes and no. He was successful and blessed when he relied on God, such as conquering Jericho with shouts and trumpets (Joshua 6:1–20). But he was not successful when he relied on his own strength, such as when the Israelites were routed by the city of Ai because of their sin (7:1–12).

Spiritual blessings. God's nonmaterial or spiritual blessings included favor, forgiveness, and protection (Psalms 5:12; 32:2; 41:2). God's blessing of grace and peace was included in one of the most well-known Old Testament blessings when Aaron blessed Israel, "The Lord bless you and keep you; the Lord make his face shine on you and be gracious to you; the Lord turn his face toward you and give you peace" (Numbers 6:24–26). Aaron was asking the Lord to show spiritual favor and blessing to Israel.

Response to blessings. When Israel was blessed by God, they responded by praising him: "Stand up and praise the LORD your God, who is from everlasting to everlasting. Blessed be your glorious name" (Nehemiah 9:5). To bless God meant to praise him, worship him, and thank him, recognizing that "every good and perfect gift is from above, coming down from the Father" (James 1:17). We should praise God for all of his blessings.

Future blessings. Israel was a blessed nation, but that didn't mean that things always went well for Israel. In fact, due to their disobedience, they were conquered by foreign nations and some of them were carried off to foreign lands. God didn't give up on them, though, and he promised future blessings. He would send the Messiah to bring his people back from captivity and make them prosperous (Jeremiah 31:23). Then, they will experience "showers of blessing" and the pouring out of his Spirit (Ezekiel 34:26; Isaiah 44:3). We will see these blessings fulfilled in the New Testament.

Blessed in the New Testament

Jesus is blessed. In fulfillment of Old Testament prophecies, Jesus is described as the Blessed One, "Blessed is he who comes in the name of the Lord" (Matthew 21:9, quoting Psalm 118:26). Throughout his ministry, Jesus blessed the poor, mourners, meek, merciful, peacemakers, and children (Matthew 5:3–11; Mark 10:16). Jesus' final action before he ascended into heaven was a blessing: "He lifted up his hands and blessed them. While he was blessing them, he left them and was taken up into heaven" (Luke 24:50–51). God's first action upon creating humans (Genesis 1:28), and Jesus' last action on earth was to bless humans. From beginning to end, God takes joy in abundantly blessing his people.

Jesus blesses God. Jesus praised God. The Bible says this about the feeding of the five thousand: "Taking the five loaves and the two fish and looking up to heaven, he gave thanks and broke the loaves" (Matthew 14:19). In Greek, "he gave thanks" is literally "he blessed." Jesus blessed, or thanked God, for the meal. Christians still do this today, as we pause to thank/bless God before eating, remembering that God graciously blesses us with our "daily bread" (Matthew 6:11).

Spiritual blessings. God has blessed us with *every* spiritual blessing: "Praise be to the God and Father of our Lord Jesus Christ, who has blessed us in the heavenly realms with every spiritual blessing in Christ" (Ephesians 1:3). In response to these spiritual blessings, Paul tells us to praise God. "Praise" is another translation for the Greek word translated "bless." We bless God—or praise him or thank him—because we know that "every good and perfect gift is from above, coming down from the Father" (James 1:17). Where would we be without God's blessings? We praise and thank him as we contemplate the dire state that we would be in without his blessings. What are you praising God for today?

Spiritual blessings include forgiveness, the Holy Spirit, salvation, peace, joy, patience, love, and contentment, among others. In a world filled with sadness, discontentedness, war, and depression, our spiritual blessings are priceless—more valuable than gold, houses, or a huge bank account. There is a sense in which we are privileged people because of God's favor and abundant blessings, even though we may be poor, mournful, or persecuted (Matthew 5:3–12).

Living Blessed Today

When we decided to enter full-time vocational ministry instead of the medical (John-Paul) and engineering
(Matt) fields, we knew there would be a financial cost. As
we look back now, decades later, there are no regrets. We
can both say that God has abundantly blessed us with
every spiritual blessing in Christ and blessed us with everything we need to fulfill his call on our lives. We have led
others to know Jesus, discipled and mentored, taught and
preached the Bible, and prayed with the needy. Our lives
are fully blessed in Jesus.

All are blessed in Jesus. Israel was the blessed nation in the Old
Testament, but now all are blessed by God: "For there is no difference
between Jew and Gentile—the same Lord is Lord of all and richly
blesses all who call on him" (Romans 10:12). The promise made to
Abraham that all nations would be blessed through him is fulfilled: "He
redeemed us in order that the blessing given to Abraham might come
to the Gentiles through Christ Jesus" (Galatians 3:14, fulfilling Genesis
12:3). God desires to bless every human being on earth.

Sharing blessings. God's desire to bless everyone is typically fulfilled through our sharing of our blessings. We should never be selfish
with our blessings or hoard them; they should be freely shared. Every
Sunday when we do our general offering, we are reminded that we are
blessed to be a blessing. When God blesses us with material blessing,
we have opportunities to share, to "invite the poor, the crippled, the
lame, the blind, and you will be blessed" (Luke 14:13–14). Those who
are privileged to receive God's material blessings "must help the weak,
remembering the words the Lord Jesus himself said, 'It is more blessed
to give than to receive'" (Acts 20:35).

Living Blessed Today

In 2022, Jackson, Mississippi, experienced a severe water crisis that caused the drinking water to be unsafe. When our (John-Paul's) church heard the news, we shared our blessings with them. We filled four big semitrucks with bottled water and had them driven from California to Mississippi. Our church responded because we wanted to share our blessings with the needy.

We are also called to share our spiritual blessings by serving others, just as Jesus did: "Heal the sick, raise the dead, cleanse those who have leprosy, drive out demons. Freely you have received; freely give" (Matthew 10:8). After Jesus modeled true servanthood by washing the disciples' feet, he said, "Now that you know these things, you will be blessed if you do them" (John 13:17). When we sacrificially serve others, not only are *they* blessed, but *we* are also blessed. Haven't you found that to be true in your own life? When you serve others, you find joy and blessing. As we've said many times, when we follow God's way (serving others), we thrive and find true life, joy, and happiness.

Blessed within trials. Even when we are enormously blessed, it doesn't mean our lives will be carefree. It is a good reminder that even Jesus experienced suffering, and he was the Blessed One of God. Paradoxically, blessings are sometimes experienced in and through our sufferings. Jesus said, "Blessed are you when people insult you, persecute you and falsely say all kinds of evil against you because of me" (Matthew 5:11). Sometimes we suffer for proclaiming the name of Jesus and doing the right thing: "Even if you should suffer for what is right, you are blessed" (1 Peter 3:14). We even bless our enemies, asking God to show them favor instead of revenge: "Bless those who persecute you; bless and do not curse" (Romans 12:14). In this sinful world, we will have trials and tribulations: "Blessed is the one who perseveres under trial" (James 1:12).

Heavenly hope. We are abundantly and spiritually blessed, but God promises more blessings in heaven. Though our present situation may be difficult, cancer, pain, suffering, and tears will all one day disappear. Jesus told us to "rejoice and be glad" even in the midst of trials and persecutions because "great is your reward in heaven" (Matthew 5:12). The book of Revelation contains the marvelous assurance of being fully blessed in heaven: "Then the angel said to me, 'Write this: Blessed are those who are invited to the wedding supper of the Lamb!'" (19:9). This "blessed hope" (Titus 2:13) allows us to keep on trusting God, even in the midst of suffering and pain, knowing that God will eventually make all things right.

Final Biblical Thoughts on Blessed

The Bible begins with a blessing for Adam and Eve. God's blessings continue throughout the Old Testament, as God blesses Abraham and Israel so they can be a blessing to every nation. The blessings were usually tangible material blessings such as wealth, children, and land, and the blessings were conditional on the Israelites' obedience to the Law of Moses. Those who were blessed responded by praising (or blessing) God for his goodness.

In the New Testament, God's blessings were extended to both Jew and Gentile. Instead of emphasizing material blessings, Jesus blessed his followers with "every spiritual blessing" (Ephesians 1:3), including forgiveness, salvation, the Holy Spirit, love, and countless other blessings. Those who are blessed respond with praise and worship to God, but they also share their blessings with the less fortunate. They share not only their financial blessings but also their spiritual blessings by serving others, imitating Jesus' example of service through washing feet, healing, driving out demons, and preaching.

Being blessed by God does not erase the possibility of suffering. In the midst of suffering, we are often able to see God's blessings more clearly, as my (Matt's) own dad experienced. It was only when he was

diagnosed with cancer that he came to finally understand God's goodness, as ironic as that sounds. In his final days, he prayed Psalm 23 over
and over again throughout the day: "The LORD is my shepherd, I lack
nothing" (v. 1). He understood that God was for him, even as his body
wasted away from cancer. In heaven, he is now cancer-free and praising
Jesus face-to-face.

One day, God will remove all suffering, and our blessing will be
eternal as we experience God's goodness, favor, and blessings face-
to-face. My dad is living that glorious truth now in heaven. No more
cancer, no more tears, no more pain—forever enjoying fellowship with
his Savior.

In one sentence, to be blessed means that you receive God's goodness and spiritual favor, allowing you to praise God and share your
blessings with others by serving them.

Finding Freedom in Jesus

Despite the fact that only God deserves blessing, he abundantly blesses
us. One of the Greek words for "blessed" can be translated as "speak well
of." When God blesses us, he "speaks well of us." Let's try that translation: "Praise be to the God and Father of our Lord Jesus Christ, who has
spoken well of us in the heavenly realms with every spiritual blessing
in Christ" (Ephesians 1:3, emphasis added). That encourages my heart.
Why? Because I know that God is so excited about me that he speaks
well of me in the heavenly realms. I remember when I (John-Paul) got
engaged. I told everybody about how great my fiancée was. God does the
same with us. He loves us and believes in us so much that he speaks well
of us. He blesses us in the heavenly realms. He is so proud of you that he
tells others about you. Those in the heavenly realms have already heard
of you because God speaks well of you.

God's blessings don't just end with words though; he blesses us with
"every spiritual blessing in Christ" (Ephesians 1:3). It is hard to believe,
but I am blessed in Christ, even though I am sinful and undeserving. It

transforms the way I think about myself when I know that the creator of the world loves me so much that he brags about me and spiritually blesses me with forgiveness, the Holy Spirit, salvation, peace, joy, hope, love, and contentment. People in Jesus' culture (and in some religions today) had to bribe the gods with prayers and offerings in order to supposedly receive their blessings.

I'm thankful that I don't have to manipulate God to bless me. He abundantly blesses me simply because he loves me. I have value in his eyes. I am compelled to worship even now as I think about it. Are you aware of God's abundant blessings in your life? One of the exercises we suggest below is to keep a gratitude journal in which you write down God's abundant blessings every day. It's a great reminder of how good and loving our God is.

Our blessings from God should lead not to selfishness but to generosity as we share our material and spiritual blessings with others. I often think of Gollum in *The Hobbit*, who said about the ring, "It is mine, I tell you. My own. My precious. Yes, my precious." We don't want to be like that. After all, every blessing—both material and spiritual—that we have comes from God. It is not our own; it has been given to us to share. And so we share our wealth with the poor; we serve those who are needy; we listen to the brokenhearted; we evangelize the lost; we serve in missions to the nations. Those who are blessed bless others. We all play a role in God's mission to bless the world.

When we recognize that every blessing we have—large and small—is from God, we are transformed from selfishness and pride to praise and gratitude in response to what God has done for us. Recognizing our blessings changes our prayer lives as we pour out our gratefulness for his goodness. We worship and honor him. Our praise delights God's heart. How can we bless or praise God? We praise God through prayer, singing, writing, and other modes of expression such as dancing and painting. One of our fondest memories as fathers was arriving home each night. Our kids would be playing, but as soon as they heard the door open, they came running down the hall and jumped into our arms, smiling and squealing with delight. What a joy! We can bring this same joy to God when we go to him in praise and gratitude—running to our Abba Father. We praise God for what he has done and for what he will do as we share our blessings with others. We bless you, Lord.

#Blessed—it's more than just a hashtag. God has blessed us. God is blessing us. God will bless us. I am abundantly blessed in Jesus!

Encouragement and Prayer by John-Paul and Matt: Point your phone's camera at the QR code and follow the link or go to youtube.com /@FindingFreedomInJesusBook.

Reflective Exercises for
Personal or Group Discussion to Embrace That You Are Blessed

1. Practice breathing exercises for three or four minutes each day. Breathe in: "blessed again and again"; breathe out: "I praise you, Jesus." If you're in a small group, do the breathing together.

2. Go to YouTube, find a worship song with the theme of "blessed" (perhaps "Doxology" by Maverick City Music), and listen to it several times each day. If you're in a small group, sing the song together.

3. Looking back at the chapter, what did you learn that you didn't know previously?

4. When you hear the word *blessed*, what definition do you have? Take some time to ponder the biblical definition of *blessed*: To be blessed means that you receive God's goodness and spiritual favor, allowing you to praise God and share your blessings with others by serving them. What part of the definition really speaks to you?

5. *Living out blessed*:

a) Give some examples of blessings in your life. Knowing that those who practice gratitude are up to 40 percent happier, are you ready to start a gratitude journal? Instead of thinking about what you *don't* have; thank God for what you *do* have. Each day, record a few things for which you are thankful. Include both small and large things, both material and spiritual blessings. Put the gratitude journal next to your bed and make this exercise the first thing you do when you wake up each morning.

b) Just as God extends his blessing to us, may we not selfishly hoard our blessings, but rather extend them to our families, friends, and neighbors, as well as to the poor, the weak, and even our enemies. What would it look like for you to share your material and spiritual blessings with others, remembering that "it is more blessed to give than to receive" (Acts 20:35). Think of two or three ways to extend your blessings to someone this week. It may be taking flowers to a neighbor, sharing the gospel with a friend, leading a Bible study, or going on a short-term mission trip.

6. Take time to meditate on and pray through Genesis 1:28; 12:2–3; Deuteronomy 28:2; Ephesians 1:3; James 1:12; and Revelation 19:9. Allow the Lord to open your heart to the truth that you are blessed in Christ. You may want to choose one of these passages to memorize.

CHAPTER 16

Alive

The thief comes only to steal and kill and destroy;
I have come that they may have life, and have it to
the full.

JOHN 10:10

As a pastor (John-Paul) who officiates quite a few funerals, I find a noticeable difference between funerals for believers and funerals for nonbelievers. You can almost feel the difference in the room before a word is said. Have you experienced that in the funerals you've attended? For believers, even though family members and loved ones are grieving and sad, there is also a spirit of celebration as they think about their loved one entering eternal bliss with Jesus. I almost always hear these words: "We are confident, I say, and willing rather to be absent from the body, and to be present with the Lord" (2 Corinthians 5:8 KJV). There is a joy in the midst of their pain that can only be explained by Jesus. For nonbelievers, though, you normally only hear about what that person did during their earthly life. Loved ones may share in general about where the person is for eternity, but it's pretty unclear. There's very little hope. For them, life is over.

As Christians, we are alive now, and we are alive for eternity. Death has been defeated. But it's more than that. Being alive in Jesus also means our lives are completely transformed here on earth to a better quality of life. Life with Jesus is better than life without Jesus.

Who am I? I am alive in Jesus. I can be transformed when I embrace that truth.

Testimony: Point your phone's camera at the QR code for a video testimony from Willa or go to youtube.com /@FindingFreedomInJesusBook.

The devastation of my father's death led me to question my faith. I thought about walking away from Jesus. Who would have guessed that it was the death of my father that led to my relationship with Jesus becoming more alive than ever? . . .

Alive in Our Culture

The word *alive* in our culture refers almost exclusively to physical life. Many people think their lives are the result of an evolutionary process—no God who created them in his image. They believe they are products of nature, a collection of cells. When someone dies, they are dead. There is no life after death. Death is the end of the story.

It's sad talking to people who believe this godless story. There is no higher purpose, no hope, and no explanation for why their lives are often filled with suffering. This life is all we get. YOLO—you only live once, so grab for everything you can. Thankfully, the Bible has a very different story to tell.

What Does the Bible Say About Being Alive?

Alive in the Old Testament

God is life. God is eternally alive and is the source of all life (Numbers 16:22; Deuteronomy 5:26). God shared that life when he breathed it into human beings: "Then the LORD God formed a man from the dust of the ground and breathed into his nostrils the breath of life, and the man became a living being" (Genesis 2:7). Due to humanity's sin, death entered humanity's story. Death didn't thwart God, who desired humans to live. From Genesis to Revelation, we learn about the ways God prioritized life for all people.

God chose the people of Israel and established a covenant relationship with them. Just before they left their wilderness wanderings and entered the promised land, God reviewed and reiterated his covenant with them. He set before them a choice between "life and prosperity" or "death and destruction" (Deuteronomy 30:15). To choose life meant they would "love the LORD your God, to walk in obedience to him, and to keep his commands," avoiding idolatry (vv. 16–17). They were to worship and follow God and God alone. Those who were alive—walking with God according to his covenant—would experience his many blessings.

What blessings came to those who were alive? Those who continued in faith and followed God's covenant were abundantly blessed with good health and longevity of life in the promised land, livestock, many children, crops, joy, and pleasure, along with rest and contentment (Deuteronomy 30:9, 20; Proverbs 4:22; 19:23; Psalm 16:11). To be "alive" meant that daily life was good, filled with God's blessings and with prosperity.

Life after death. In the Old Testament, the term *alive* emphasized physical life in this world. There were, however, a few allusions to life after death. Hints of life eternal were found at the very beginning of creation. In the Garden of Eden, Adam and Eve were told that if they ate from the "tree of life," they would "live forever" (Genesis 3:22). There were also hints of life after death in the Prophets. They declared that death would not be the end of life for the coming Messiah. "After he has suffered, he will see the light of life" (Isaiah 53:11). The prophet Ezekiel alluded to life after death when he shared a vision of dry bones coming back to life (Ezekiel 37:1–14)). As the Old Testament came to end, it wasn't clear what life after death would look like—a reality that wouldn't be explained until the New Testament.

Alive in the New Testament

Jesus is life. Just as the Old Testament reveals God as the source of life, the New Testament presents Jesus as the source of life: "As the Father has life in himself, so he has granted the Son also to have life in himself" (John 5:26). Jesus fulfilled the Old Testament expectation of a coming Suffering Messiah: "I am the good shepherd. The good shepherd lays down his life for the sheep" (John 10:11). Although Jesus died on the cross, death did not end his life. On the third day, he was raised back to life (Matthew 17:23). His death on the cross brought life to human beings.

Jesus brings life. While the Old Testament terms for life emphasized *physical* prosperity and blessing, the New Testament terms for life highlight abundant *spiritual* blessings. Satan came to bring death, but Jesus came to bring life: "The thief comes only to steal and kill and destroy; I have come that they may have life, and have it to the full" (John 10:10). Jesus is "the bread of life," "the resurrection and the life," and "the way and the truth and the life" (John 6:48; 11:25; 14:6). Jesus is life and brings life.

Finding life. We are made alive in Jesus through faith. The one who "believes in the Son has eternal life" (John 3:36). Jesus brought life to believers even while trapped by sin: God "made us alive with Christ even when we were dead in transgressions—it is by grace you have been saved" (Ephesians 2:5). What does it mean to be alive with Jesus? Christians are alive in two ways: quantity and quality.

QUANTITY OF LIFE. Life in Jesus will last eternally—a *quantity* of time. Just as Jesus is "alive for ever and ever" (Revelation 1:18), believers will live eternally in heaven: "The one who believes in me will live, even though they die" (John 11:25). We will physically die but will never spiritually die. Jesus' resurrection is the promise that Christians will also be resurrected to live forever: "In Christ all will be made alive. But each in turn: Christ, the firstfruits; then, when he comes, those who belong to him" (1 Corinthians 15:22–23).

QUALITY OF LIFE. To be alive with Jesus also means the *quality* of our life is better *right now* here on earth. The Bible says that eternal life is a *present* possession. Clearly, our quality of life in heaven will be infinitely superior, but the Bible teaches that Christian life has a better quality here and now because we are living life the way God intended for us to live. Through the power of the Holy Spirit and by faith in Jesus, our lives on earth are transformed for the better in comparison to those who do not follow Jesus. Those who believe in Jesus find abundant and full life (John 10:10).

Christians experience eternal life *now*, a better *quality* of life, and *later* when they are raised to life with Christ forever, a *quantity* of life. Now and later. Quality and quantity.

Abundant life. What does it mean that our quality of life is better here on earth? Jesus said, "The thief comes only to steal and kill and destroy; I have come that they may have life, and have it to the full." Some Christians in our country have made this verse solely about material possessions, perhaps due to a misunderstanding of the translations that use the word *abundantly*: "I came so that they would have life, and have *it* abundantly" (John 10:10 NASB). In the context of John's gospel, abundant life isn't about abundant material blessings, but rather about the abundant spiritual blessings experienced by Christians, such as forgiveness of sins, removal of shame, and the provision of hope, joy, peace, love, and purpose.

In Paul's letters, eternal life means that our character is transformed from harmful and destructive acts like sexual immorality, hatred, anger, jealousy, and selfishness to life-giving actions reflecting the fruit of the Spirit: "love, joy, peace, forbearance, kindness, goodness, faithfulness, gentleness and self-control" (Galatians 5:19–23). Alive in Christ means that believers are Holy Spirit–empowered to live a different and better quality of life here on earth because of Jesus' presence in our life. Christians are enabled to choose God's way over the world's way. Christians shine in this dark world because we are filled with the fruit of the Spirit in order to love and serve our neighbors.

Living Alive Today

I (John-Paul) recently went to the post office (not really my favorite place to visit). As I waited in line to be helped, I noticed three workers, two of whom didn't look like they were having a good day. One stood out to me. She had a radiant smile and intentionally engaged with the customers. As she called me up to her window, she embodied the fruit of the Spirit as she interacted with me. She was patient, kind, gentle, and loving. She genuinely cared. I later learned she was a Christian, but I should have known it—her kindness was right there before my eyes. Her quality of life was different because Jesus had transformed her and brought her eternal life, and I could see it in the joy and kindness that radiated from her.

Sin kills life. Sin is the opposite of an abundant life; instead of life, it brings death: "The wages of sin is death" (Romans 6:23). Sin deceives us and destroys our joy, peace, and life. God "called us to a holy life" (2 Timothy 1:9) because only when we follow God in obedience do we find true, abundant life. The Bible tells us it won't be easy to choose God's way and find life: "Wide is the gate and broad is the road that leads to destruction, and many enter through it. But small is the gate and narrow the road that leads to life, and only a few find it" (Matthew 7:13–14).

Heavenly hope. Since the Garden of Eden, humans have desired to eat of the "tree of life" and live forever with their Creator God (Genesis 2:9). Through faith in Jesus, this hope became a reality: "I will give the right to eat from the tree of life, which is in the paradise of God" (Revelation 2:7). We will be warmly welcomed into heavenly bliss to live with Jesus forever, entering into the fullness of life because our names have been written in the Lamb's book of life (Revelation 3:5). Just as the father in the parable of the prodigal son rejoiced and celebrated that "this son of mine was dead and is alive again" (Luke 15:24), God rejoices that we are alive in Jesus. When we came to faith, there was a celebration in heaven (Luke 15:7)—a celebration that will never end. We are alive in Jesus . . . for ever and ever!

Final Biblical Thoughts on Alive

God, who is eternally alive, breathed life into humans. In the Old Testament, those who followed God found life in physical prosperity. They received long life, health, children, crops, and joy. Life in the Old Testament typically referred to life on earth, but the prophets occasionally hinted at life after death.

In the New Testament, Jesus is the source of life who brings abundant and full spiritual life. Jesus was raised back to life after death to show that all who believe in him will also be raised to eternal life. Death has been defeated—there is more than just life here on earth. The phrase "eternal life" in the Gospels means both a better *quality* of life now and a *quantity* of life that lasts forever. Christians are abundantly blessed on earth with the fruit of the Spirit. The *quality* of their life is transformed from the dark deception of sin and death to a joy-filled, abundant life in the Spirit. One day, just as Jesus lives eternally in heaven, those who believe in him will eat from the tree of life and spend eternity with Jesus. We are alive in Jesus now (quality) and forever (quantity).

In one sentence, to be alive means that you thrive right now in this life with abundant spiritual blessings and will live forever in heavenly bliss—quality and quantity of life.

Finding Freedom in Jesus

Before coming to faith in Jesus, we were like stone statues, cold and dead, held captive by sin. The enemy tried to lie, steal, kill, and destroy us, but Jesus came to bring us abundant spiritual life. Through faith, we are alive in Jesus. We are transformed from the traits of the world (such as anger, sexual immorality, greed, and discontent) to the attributes of the Holy Spirit (such as love, joy, peace, patience, and hope).

Jesus offers life to the full—an abundant, satisfying life as we walk with him. Sometimes, though, we are tempted to choose the world's ways. For example, many people are tempted to trade love for lust. A 2001 study from Rutgers University's National Marriage Project stated that 94 percent of adults desire a soulmate to share life with.[1] Humans long for one partner, someone who knows them intimately and loves them, which is also God's design. And yet many choose the world's way. "Starter marriages" have become more and more popular. The American Psychological Association (APA) notes some terrifying divorce rates: 41 percent of first marriages and 60 percent of second marriages will end in divorce.[2] And many are choosing pornography even though pornography has been shown to destroy the brain in so many ways—loneliness, shame, depression, dissatisfied marriages, and a disconnect from the real world. In a 2020 study, the National Institute of Health estimated that 91 percent of men and 60 percent of women had consumed pornography in written, picture, or video form in the past month.[3] We desire a soulmate, but we are trading that for a lustful moment or a short-term marriage, not realizing that we are slowly being destroyed. Choosing pornography over God's sexual plan is like trading a juicy filet mignon for a dry, moldy piece of bread. We are given life in Jesus. Why would we choose sin and destroy that? Are there areas in which you are tempted to choose the second best instead of full life in Jesus?

Statistics on suicide from the Centers for Disease Control and Prevention indicate that far too many people are choosing death over life. In 2023, an estimated 13.2 million Americans considered suicide, and after 1.6 million suicide attempts, nearly 50,000 Americans died (1 every 11 minutes).[4] Shockingly, suicide is the eleventh leading cause of death in the United States. These statistics are horrifically sad, especially for those of us who have had family members or friends take their own lives. Too often, people have never heard the good news of *life* in Jesus. They remain unaware of the life-giving transformation, purpose, and freedom that Jesus brings. Their lives can be transformed from literal physical death and spiritual death to eternal life in Jesus. They can be alive in Jesus and find a better quality of life now and eternal life forever. The Lord has chosen you to share life with those around you.

Full and satisfying life is found only in Jesus. We pray that you will choose Jesus over the temptations that so easily entangle. We also pray that you will find joy in helping others to become truly alive in Jesus as you share this good news with your family, friends, and neighbors.

Encouragement and Prayer by John-Paul and Matt: Point your phone's camera at the QR code and follow the link or go to youtube.com /@FindingFreedomInJesusBook.

Reflective Exercises for
Personal or Group Discussion to Embrace That You Are Alive

1. Practice breathing exercises for three or four minutes each day. Breathe in: "abundant life now"; breathe out: "alive forever." If you're in a small group, do the breathing together.

2. Go to YouTube, find a worship song with the theme of "alive," and listen to it several times each day. If you're in a small group, sing the song together.

3. Looking back at the chapter, what did you learn that you didn't know previously?

4. Take some time to ponder the biblical definition of *alive*: To be alive means that you thrive right now in this life with abundant spiritual blessings and will live forever in heavenly bliss—quality and quantity of life. What part of the definition really speaks to you?

5. *Living out alive*:
   a) Can you remember a time when you were dead in your sin? What was it like? How is it different now? Spend time thanking and praising God for the abundant spiritual blessings of being transformed from death to life in Jesus.
   b) Did you know that eternal life involves a better *quality* of life right now in the present? Being alive in Jesus includes resisting the world's way and

choosing to live God's way, which brings true joy, peace, and love. Are you experiencing this? If you are struggling to experience this abundant life now, are you ready to seek out a pastor or friend and ask for encouragement and help? Transformation is easier when we are in community.

c) Do you have friends or family members who have not yet found life in Jesus? Are you praying for them? How can you begin to share your life story with them?

6. Take time to meditate on and pray through Deuteronomy 30:15; Psalm 16:11; Luke 15:24; John 3:36; 10:10; 11:25; and Ephesians 2:5. Allow the Lord to open your heart to the truth that you are alive in Jesus. You may want to choose one of these passages to memorize.

CHAPTER 17

Empowered

"Not by might nor by power, but by my Spirit," says the LORD Almighty.

ZECHARIAH 4:6

I(Matt) remember when my toddler son used to say, "I do it," even though he really couldn't do it. But we adults sometimes think that way too, don't we? We think we can do it ourselves. Jesus said, "By myself I can do nothing" (John 5:30). If that was true for Jesus, how much more is it true for us?

Ready for the good news? Although we are weak, God is omnipotent, which is a theological word for "all-powerful." In his goodness, he shares his power with us. God wants to reach the world with the good news about Jesus, so he empowers us by the Holy Spirit so we can participate in his mission. Yes, we are weak, insufficient, and sinful, but we are also empowered by the Spirit to do amazing and miraculous things for God, especially when we consider that we are not alone in this. We are surrounded by other empowered Christians in the church. Together as an empowered church, we can do amazing things to fulfill his mission.

Who am I? I am empowered in Jesus. I can be transformed when I embrace that truth.

Testimony: Point your phone's camera at the QR code for a video testimony from Clark or go to youtube.com /@FindingFreedomInJesusBook.

When the world shut down due to COVID-19, I was concerned for kids who were stuck inside and all alone. I felt that God was calling me to start a summer camp for them, but I was only sixteen years old . . .

Empowered in Our Culture

Power in our culture is often defined as influence, wealth, or military might. Unfortunately, power is frequently used as an instrument for evil. People abuse power and lie, intimidate, criticize, or coerce others for their own selfish desires. Corrupt power is found in our governments, schools, gangs that rule the streets of our cities, and sometimes even among church leadership. Power seems to be more important than morality. Few ask what the right thing is, as they greedily grab and fight for what they want.

God's followers are empowered, but not to use it selfishly or to abuse others. The empowered Christian is asked to sacrificially and humbly serve, using their power for good, not evil. What a difference from the way power is exercised in our culture!

What Does the Bible Say About Being Empowered?

Empowered in the Old Testament

God shares power. God's power is all-encompassing and unstoppable: "Sovereign LORD, you have made the heavens and the earth by your great power and outstretched arm. Nothing is too hard for you" (Jeremiah 32:17). After he created humans, God shared his power and gave them authority to rule over creation (Genesis 1:26). Throughout the Old Testament, God anointed and empowered groups of leaders to help his people—judges, kings, priests, and prophets.

Empowered judges. God empowered judges to deliver the people of Israel from their enemies. Samson, perhaps the most well-known judge, was empowered by God's Spirit to kill a lion with his bare hands and to overcome the enemy Philistines (Judges 14:6; 15:14). However, Samson struggled with abuse of power along with using it for good. Deborah was another judge who delivered Israel. She prophesied exactly where to go and when to act so that Israel was delivered from the enemy Canaan. Deborah's victory led to peace in the land for forty years (Judges 4–5).

Empowered kings. Israel's first kings—Saul, David, and Solomon— were anointed with oil (1 Samuel 10:1; 16:13; 1 Kings 1:39). This physical anointing symbolized the deeper spiritual truth that they were empowered by the Holy Spirit: "Samuel took the horn of oil and anointed him in the presence of his brothers, and from that day on the Spirit of the LORD came powerfully upon David" (1 Samuel 16:13). The kings were empowered by the Spirit to lead the nation and to win military victories (2 Samuel 22:51): "The LORD gives victory to his anointed. He answers him from his heavenly sanctuary with the victorious power of his right hand" (Psalm 20:6). The king's anointing and empowering were necessary politically too. Solomon is credited as expanding Israel's territory and wisely dealing with the neighboring nations (1 Kings 4:34).

Empowered priests. Priests were also anointed to lead, beginning with Aaron: "Anoint them just as you anointed their father [Aaron], so they may serve me as priests. Their anointing will be to a priesthood that will continue throughout their generations" (Exodus 40:15). While the kings led Israel politically, the priests led them spiritually in their relationship with God.

Empowered prophets. Finally, Israel's prophets were empowered by God to hear God's message and proclaim it to Israel. Prophets often warned Israel of coming judgment and called them to repent and to keep their faith in God despite difficult times. God spoke to the prophets through the Spirit, which enabled them to speak God's words to the people, such as the prophet Ezekiel: "The Spirit came into me and raised me to my feet, and I heard him speaking to me" (Ezekiel 2:2). The phrases "this is what the LORD says" and "this is what the LORD commands" appear more than four hundred times in the Old Testament.

Some prophets were also empowered to perform miracles. Moses was able to perform his miracles because he had "the power of the Spirit" (Numbers 11:17). Elisha the prophet even miraculously raised a child from the dead (2 Kings 4:34).

Leaders were anointed and empowered by God to do amazing things. However, they could do nothing—no victory, no miracles, no prophecy—by their own power. These mighty acts were only possible through the Spirit's empowerment: "Not by might nor by power, but by my Spirit" (Zechariah 4:6).

Empowered service. These leaders were not empowered by God to selfishly manipulate others or make mini-kingdoms for themselves. No, they were empowered to sacrificially serve the nation of Israel. I don't know of anything more countercultural than this commitment to service. In the ancient culture as well as in ours, those who have power typically want to be served. They want the first-class seats, the power suit, the maid, the servants. God asked Israel's empowered leaders to serve and sacrifice for others.

Hope for a Messiah. Although God's empowered prophets warned the Israelites, they rebelled against God and were exiled to foreign lands. The empowered prophets began to talk about the future, when God's

Messiah would lead them. The Hebrew term for Messiah, *mashiah*, means "Anointed One." Isaiah prophesied, "The Spirit of the Sovereign LORD is on me, because the LORD has anointed me to proclaim good news to the poor. He has sent me to bind up the brokenhearted, to proclaim freedom for the captives and release from darkness for the prisoners, to proclaim the year of the LORD's favor" (Isaiah 61:1–2). The Messiah would be the greatest of all those anointed and empowered by the Holy Spirit, and yet his ministry was to be one of service as he brought salvation, preached the good news, and brought freedom and "justice to the nations" (42:1). Jesus himself said that he "did not come to be served, but to serve" (Mark 10:45).

When the Messiah arrived, the Spirit would be given to *all* people to empower them, not just the leaders (Ezekiel 39:29). All people would be Spirit-empowered and able to hear the Lord's voice: "Afterward, I will pour out my Spirit on all people. Your sons and daughters will prophesy, your old men will dream dreams, your young men will see visions" (Joel 2:28).

Empowered in the New Testament

Jesus was empowered. Jesus fulfilled the Old Testament prophecies as the "Anointed One," translated as "Messiah" (Hebrew, *mashiah*) or "Christ" (Greek, *christos*). Jesus fulfilled all of the anointed and empowered leadership roles found in the Old Testament—judge, king, prophet, and priest (John 5:22; Matthew 27:11; 21:11; Hebrews 3:1). Just like the Israelite leaders, Jesus was empowered by the Holy Spirit: "God anointed Jesus of Nazareth with the Holy Spirit and power" (Acts 10:38).

Why was Jesus empowered? In our world, power is often abused and self-seeking. Jesus, though, was empowered to serve and to do good by healing and casting out demons: "God anointed Jesus of Nazareth with the Holy Spirit and power, and how he went around doing good and healing all who were under the power of the devil" (Acts 10:38). Jesus quoted and fulfilled Isaiah's prophecy (Isaiah 61:1–2) in one of his first sermons: "The Spirit of the Lord is on me, because he has anointed me to proclaim good news to the poor. He has sent me to proclaim freedom for the prisoners and recovery of sight for the blind, to set the oppressed free, to proclaim the year of the Lord's favor" (Luke 4:18–19).

Jesus was empowered by the Holy Spirit to do good, heal the sick, preach the gospel, and set prisoners free. The word *prisoners* is a metaphor for demonized people: "With authority and power he gives orders to impure spirits and they come out" (Luke 4:36). Jesus drove out demons, or impure spirits, and released them from their spiritual prison. Jesus did not selfishly abuse his power. He served and set free those who were physically and spiritually oppressed.

Sometimes we think that Jesus was able to perform miracles because he is God. Please do not misunderstand us. Jesus is God; but the Bible teaches that Jesus ministered through the power of the Holy Spirit: "Jesus returned to Galilee in the power of the Spirit" (Luke 4:14), and "It is by the Spirit of God that I drive out demons" (Matthew 12:28). Jesus fulfilled his ministry of preaching, healing, and driving out demons through the Spirit's empowerment. He is fully divine and fully human. As a man, he was empowered by the Spirit to perform miracles. This truth is important because the same Spirit that empowered Jesus and empowered the first believers in the book of Acts now empowers Christians today.

Empowered by Jesus. Just before Jesus' ascension into heaven, he anointed and empowered his disciples and sent them to continue his mission to this lost world: "You will receive power when the Holy Spirit comes on you; and you will be my witnesses in Jerusalem, and in all Judea and Samaria, and to the ends of the earth" (Acts 1:8). This promise was fulfilled on the Day of Pentecost, when all the believers "were filled with the Holy Spirit" (2:4).

Christians minister not through their own power but through the Holy Spirit's power. Paul prayed that God will "strengthen you with power through his Spirit" (Ephesians 3:16). Christians are anointed and empowered by the Holy Spirit, just as Jesus was, but it doesn't mean we ourselves are powerful. After healing a lame beggar, Paul said that the power to heal was not his own, but the Lord's: "Why do you stare at us as if by our own power or godliness we had made this man walk?" (Acts 3:12). We do ministry in and through God's power, not our own, which leaves no room for pride.

Sent by Jesus. After empowering his followers with the Spirit, Jesus sent them to continue his mission to reach the lost with the message of hope: "As [the Father] sent me into the world, I have sent them into the world" (John 17:18). Followers of Jesus are empowered to do good, heal the sick, preach the gospel, and set prisoners free: "Anyone who believes in me will do the same works I have done, and even greater works, because I am going to be with the Father" (John 14:12 NLT).

Our empowered ministry is a teaching and doing ministry, or as we used to say in elementary school, a show-and-tell activity. We tell people about Jesus, and we show them the truth through our loving actions and, if God sovereignly chooses and gifts us, through miraculous signs and driving out demons, just as we see in Jesus' ministry and his disciples' ministry in the book of Acts.

Empowered for a purpose. The Holy Spirit's empowerment always comes with a purpose—to fulfill the mission of God. In order to stay empowered, we must stay connected to Jesus, the Vine: "I am the vine; you are the branches. If you remain in me and I in you, you will bear much fruit; apart from me you can do nothing" (John 15:5). As Jesus himself said, "By myself I can do nothing" (John 5:30). We are empowered by the Spirit, connected to Jesus the Vine, in order to continue Jesus' mission of reaching the lost and bearing much fruit.

Examples of empowered ministry. The New Testament is a story of God working through ordinary everyday Christians who were Spirit-empowered to continue Jesus' ministry. Here are a few examples:

STEPHEN. He was the first martyr in the book of Acts, and he was empowered to do miracles: "Stephen, a man full of God's grace and power, performed great wonders and signs among the people" (Acts 6:8).

PAUL. This apostle performed miracles "by the power of signs and wonders, through the power of the Spirit of God" and "fully proclaimed the gospel of Christ" (Romans 15:19). Paul did not just evangelize with words; his preaching included miracles to prove the truth of the gospel: "My message and my preaching were not with wise and persuasive words, but with a demonstration of the Spirit's power" (1 Corinthians 2:4). He had a show-and-tell ministry, just like Jesus.

BARNABAS. He was one of Paul's coworkers in the gospel: "He was a good man, full of the Holy Spirit and faith, and a great number of people were brought to the Lord" (Acts 11:24). Barnabas was powerfully gifted in evangelism.

Empowered gifts. Although the men and women in the Bible did amazing works through the Spirit's power, we must remember that we are not empowered to do anything and everything. God sovereignly chooses how to empower each believer with specific spiritual gifts. Paul emphasized that we do not receive all of the gifts. In the Greek language, the way Paul asked questions about the reception of gifts assumes a "no" answer: "Are all apostles? Are all prophets? Are all teachers? Do all work miracles? Do all have gifts of healing? Do all speak in tongues? Do all interpret?" (1 Corinthians 12:29–30). The answer to all of these questions in Greek is "no." Not all will heal. Not all will prophesy. Not all will work miracles. Not all will speak in tongues.

An individual does *not* receive all of the gifts. The gifts are sovereignly distributed to each one of us, just as *God* determines. As elementary school children learn from their teachers, "You get what you get, and you don't throw a fit." God has empowered you with just the right gift for your ministry. You don't necessarily get the gift you desire, but you *always* get the gift that God desires you to have. Since God is all-knowing, or omniscient, he knows exactly what we need to fulfill his mission. We can trust him.

It would be impossible for our churches to have the impact we are seeing today in our communities without empowered and committed people who faithfully serve every week. We need everyone's gifts. We need evangelists to bring people in; we need teachers to teach them; we need those with hospitality to make them feel welcomed; and so on.

Every gift is important. No gift is "less than" because God sovereignly gives just the right gifts so the church can be built up.

Empowered in weakness. Christians are empowered to do amazing works, but this power often comes in weakness. If you ever think you are too weak to operate as a Holy Spirit–empowered believer, remember the Lord's words to Paul: "My power is made perfect in weakness" (2 Corinthians 12:9). We see power in weakness displayed on the cross, the ultimate demonstration of Jesus' suffering. At his weakest moment, as he hung on a cross and died, Jesus powerfully *triumphed* over Satan; Jesus "disarmed the powers and authorities, [and] he made a public spectacle of them, triumphing over them by the cross" (Colossians 2:15). It didn't seem that Jesus had much power on the cross, did it? But it was on the cross that his most powerful work was done as he defeated Satan, sin, and death. We are empowered in Jesus, even in our weakness and suffering, to proclaim the gospel in both word and works to a needy world.

Final Biblical Thoughts on Empowered

In the Old Testament, only God was all-powerful, but he chose to share his power with frail humans to fulfill his purposes and mission in the world. Judges, kings, priests, and prophets were anointed and empowered by the Spirit for leadership roles. They were empowered not to selfishly control others or make mini-kingdoms for themselves but to serve the nation of Israel.

The Old Testament prophesied that a powerful Messiah, or Anointed One, would come to bring salvation, freedom, and justice and to preach the good news. When the Messiah arrives, all people will be empowered, not just the leaders (Joel 2:28).

In the New Testament, Jesus perfectly fulfilled all of the Old Testament roles of judge, prophet, priest, and king as the "Anointed One." He was Holy Spirit–empowered to do good, heal the sick, preach the gospel, drive out demons, and set the prisoners free.

Jesus gave the Holy Spirit to all Christians to empower and anoint them for ministry. The New Testament contained examples in Stephen, Paul, Barnabas and others to show that Christians continue Jesus' mission of preaching the gospel, doing miraculous deeds according to one's spiritual gifts, and setting free those imprisoned by Satan. As we stay connected to Jesus the Vine, walk in step with the Spirit, and stay persistent in prayer, we are empowered to sacrificially serve and minister to others through our spiritual gifts. Christians are empowered, not to "lord it over" others (Mark 10:42) but to selflessly serve, even in times of weakness and suffering.

In one sentence, to be empowered in Jesus means that you are supernaturally enabled and gifted by the Holy Spirit to sacrificially serve in ministry in both word and works.

Finding Freedom in Jesus

The omnipotent God of the universe anointed and empowered *you* with a God-given purpose. Have you ever wondered why you are here? Do you sometimes think there might be more to life than just going to school or work, raising a family, making money, or climbing the corporate ladder? There is so much more! We are privileged to continue Jesus' mission—preaching the gospel, healing the sick, setting free those imprisoned by Satan—all according to our giftedness through the Holy Spirit's power. Think of all of the people you know who are hurting and need Jesus. God has empowered *you* to preach the gospel and help set them free. Look around today and see how God might use you. Are you ready to continue Jesus' ministry through your gifts?

But remember, just like Jesus, you can do nothing on your own. God gives you spiritual gifts to fulfill *his* mission, not yours. It's all about him, not you. You will not receive all the gifts, but the gift(s) you do receive is (are) perfect for you and your ministry. Are you aware of the gifts God has given to you? How are you using them to advance Jesus' kingdom?

Encouragement and Prayer by John-Paul and Matt: Point your phone's camera at the QR code and follow the link or go to youtube.com /@FindingFreedomInJesusBook.

Reflective Exercises for
Personal or Group Discussion to Embrace That You Are Empowered

1. Practice breathing exercises for three or four minutes each day. Breathe in: "Spirit-empowered"; breathe out: "gifted to minister." If you're in a small group, do the breathing together.

2. Go to YouTube, find a worship song with the theme of "empowered," and listen to it several times each day. If you're in a small group, sing the song together.

3. Looking back at the chapter, what did you learn that you didn't know previously?

4. Take some time to ponder the biblical definition of *empowered* in Jesus: To be empowered means that you are supernaturally enabled and gifted by the Holy Spirit to sacrificially serve in ministry in both word and works. What part of the definition really speaks to you?

5. *Living out empowered:*

  a) Do you believe you have a purpose, like we heard in Clark's video testimony? Are you bored or wondering what life is all about? Do you believe that God has empowered you with spiritual gifts to continue Jesus' mission of setting free the lost? Take time to pray for guidance.

  b) What are your gifts? It may be helpful to ask trustworthy friends who know you for their insights. Are there gifts you are ignoring or underutilizing? How can you use these spiritual gifts?

  c) God anoints and empowers Christians in their weakness. Does this describe you? How can you minister to someone this week in your weakness? Take a moment in prayer and think of a couple of examples.

6. Take time to meditate on and pray through Isaiah 61:1–2; Zechariah 4:6; John 15:5; Acts 1:8; 10:38; and Ephesians 3:16. Allow the Lord to open your heart to the truth that you are empowered in Jesus. You may want to choose one of these passages to memorize.

CHAPTER 18

Victorious

Death has been swallowed up in victory.
Where, O death, is your victory?
Where, O death, is your sting?

1 CORINTHIANS 15:54–55

I (John-Paul) have the blessing and privilege of being the fourth pastor of Faithful Central Bible Church in Inglewood, California, founded in 1936. My predecessor, Bishop Kenneth Ulmer led this congregation for more than forty years. The church has a motto that serves as our mission: "Building Champions for Victorious Living." We intentionally reach out to our community and the inner city of Los Angeles to find those who need to know they can become champions in Jesus. This community engagement helps our church have an enormous influence in Los Angeles by helping meet the city's significant physical and spiritual needs. There's no other way to live victoriously than through following Jesus.

The biblical truth is that there is a champion in every believer because we have become *victorious* in Christ. Since Jesus was victorious over Satan, sin, and death, we can live a victorious life through the transforming power of the Holy Spirit.

Who am I? I am victorious in Jesus. I can be transformed when I embrace that truth.

First Testimony: Point your phone's camera at the QR code for a video testimony from Bishop Kenneth C. Ulmer or go to youtube.com /@FindingFreedomInJesusBook.

I was done! I had failed in marriage. I had failed in life. I felt like I had lost the battle in life . . .

Second Testimony: Point your phone's camera at the QR code for a video testimony from Dr. J. P. Moreland or go to youtube .com/@FindingFreedomInJesusBook.

I have a rare form of cancer. In the last ten years, I have had twenty-one surgeries, two rounds of chemo, and three rounds of radiation . . .

Victorious in Our Culture

Victory in our culture is defined by winning—in sports, wars, elections, or arguments. "Might makes right" and "only the strong survive" are the mottos of our age. For many, it doesn't matter if you have to cheat to gain victory, as long as you win, whether it means taking performance-enhancing drugs, being unethical at work, or cheating on tests. It's victory at all costs. Ricky Bobby in the movie *Talladega Nights* captured our cultural vibe when he said, "If you ain't first, you're last." What a stark contrast from what the Bible teaches: "The last will be first, and the first will be last" (Matthew 20:16).

What Does the Bible Say About Being Victorious?

Victorious in the Old Testament

Victorious through God's power. In the Old Testament, the word *victorious* was typically used to describe a victory in battle. After being liberated from Egypt, the Israelites had to conquer foreigners in order to enter and live in the promised land. God assured them that the same power that miraculously rescued them from Egypt would be with them in their battles: "The LORD your God is the one who goes with you to fight for you against your enemies to give you victory" (Deuteronomy 20:4). No victory came through their own power; it was all through God's power and support. God gave them victory over enemies who were sinful and openly defied the Lord. So in conquering the physical enemy, they were also gaining spiritual victory over sin's influence in the world.

The Israelites learned the lesson of their dependence on God for victory very quickly. The first city they conquered was Jericho. God promised victory to them: "I have delivered Jericho into your hands" (Joshua 6:2). Isn't it funny that they defeated Jericho through shouting and blowing trumpets, not through their military? God wanted them to know that victory was found in him and in him alone. In their second battle, though, they learned that winning wasn't a guarantee. They were easily defeated in Ai because of their sin (Joshua 7). It was only after they dealt with their sin that they achieved victory, because God gives victory to those who follow him obediently (Joshua 8:2).

Later, the Israelite kings learned that their successes in battle were because of the Lord's help (2 Chronicles 13:18). Human swords didn't win wars; God alone gave victory (Psalm 44:3). Although King David was powerful and victorious in many battles, he said, "Now this I know: The LORD gives victory to his anointed. He answers him from his heavenly sanctuary with the victorious power of his right hand. Some trust in chariots and some in horses, but we trust in the name of the LORD our God" (Psalm 20:6–7). This is a great lesson for us today. We often think we are going to advance in school or in our careers based on our own strength. Psalm 20 reminds us that we are victorious *only* when we trust in God.

Future victory. Israel was victorious when they relied on God, but throughout their history we see how their idolatry and sin led to defeat and exile. But all hope was not lost. The prophets talked about a coming victorious king in the line of King David: "Rejoice greatly, Daughter Zion! Shout, Daughter Jerusalem! See, your king comes to you, righteous and victorious, lowly and riding on a donkey, on a colt, the foal of a donkey" (Zechariah 9:9). This hope of a coming messianic King—powerful and victorious—was fulfilled in Jesus. But what kind of victory would this Messiah bring?

Victorious in the New Testament

Near the end of his earthly ministry, Jesus entered Jerusalem riding on a donkey amid shouts of "Hosanna! Blessed is he who comes in the name of the Lord! Blessed is the king of Israel!" (John 12:13). The Jewish crowds recognized Jesus as the expected messianic King, the Son of David. They expected him to begin a military revolt and be victorious over the Romans, like King David was victorious in battle. However, Jesus' enemy was Satan rather than Rome, and he was spiritually victorious over Satan through his death on the cross.

Jesus was victorious over Satan. Jesus' victory over Satan was seen every time he drove out demons: "If I drive out demons by the finger of

God, then the kingdom of God has come upon you" (Luke 11:20). Jesus set free those who were demonized (Mark 1:25). Jesus "disarmed the powers and authorities, [and] he made a public spectacle of them, triumphing over them by the cross" (Colossians 2:15). Jesus triumphed over Satan on the cross, and also was victorious over death: "Death has been swallowed up in victory. Where, O death, is your victory? Where, O death, is your sting?" (1 Corinthians 15:54–55). Jesus redefined *victorious* by his victory over death. Death died as a result of Jesus' death on the cross. Jesus never raised a sword to gain a military victory, but he was spiritually victorious in defeating Satan and his demonic forces on the cross.

Victorious over demons. Because of Jesus' victory, Christians are victorious in at least four areas. First, our main enemy on earth is Satan and his demons, just as it was for Jesus. Jesus was victorious over the world and Satan, and Jesus' followers share in his victory. Never forget that God's power in us is greater than any power of Satan: "You, dear children, are from God and have overcome them, because the one who is in you is greater than the one who is in the world" (1 John 4:4). We face a spiritual enemy who has no authority over our lives, and thus can be victoriously resisted since he is already defeated through our faith in Jesus: "The God of peace will soon crush Satan under your feet" (Romans 16:20). Notice that Paul used "*your* feet," not "Jesus' feet." We have been given victorious power over Satan, and we share in Jesus' victory over him through our faith.

Not only should Satan be resisted in our own lives, but we strive to set others free from demonic influences, just as Jesus did. Jesus instructed his disciples to "drive out demons" (Matthew 10:8). The disciples experienced this: "Impure spirits came out of many" (Acts 8:7). Christians continue Jesus' ministry of overcoming Satan and his demonic forces by being involved in spiritual warfare. We can be victorious in Christ. Spiritual warfare isn't always easy, but we are assured victory.

Living Victorious Today

A young woman who had been assaulted came to talk to me (Matt). After a long discussion, we prayed and asked Jesus to heal that memory and any lingering effects from it. Then she decided to forgive the man who had assaulted her. (See chapter 9 on "forgiven." This didn't mean the man got away with this cruel assault; Jesus believes in justice.) She forgave him, and then she tried to command any demons that might be harassing her as a result of the assault to leave her. I waited about a minute. Silence. I asked her if she was okay. She said, "I can't talk. I literally can't move my tongue." The demons were trying to scare her. We reminded them that they were under Jesus' authority and had no power over her because of her allegiance to Jesus. I asked her to try telling the demons to leave again, and she did so. She immediately felt a peace that she hadn't in a long time. Satan tries to scare us, but we are powerful and victorious because we walk in Jesus' name.

Victorious over sin. Second, Christians are victorious over sin and the world: "Everyone born of God overcomes the world. This is the victory that has overcome the world, even our faith" (1 John 5:4). We are victorious, but only because we are in Christ: "Thanks be to God! He gives us the victory through our Lord Jesus Christ" (1 Corinthians 15:57). Every time we resist sin and choose God's way, it is a victory. Instead of evil, we do good deeds for others: "Do not be overcome by evil, but overcome evil with good." One way to do this, Paul explained, is this: "If your enemy is hungry, feed him" (Romans 12:20–21). Continuing to love God, resist sin, and help even our enemies is victory.

Victorious over injustice. Third, like Jesus, we are victorious over injustice: "In faithfulness [Jesus] will bring forth justice; he will not falter or be discouraged till he establishes justice on earth" (Isaiah 42:3–4, fulfilled in Matthew 12:20). Jesus' messianic role was to bring justice to the world, stamping out all forms of injustice. Followers of Jesus should also be passionate about establishing justice everywhere we can.

Victorious over suffering. Fourth, to be victorious also means Christians are victorious over the suffering and challenges we experience in this world. After Paul's long list of his troubles, including persecution, famine, danger, and sword, he writes, "In all these things we are more than conquerors through him who loved us" (Romans 8:37). How could Paul say that? He suffered so much! It didn't seem like he was a victorious conqueror. Victory for Paul wasn't avoiding trouble but about persevering *through* trouble by maintaining his faith and love for Jesus (Romans 8:38–39). We are victorious when we stand up to trials in our lives through the Spirit's powerful help.

It is crucial to remember that Christians aren't immune from danger, suffering, and persecution, just as Jesus and the early Christians weren't. Jesus suffered and died on a cross. John the Baptist was imprisoned and beheaded. Stephen and most of the twelve apostles were martyred. Paul was persecuted. We will have challenges in this life, but we can be victorious *through* them as we rely on God. The key is to keep our eyes on Jesus in the midst of trials, just as Stephen did as he was being stoned: "Stephen, full of the Holy Spirit, looked up to heaven and saw the glory of God, and Jesus standing at the right hand of God" (Acts 7:55).

The book of Revelation implies that suffering will get worse as the end of the world draws near. Will Christians be victorious through these challenges, or will they turn their backs on God? After the seven plagues come to an end, we read, "Those who had been victorious over the beast . . . held harps given them by God" and sang a song of praise (Revelation 15:2–4). Despite the horrible suffering they had witnessed and experienced, they worshiped God. They were victorious! The beast and kings will fight against Jesus and Christians, but "the Lamb will triumph over them because he is Lord of lords and King of kings—and with him will be his called, chosen and faithful followers" (17:14). The victory belongs to Jesus, and Christians share in that victory—both now and at the end of the world.

Heavenly hope. Jesus was victorious, but wouldn't you agree that we don't presently see or experience enough victories in our day-to-day lives? It seems that the world is winning and that Satan and demons still have much influence in our world. As we said often, we can remain hopeful even in the midst of suffering because we know that God will eventually make all things right for all eternity. Satan will be completely defeated: "The devil, who deceived them, was thrown into the lake of burning sulfur, where the beast and the false prophet had been thrown. They will be tormented day and night for ever and ever" (Revelation 20:10). Evil will not win. Satan's doom is sure. We've read the end of the story, and God wins!

"It's Friday, but Sunday's coming," as Christians say on Good Friday—the day Jesus was crucified—as we look forward to his resurrection on Easter Sunday. The apparent victories that the evil one wins in this world are temporary. You are victorious and hopeful in Jesus. Hang in there, my friend—remain faithful in your love for Jesus because "those who are victorious will inherit all this, and I will be their God and they will be my children" (Revelation 21:7).

When we compete in sports, fans on the sidelines cheer us on to victory, "Go. You can do it. Don't give up." Jesus is doing the same for us as he awaits our arrival on the shores of heaven: "Go. You can do it. Don't give up." There will come a day when the "not yet" turns into "now." You are victorious in Jesus.

Final Biblical Thoughts on Victorious

Israel was victorious in battle only when they relied on God's power. But they did not always rely on God, and as a result, they were defeated and taken into exile. They expected a coming Messiah, in the line of King David, who would bring them victory over their enemies.

In the triumphal entry, Jesus entered Jerusalem on a donkey to shouts of "Hosanna," "Son of David," and "king of Israel." They expected him to be victorious over their enemy, Rome. They expected a military victory, much as King David had achieved in the Old Testament. Jesus, though, defeated the real enemy, Satan. It was a surprising victory. Jesus triumphed over the demonic forces on the cross—defeating sin, evil, Satan, and death. This final defeat of Satan was foreshadowed throughout Jesus' ministry as he drove out demons.

Christians now share in Jesus' victory by continuing his mission on earth. Like Jesus, we can be victorious over sin, Satan, and demonic forces and can establish justice on earth. We can overcome evil by doing good deeds for others. We can persevere through challenges and suffering as we faithfully keep on loving God. Our final reward for being victorious includes eternal life and reigning with Jesus in the new creation.

Jesus' victory on the cross means we are victorious in Christ. Jesus is in our corner, cheering us on to live out the victory every day as we resist the influence of sin and Satan and live a holy life, being transformed more and more into his image.

In one sentence, to be victorious means that you face a spiritual enemy that has no authority over your life, can be victoriously resisted, and is already defeated because of your place in Christ.

Finding Freedom in Jesus

We are already victorious because we share in Jesus' victory, but the battle continues, doesn't it? The devil continues to tempt and accuse us, so how do we fight him? Paul's made it clear: "Put on the full armor of God, so that you can take your stand against the devil's schemes." After listing various parts of the armor, he concluded, "Pray in the Spirit on all occasions with all kinds of prayers and requests" (Ephesians 6:11–18). Have you ever struggled in your prayer life? If prayer is our main weapon to gain victory over the enemy's temptations, is it any wonder that prayer is difficult? Prayer is battle. Prayer is spiritual warfare. Through prayer comes victory. Keep on praying even when it's hard to do; that is where the fight is.

When we understand that we are victorious in Jesus, our lives are transformed. It's a bit like watching a movie for which we already know the ending. We will live and reign forever in heaven with Jesus the Victor. Knowing the ending helps us be victorious on earth, despite challenges and sufferings.

Are you experiencing victory over your enemy Satan? Are you facing spiritual warfare in your life, and helping others who experience spiritual warfare, with the confidence that you are victorious because of the cross? Are you relying on God's greater power to help you to overcome evil by doing good? Are you praying for those who persecute you? As we rely on Jesus' example and the Holy Spirit's strength, we can experience victory in our lives.

Jesus was victorious over injustice and asks his followers to establish justice wherever possible. Where do you see injustice in your neighborhood and city? What specific steps could you take to bring about justice? You may not have much influence to bring change by yourself, but by working with your church or friends and neighbors, your influence can increase.

One of my (John-Paul's) greatest joys as a pastor is watching church members become victorious as they put their trust in God. Some have experienced opposition at home, at work, with friends, with health, and with strong temptations, but God has given them the ability to be victorious through his power. He can do the same for you when you rely on his strength instead of your own.

The trials of this life are not the final story. Jesus is still sitting victoriously on the throne, and he will come again to make all things right. In the meantime, he is cheering you on to victory.

Encouragement and Prayer by John-Paul and Matt: Point your phone's camera at the QR code and follow the link or go to youtube.com /@FindingFreedomInJesusBook.

Reflective Exercises for
Personal or Group Discussion to Embrace That You Are Victorious

1. Practice breathing exercises for three or four minutes each day. Breathe in: "victorious in Christ"; breathe out: "overcoming the world." If you're in a small group, do the breathing together.

2. Go to YouTube, find a worship song with the theme of "victorious," and listen to it several times each day. If you're in a small group, sing the song together.

3. Looking back at the chapter, what did you learn that you didn't know previously?

4. Take some time to ponder the biblical definition of *victorious*: To be victorious means that you face a spiritual enemy who has no authority over your life, can be victoriously resisted, and is already defeated because of your place in Christ. What part of the definition really speaks to you?

5. *Living out victorious:*

a) Reflect on the times you were stuck in hardship, suffering, or sin. How did Jesus bring you victory over those difficult times?

b) What challenges are you facing today? How can reflecting on Jesus' victory over sin, evil, death, and Satan on the cross empower and motivate you to be victorious today—remembering that "victorious" doesn't always mean that Jesus takes away suffering, but that he is with you in the suffering to empower you to remain in God's love.

c) We are victorious when we overcome evil with good. Where is the evil and injustice in your world? Where are the oppressed, the needy, the poor, and the downtrodden in your community? Try to think of one thing you can do this week to help someone else.

6. Take time to meditate on and pray through Psalms 20:6–7; 60:12; 1 Corinthians 15:54–55; 1 John 4:4; 5:4–5; and Revelation 3:21. Allow the Lord to open your heart to the truth that you are victorious in Jesus. You may want to choose one of these passages to memorize.

CHAPTER 19

Adopted

*To all who did receive him, to those who believed
in his name, he gave the right to become children
of God.*

JOHN 1:12

When you hear the word *father*, does it stir up good feelings or bad feelings in you? While some people are fortunate to have caring and loving fathers, others have faced the pain of abandonment, abuse, alcoholism, neglect, or indifference. The U.S. Census Bureau stated in 2023 that 25 percent of children grow up without a father.[1] When we consider what it means to be adopted into the family of God, with God as our Father, our experiences (or lack of experiences) with our earthly fathers impact how we view God as Father. If your dad didn't have time for you, you may conclude that God doesn't have time for you either.

As we reflect on adoption in Jesus, one of our primary goals is to recognize the goodness of our heavenly Father and to understand that being embraced into his family is a truly positive experience. God loves and cares for me. He intentionally chose me. He adopted me. Understanding the truth that we are adopted by a loving Father can transform our identity.

Who am I? I am adopted in Jesus. I can be transformed when I embrace that truth.

Testimony: Point your phone's camera at the QR code for a video testimony from Pastor Brian Moore or go to youtube .com/@FindingFreedomInJesusBook.

At the age of forty, I learned that my dad was not my biological dad. My real dad was a drug dealer . . .

Adopted in Our Culture

In the United States, there is an epidemic of children in need of adoption. Of the 400,000 children in foster care, about 117,000 are waiting to be adopted.[2] Common reasons that children enter the foster system include neglect, abuse, and abandonment. In Los Angeles County alone, more than one hundred kids per day are placed in foster care—each day! Looking at statistics worldwide is even more heartbreaking. It is estimated that there are 147 million orphans in our world, and 20 million of these children are awaiting adoption.[3]

Parents who adopt children assume permanent legal responsibility for those children. They care for, provide, protect, and love them as their very own. Adopted children become members of the family. In the same way, when we believe in Jesus, we are adopted as children of God and become a part of his family (John 1:12). Therefore as believers, we must embrace what it truly means to be adopted by God, our good, good Father.

What Does the Bible Say About Being Adopted?

Adopted in the Old Testament

One of the earliest instances of adoption in the Bible is seen when Pharaoh's daughter adopted Moses (Exodus 2:10). Much later in the Old Testament, Esther was adopted by her cousin, Mordecai (Esther 2:7). And David was spiritually adopted by God: "I will be his father, and he will be my son" (2 Samuel 7:14).

God adopts Israel. God chose the people of Israel and adopted them: "Israel is my firstborn son" (Exodus 4:22). After their rescue from Egypt, God told them, "I will take you as my own people, and I will be your God" (Exodus 6:7). God told the prophet Hosea that the Israelites "will be called 'children of the living God'" (Hosea 1:10). God adopted the Israelites as his own children.

Israel's benefits as adopted. In any adoption, there are benefits and responsibilities. As the adopting Father, God took on responsibilities such as guiding and protecting the Israelites: "I will lead them beside streams of water on a level path where they will not stumble, because I am Israel's father" (Jeremiah 31:9). God also loved and cared for Israel: "The Lord your God carried you, as a father carries his son" (Deuteronomy 1:31). As a Father, God accepted these responsibilities, and Israel, his adopted child, benefited from his love, guidance, and protection.

Israel's responsibilities as adopted. What responsibilities did the Israelites have as adopted children of God? To become more and more like their Father God. But before stating their responsibilities, God provided the theological foundation of their adoption: "You are the children of the Lord your God. You are a people holy to the Lord your God" (Deuteronomy 14:1–2). Just as children naturally imitate their fathers, Israel was called to imitate their Father: "Be holy because I, the Lord your God, am holy" (Leviticus 19:2).

What did holiness require? Many of us know about the Ten

Commandments, but did you know that there are 613 commandments in the Law of Moses? There are 365 negative commandments ("don't . . .") and 248 positive commandments ("do . . ."). These laws weren't intended to ruin the Israelites' lives; obeying them would lead to being blessed with true life and freedom. God reminded the Israelites before they entered the promised land, "All these blessings will come on you and accompany you if you obey the LORD your God" (Deuteronomy 28:2). A point worth repeating here is that true freedom, joy, blessing, and contentment are *only* found when we live the way God designed us to live.

Fatherly discipline. Israel did not always live up to their responsibilities as God's adopted children. They disobeyed him and committed idolatry by following other gods (Isaiah 1:2). As a result, like any good and loving father, God disciplined them. The nation of Israel was conquered and carried away to foreign countries. Many skeptics point to the exile as proof that God is evil and doesn't care for his people, but the opposite is true. If abundant life and freedom are found only in following God's commandments, then the exile should be understood as discipline and not punishment. The goal of the exile was to bring Israel back to God their Father: "The Lord disciplines those he loves, as a father the son he delights in" (Proverbs 3:12). God the Father always desires to welcome back his adopted children.

Future hope. Even in the exile, after Israel had sinned and rejected God over and over again, God did not abandon or disown his adopted children. God's fatherly, unconditional love was seen in his promise that his people would return from exile and be restored. They would once again experience a close relationship with God: "So you will be my people, and I will be your God" (Jeremiah 30:22). These prophecies were fulfilled in the New Testament.

Adopted in the New Testament

The New Testament speaks more specifically to how believers in Jesus are adopted into God's family: "To all who did receive him, to those who believed in his name, he gave the right to become children of God" (John 1:12). God chose to adopt because he delighted in us: "He predestined us for adoption to sonship through Jesus Christ, in accordance with his pleasure and will" (Ephesians 1:5). God wants you to be part of his eternal family and he wants to be your adoptive heavenly Father.

Abba, Father. Jewish children called their father *Abba*, which signified authority as well as intimacy. Our heavenly "Papa" welcomes us. We can call out to him day or night for help and assurance, just as Jesus did in Gethsemane in his time of sorrow: "My Father, if it is possible, may this cup be taken from me" (Matthew 26:39). Remember that Jesus taught his disciples to pray to "*our* Father" (Matthew 6:9). God is *our* Father, just as much as he is Jesus' Father. As adopted sons and daughters, we have an intimate, loving relationship with our *Abba*, Father: "The Spirit you received brought about your adoption to sonship. And by him we cry, 'Abba, Father'" (Romans 8:15). No matter what your relationship with your earthly father is like, don't be afraid to rest your head on your heavenly Father's shoulder and tell him all your troubles. He delights in you.

Christian benefits of adoption. In any adoption, there are both benefits and responsibilities. What benefits do Christians receive as adopted children of God? As God's children, Christians become God's *heirs.* We will receive "an inheritance that can never perish, spoil or fade . . . kept in heaven for you" (1 Peter 1:4). Through adoption, we are transformed from being bound by sin to being co-heirs with Christ (more on that in the next chapter on "co-heir").

Another benefit of being adopted by God is that we receive his *abundant love*: "See what great love the Father has lavished on us, that we should be called children of God! And that is what we are" (1 John 3:1). As a loving Father, he *protects* his children: "I protected them and kept them safe by that name you gave me" (John 17:12). Adoption into God's family means we are adopted into a loving and protecting family— something that many of us did not have growing up. Our Father wants the best for us and always has our backs.

There is a *community* aspect to adoption as well. We have an estimated 2.4 billion Christian brothers and sisters worldwide who were also adopted into God's family. There is something unique and special about the family of God. Loneliness is widespread in our society, and we often feel like we don't belong. But those adopted in Jesus can travel anywhere in the world and instantly find common ground with brothers and sisters in Christ, no matter the culture, race, or ethnicity. We are members of a family that is called to love one another (1 Thessalonians 4:10). How great is it that I have friends from literally all over world because we have the same heavenly Father? The outcasts and outsiders have found a home in God's family.

Living Adopted Today

I (Matt) have a friend who was orphaned as a child in Kenya. He grew up begging on the streets. One day, he heard about a church that was handing out food, so he went. He ended up receiving much more than food; he found Jesus. He was adopted by a Christian family and moved in with them. He went from homeless, hungry, and hopeless to a man of God with a home, food, parents, brothers and sisters, and hope. He recently graduated from Biola University and is now married to a wonderful Christian woman.

Christian responsibilities of adoption. What are the responsibilities of God's adopted children? It's natural for children to follow family rules, right? Just as we saw in the Old Testament, we are called to be *holy*, to live differently from the way those in the world live (1 Peter 1:15). Children naturally become like their Father. Those adopted in Jesus love God and carry out his commands (1 John 5:2). God's adopted children seek to "become blameless and pure, 'children of God without fault in a warped and crooked generation'" (Philippians 2:15).

We are also called to be peacemakers: "Blessed are the peacemakers, for they will be called children of God" (Matthew 5:9). In our divided world, where hate speech is prevalent, especially on social media, Christians are pure, loving, and conciliatory. We are called to live as Christian children, but this change of character and behavior is not done in our own effort. We receive and are "led by the Spirit of God" (Romans 8:14).

God's loving discipline. Despite this call to be loving and holy, we continue to struggle with sin, don't we? When we sin, does God abandon us or disown us? No, just as we saw in the Old Testament, he calls us back to himself. Sometimes, as good fathers do, he needs to discipline us to bring us back: "For what children are not disciplined by their father? If you are not disciplined—and everyone undergoes discipline—then you are not legitimate, not true sons and daughters at all"·(Hebrews 12:7–8). Discipline is not punishment. It is lovingly designed to bring us back to God: "Those whom I love I rebuke and discipline. So be earnest and repent" (Revelation 3:19). He disciplines us because he loves us too much to let us continue going down the wrong path that leads to pain and destruction. Our Father wants us to return to living an abundant life, which is found only in following him.

Heavenly hope. When I (Matt) was a kid, I loved buying the candy called Now and Later because I could eat some right now, but there was plenty to look forward to eating later. Adoption is like that candy—we are adopted into God's family now with heaps of benefits, but the fullness of adoption will be experienced later for all eternity: "Dear friends, now we are children of God, and what we will be has not yet been made known. But we know that when Christ appears, we shall be like him, for we shall see him as he is" (1 John 3:2). Our identity in Christ as adopted sons and daughters and our relationship with our Father God will be perfect and fully experienced in heaven. We shall see Jesus face-to-face. We will be like him. I can't wait!

Final Biblical Thoughts on Adopted

In the Old Testament, God adopted Israel and gave her both benefits and responsibilities. In the New Testament, Christians receive those same benefits and responsibilities when we believe and are adopted in Jesus. We are adopted out of captivity to sin and into the family of God. We now have billions of adopted brothers and sisters in Christ, along with an intimate relationship with our *Abba*, Father, who loves, cares, protects, and guides us. Because our Father fully loves and knows us, we can cry out to him day or night, *"Abba*, Father." We can talk to him about all of our concerns, anxieties, and troubles. He has time for us. As adopted sons and daughters, we are fully functioning members of God's family. As such, we have a responsibility to follow God's ways, but we also have an inheritance awaiting us in heaven as a co-heir with Christ.

In one sentence, to be adopted in Jesus means that you are now a son or daughter of God, adopted by faith in Christ into a rich and eternal inheritance.

Finding Freedom in Jesus

Did you have a good earthly dad? Our relationship with our dad influences how we view God the Father. If your dad told you to "stop crying like a baby," you may be hesitant to go to God with your feelings. Or maybe your dad was too harsh, and now you think that God likes you only when you read your Bible consistently and do the right thing. We pray that this summary of our adoption in Jesus has shown you that God is a very good, loving, and patient Father. He desires the best for you and always has your back. In the reflection questions, we will talk about the need to renounce any lies you may believe about the character of God the Father based on your experience with your earthly father. We've seen too many people misunderstand and mischaracterize God based on lies and bad experiences. The father of lies, Satan, loves it when we continue to believe those lies. We urge you to take time to pray and work through this issue.

In order to avoid the lies of the evil one, we need to continually remind ourselves of the great honor and gracious gift it is to be an adopted son or daughter of God. God is good and graces us with many blessings, including an intimate relationship with *Abba*, Father; the presence of the Holy Spirit to guide and empower us; and an amazing inheritance as a co-heir in Christ. In addition, we are known, cared for, protected, and given purpose, peace, and an abundant life.

Encouragement and Prayer by John-Paul and Matt: Point your phone's camera at the QR code and follow the link or go to youtube.com /@FindingFreedomInJesusBook.

Reflective Exercises for
Personal or Group Discussion to Embrace That You Are Adopted

1. Practice breathing exercises for three or four minutes each day. Breathe in: "adopted son/daughter"; breathe out: "loved as his own." If you're in a small group, do the breathing together.

2. Go to YouTube, find a worship song with the theme of

"adopted," and listen to it several times each day. If you're in a small group, sing the song together.

3. Looking back at the chapter, what did you learn that you didn't know previously?

4. Take some time to ponder the biblical definition of *adopted*: To be adopted in Jesus means that you are now a son or daughter of God, adopted by faith in Christ into a rich and eternal inheritance. What part of the definition really speaks to you?

5. *Living out adopted*:

   a) What negative experiences and memories of your earthly father do you have? In what way(s) have these experiences affected your view of God? Satan, the father of lies, wants you to believe lies about your heavenly Father. We need to unravel any lies we project onto our heavenly Father. Please take time to pray through these memories, asking God to heal them and replace any lies with truth. If you harbor any unforgiveness toward earthly parents, see chapter 9 on "forgiven" so you can work through that.

   b) What does the truth that you are an adopted son or daughter of the King of kings say about your value and self-worth? Do you struggle with low self-image? Spend some time reflecting on God's view of you as a beloved son or daughter. He delights in you and sings over you! Allow Jesus to speak truth into your life.

c) Being adopted in Jesus also brings responsibilities. My (Matt's) father-in-law was a judge in a small town. My wife was often told as a child, "Remember, you are a Barber." (Barber was her last name, not her occupation.) She wasn't supposed to do anything to dishonor the family name. It's the same for us as God's adopted children. Our behavior should bring honor, not shame, to our Father God. Can you think of ways to bring God honor by the way you live? Are there any habits or hang-ups that need to change because they are bringing dishonor to God?

6. Take time to meditate on and pray through Exodus 6:7; Leviticus 19:2; Jeremiah 31:9; John 1:12; Romans 8:14–17; and 1 John 3:1. Allow the Lord to open your heart to the truth that you are adopted in Jesus. You may want to choose one of these passages to memorize.

CHAPTER 20

Co-Heir

Now if we are children, then we are heirs—heirs of
God and co-heirs with Christ.

ROMANS 8:17

Every now and then, we read about someone's rich uncle dying and leaving them everything. All of a sudden, they inherit a fortune and become rich. We all secretly hope for that, right? Well, I've got even better news. The God of the universe has named *you* as his heir. When we believe in Jesus, God adopts us into his family as sons and daughters, as we saw in the last chapter. One of the benefits of being adopted is that we become heirs of God, co-heirs with Christ. Does that mean you will inherit millions of dollars? Nope, sorry, you can't go buy that new car or house. What we will inherit from God is even *better* than a pile of money!

Who am I? I am a co-heir with Jesus. I can be transformed when I embrace that truth.

Testimony: Point your phone's camera at the QR code for a video testimony from Udo or go to youtube.com /@FindingFreedomInJesusBook.

I experienced tragedy in the death of my father at the age of nine. I didn't know how I could ever heal from this. I was fatherless . . .

Co-Heir in Our Culture

An heir is a person who is legally entitled to inherit the property of someone after that person dies. A co-heir is a person who shares the inheritance with someone else. Someday, when my (Matt) mother passes away, my brother and I will be co-heirs of her assets. In 2022, when Queen Elizabeth II passed away, her son Charles inherited her fortune, estimated to be worth more than $500 million, including castles and the Crown Jewels. Is our inheritance as Christians really better than this? Well, let's turn to the Bible and see.

What Does the Bible Say About Being a Co-Heir?

Co-Heir in the Old Testament

Physical inheritance. What inheritance did the people of God receive in the Old Testament? They inherited physical blessings from God, such as the promised land of Canaan: "I will give your descendants all this land I promised them, and it will be their inheritance forever" (Exodus

32:13). The land was good, described as "a land flowing with milk and honey" (Leviticus 20:24). Biblical scholars think this meant the land was fertile for growing fruits and vegetables and for raising livestock. In that culture, a rich person was someone who owned a lot of animals. God blessed the Israelites with the rich inheritance of the promised land so they could prosper.

Spiritual inheritance. A few Bible passages describe a spiritual rather than physical inheritance. Noah became an "heir of the righteousness that is in keeping with faith" (Hebrews 11:7). Proverbs said, "The wise inherit honor" (Proverbs 3:35). King David said that God's commands were his inheritance and joy (Psalm 119:111 NASB). We may at times view God's laws as burdensome, but David rejoiced in them and found comfort in them. God's commands were the guardrails that kept David from veering off the path and over a cliff. David treasured God's law as his inheritance. Psalm 119 described many benefits that come from obeying God's commands, including life and prosperity. The people of God in the Old Testament had an amazing inheritance from God—rich land, righteousness, honor, and joy. These gifts are much more valuable than all of Great Britain's vast wealth.

As we will see in the New Testament, Christians become heirs through faith in Jesus, and our inheritance is far more valuable than land or gold.

Co-Heir in the New Testament

Co-heir with Jesus. Jesus is the "heir of all things" (Hebrews 1:2), but he lovingly chooses to share his inheritance with us. Since we are adopted into his family, we become his co-heirs: "Now if we are children, then we are heirs—heirs of God and co-heirs with Christ" (Romans 8:17). Stop and let that sink in: We are co-heirs with Jesus. That's amazing, isn't it?

Jew and Gentile. Although the Gentiles were mostly excluded as heirs in the Old Testament, they are now included: "This mystery is that through the gospel the Gentiles are heirs together with Israel, members together of one body, and sharers together in the promise in

Christ Jesus" (Ephesians 3:6). The racial division was demolished. Jews and Gentiles are co-heirs together.

Spiritual inheritance. Although the inheritance in the Old Testament usually referred to a physical inheritance, the term *heir* was typically used in a spiritual sense in the New Testament. Our inheritance includes salvation (Hebrews 1:14), along with an abundant and full life, now and for all eternity (John 10:10). God saved us, "so that, having been justified by his grace, we might become heirs having the hope of eternal life" (Titus 3:7). The inheritance of eternal life means we receive joy, peace, purpose, forgiveness, hope, love, and the removal of shame. We are empowered by the Spirit to leave behind old behaviors like greed, lust, selfishness, and impatience and now experience a better quality of life in Jesus. Our inheritance is not just reserved for us in heaven but is received *now* in this present life.

Living Co-Heir Today

A woman who was living in sexual immorality would sometimes come to our (John-Paul's) church's Bible study smelling like marijuana. Over time, I watched God transform her life. She fully surrendered to Christ and became a co-heir with Christ. The richness of her spiritual inheritance was evident to all of us. She joined a life group and our prayer team. She was spiritually rich, no longer chasing money, sex, or smoking to numb her pain. She was experiencing the richness of her spiritual inheritance!

Co-heirs reign. As co-heirs, we inherit the kingdom of God (Matthew 25:34), which is a spiritual kingdom in which King Jesus reigns. Although we Christians do not inherit a physical throne, like King Charles III of Great Britain did, part of our inheritance is to reign alongside God over creation: "You have made them to be a kingdom and priests to serve our

God, and they will reign on the earth" (Revelation 5:10). We may not be kings and queens ruling over countries, but we are ambassadors of King Jesus, representing him everywhere we go, administering love, justice, and peace throughout the spiritual kingdom of God.

A family of heirs. One of the greatest blessings of being adopted into God's family as co-heirs with Jesus is that we are also co-heirs with all 2.4 billion fellow believers (see Colossians 1:12). We have fellowship and community with believers worldwide since we all are members of God's family. We are all co-heirs together with Jesus—one big family of God.

The cost. Our inheritance is priceless, obtained freely by faith in Jesus, but there is also a cost. Paul said, "Now if we are children, then we are heirs—heirs of God and co-heirs with Christ, if indeed we share in his sufferings in order that we may also share in his glory" (Romans 8:17). Paul wasn't saying that if we suffer we will become co-heirs. No, we become co-heirs when we believe and follow Jesus. Living out our faith as co-heirs in this cruel, evil world will include suffering, just as it did for Jesus. So don't be surprised when suffering comes to you. Jesus suffered, and he is with us when we suffer. His presence through tough times is part of our inheritance.

Jesus may even ask us to leave family or jobs to be an ambassador or missionary in another place. As difficult as it may be to do so, there is even an inheritance in going: "And everyone who has left houses or brothers or sisters or father or mother or wife or children or fields for my sake will receive a hundred times as much and will inherit eternal life" (Matthew 19:29).

Heavenly hope. We are co-heirs with Christ right now. We have already inherited an abundance of blessings, but there is more to come. We will experience our full inheritance after our death when we receive our heavenly inheritance. The Holy Spirit's presence within us is a promise guaranteeing that one day we will inherit everything without limit (Ephesians 1:14), "an inheritance that can never perish, spoil or fade. This inheritance is kept in heaven for you" (1 Peter 1:4). It's a guarantee; our heavenly inheritance is waiting for us.

Final Biblical Thoughts on Co-Heir

The Israelites inherited the prosperous promised land, but the Old Testament did not talk much about a spiritual inheritance. The New Testament fulfilled and made the spiritual inheritance explicit. Both Jews and Gentiles can now be adopted into the family of God through faith in Jesus and become co-heirs with Christ. We inherit an abundance of spiritual blessings, including eternal life, salvation, and the fruit of the Spirit. As heirs of the kingdom of God, we reign on earth as we administer justice.

Even though we are heirs with a prized inheritance, we will still undergo suffering. But all of the suffering will go away when we receive the fullness of our inheritance in heaven. Until then, we have the Holy Spirit within us who guarantees our inheritance and empowers us to enjoy life with Jesus, our co-heir, in the family of God.

In one sentence, to be a co-heir with Christ means that God our Father has blessed you here on earth and later in heaven with a rich inheritance of abundant life.

Finding Freedom in Jesus

Have you thought today about all that you have inherited in Christ? I usually don't. I get caught up in the material possessions I desire much more than the spiritual inheritance I have already received. When we trust in Jesus, we become co-heirs with Christ because we are adopted into the family of God. Our Father God lovingly and joyfully shares his inheritance with us. Be sure to meditate daily on the present blessings that God has given to you—eternal life, salvation, and entrance into his kingdom. God is good all the time.

Hope. I love the word *hope*. We live in a country where a rising number of adults experience anxiety or depression each year.[1] When I (Matt) talk with people struggling with mental health issues (as have I), I always emphasize the word *hope*. Looking to the future can brighten a stormy day. We are not only heirs of amazing blessings right now, but we also have the hope of a future inheritance. We are not hopeless, but rather hopeful. *Hope* can be defined this way: <u>H</u>old <u>O</u>n <u>P</u>ain <u>E</u>nds. Hope can transform our perspective here on earth when suffering arrives. Hope means that things are going to get better—perhaps not in our life here but certainly in heaven. Keep hope alive in your life by thinking often about your eternal inheritance, as well as your present spiritual inheritance. In heaven, there will be no more suffering, anxiety, or depression. Our heavenly inheritance can help us maintain hope and hold on in difficult times.

God must really love us, right? Look at our inheritance as co-heirs with Christ. He has blessed us "with every spiritual blessing in Christ" (Ephesians 1:3), including an inheritance of salvation, hope, and the promise that we will reign with Jesus for all eternity. I certainly don't feel worthy of such an inheritance, which is why the truth that I am a co-heir is so powerful. It does not depend on my feelings, but rather on the truth of Scripture.

Who am I? I am a co-heir with Christ.

Encouragement and Prayer by John-Paul and Matt: Point your phone's camera at the QR code and follow the link or go to youtube.com /@FindingFreedomInJesusBook.

Reflective Exercises for
Personal or Group Discussion to
Embrace That You Are a Co-Heir

1. Practice breathing exercises for three or four minutes each day. Breathe in: "co-heir with Christ"; breathe out: "abundant blessings." If you're in a small group, do the breathing together.

2. Go to YouTube, find a worship song with the theme of "co-heir," and listen to it several times each day. If you're in a small group, sing the song together.

3. Looking back at the chapter, what did you learn that you didn't know previously?

4. Take some time to ponder the biblical definition of *co-heir*. To be a co-heir with Christ means that God our Father has blessed you here on earth and later in heaven with a rich inheritance of abundant life. What part of the definition really speaks to you?

5. *Living out co-heir.*
   a) Compare the inheritance of King Charles III of Great Britain to your spiritual inheritance in Jesus. Would you rather be an heir of the throne of England or of God's heavenly throne? Why? Take some time to list your spiritual inheritance in Jesus and to thank God for it.
   b) It is crucial to fully embrace our identity in Christ. All too often, we allow our feelings to dictate our

lives. You are a co-heir with Christ. That is who you are. Allow that truth to transform your self-image today. Look in the mirror and imagine that Jesus, your co-heir, is standing beside you, handing your inheritance to you. What would he say to you?

c) As a co-heir, you have brothers and sisters in Christ who are also co-heirs. How does this truth cause you to love them and seek fellowship with believers even more?

6. Take time to meditate on and pray through Exodus 32:13; Psalm 8:4–6; Romans 8:17; Ephesians 5:5; and Revelation 21:7. Allow the Lord to open your heart to the truth that you are a co-heir with Christ. You may want to choose one of these passages to memorize.

CHAPTER 21

Hopeful

Those who hope in the LORD
will renew their strength.
They will soar on wings like eagles;
they will run and not grow weary,
they will walk and not be faint.

ISAIAH 40:31

Let's face it, life is tough. That being said, nearly every Old Testament section in this book ends with the hope of a coming Messiah who will bring restoration, and nearly every New Testament section ends with the hope of a bright future in heaven. It is our hope (pun intended) that this summary chapter will help us trust in the Lord and find rest in him, even in the darkest of times and tribulations.

A few years ago, I (Matt) struggled with anxiety that resulted from an inner ear problem. For a couple months, I lost hope that things would ever get better. I was stuck on a mattress in my living room, convinced I would never return to teaching or to any sort of normal life again. I understand the tragedy and darkness of losing hope. It was a rough time, with a lot of dark, sleepless, tear-filled nights. Thanks to counseling, prayer, and meditating on God's Word, I also understand the positive outlook of an expectant confidence and the hope of a brighter future. The Lord has brought me back from the edge.

Have you lost hope in your life? We are praying that this chapter reminds you that your faithful and trustworthy God has promised you a future and a hope.

Who am I? I am hopeful in Jesus. I can be transformed when I embrace that truth.

Testimony: Point your phone's camera at the QR code for a video testimony from Dr. John-Paul Foster or go to youtube .com/@FindingFreedomInJesusBook.

I had great hopes of playing collegiate basketball and studying medicine, but when I injured my ankle, it destroyed my hope. I felt hopeless and angry with God . . .

Hopeful in Our Culture

In our culture, *hopeful* means we *want* something to happen or be true, and we have a pretty good reason for thinking it might happen. Some hope to win the lottery, a free trip to an exotic part of the world, or a new car at a raffle. How much hope a person has is based on how much trust one has in themselves or in someone else to make it happen.

Hope in our culture is not based on a solid foundation. It is wishful thinking more than expectant confidence. Christian hope is different.

Our hope is built on nothing less than Jesus, the unchanging and faithful Rock, a solid foundation, which is far better than any hope the world can offer.

What Does the Bible Say About Being Hopeful?

Hopeful in the Old Testament

Abraham's hope. Abraham is the model of hope in the Old Testament. God called Abram at the age of seventy-five to "go from your country, your people and your father's household to the land I will show you. I will make you into a great nation, and I will bless you . . . and all peoples on earth will be blessed through you" (Genesis 12:1–3). Abraham obeyed God—but then he went through a famine and twenty-five years of an inability to father a child with his wife Sarah. He was now a hundred years old. Would God fulfill his promises? Could Abraham continue to be hopeful? In these difficult circumstances, he seemingly lost hope: "Abraham fell facedown; he laughed and said to himself, 'Will a son be born to a man a hundred years old?'" (17:17).

The Lord reminded Abraham, "Is anything too hard for the LORD?" (Genesis 18:14). Abraham struggled and yet continued to believe in God and remain hopeful until finally, "Sarah became pregnant and bore a son to Abraham in his old age, at the very time God had promised him" (21:2). The apostle Paul summarized Abraham's story: "Against all hope, Abraham in hope believed and so became the father of many nations, just as it had been said to him" (Romans 4:18). Despite temporary doubt, Abraham was hopeful in God's promises when all looked hopeless.

The Israelites' hope. The Israelites were not hopeful in their own power, wealth, or strength: "Some trust in chariots and some in horses, but we trust in the name of the LORD our God" (Psalm 20:7). They were hopeful because of the Lord's help and strength: "Israel, put your hope in the LORD, for with the LORD is unfailing love and with him is full redemption" (Psalm 130:7). They could be hopeful in God because "The

LORD is trustworthy in all he promises and faithful in all he does" (Psalm 145:13). God is faithful. When God says it, I believe it!

God's people could also be hopeful and confidently trust in God because of his promise to always be with them: "When you pass through the waters, I will be with you" (Isaiah 43:2). In fact, all of Isaiah 43 gave reasons for Israel to hope in God: "I have summoned you by name; you are mine" . . . "You are precious and honored in my sight, and . . . I love you" . . . "I, even I, am the LORD, and apart from me there is no savior" (Isaiah 43:1, 4, 11). God reminded them of his love and care for them in the past and promised to continue to care for them in the future. They could hope in God's promises. Sometimes it takes looking backward to look forward. Looking back at God's faithfulness gives us hope as we look forward to his never-ending faithfulness.

Job's and Daniel's hope. Being hopeful in the Old Testament didn't mean that life was without struggles, as we saw in Abraham's story. Just look at Job. He lost his property, his children died, and he experienced great physical agony, and yet Job confidently stated, "Though he slay me, yet will I hope in him" (Job 13:15). Daniel was thrown into the lions' den, and yet "when Daniel was lifted from the den, no wound was found on him, because he had trusted in his God" (Daniel 6:23). How could Job and Daniel continue to hope in God?

Jeremiah's hope. When the city of Jerusalem was destroyed, it appeared that all hope was lost for Israel, and yet the prophet Jeremiah continued to hope and trust in the Lord: "Yet this I call to mind and therefore I have hope: Because of the LORD's great love we are not consumed, for his compassions never fail. They are new every morning; great is your faithfulness. I say to myself, 'The LORD is my portion; therefore I will wait for him'" (Lamentations 3:21–24). How could Jeremiah continue to hope in God?

Shadrach's, Meshach's, and Abednego's hope. These three exiles were thrown into a furnace that was heated seven times hotter than normal. When King Nebuchadnezzar looked into the fiery furnace, he saw four men instead of the three he had thrown into the fire, and "the fourth looks like a son of the gods" (Daniel 3:25). Biblical scholars debate as to whether the fourth "man" was an angel or a manifestation of Jesus, but what is certain is that the three men were not alone in their time of need. God's presence was there to give them hope. How could these three men continue to hope in God?

Despite difficult circumstances, God continued to love, to make promises, to be gracious, to be Israel's God. God's people remained hopeful because they experienced God's presence in the midst of their suffering. God's faithfulness to fulfill his promises gave hope to the hopeless. God is trustworthy. Being hopeful transforms our strength: "Those who hope in the LORD will renew their strength. They will soar on wings like eagles; they will run and not grow weary, they will walk and not be faint" (Isaiah 40:31).

Future hope. When Jerusalem was destroyed and the people were carried off into foreign lands, hope seemed to be lost, and yet God promised to restore them. The story was not over. The Lord still had a future for them: "'I know the plans I have for you,' declares the LORD, 'plans to prosper you and not to harm you, plans to give you hope and a future'" (Jeremiah 29:11). The exiled nation continued to hope because God promised that they would return home to their own land (Jeremiah 31:17). Don't give up; keep on hoping!

Although they were prisoners in foreign lands, God made a promise: "Return to your fortress, you prisoners of hope; even now I announce that I will restore twice as much to you" (Zechariah 9:12). God's promises brought hope even in the midst of suffering. God called his people to rejoice, trust, and be hopeful. The Messiah would come; God would restore. They could be hopeful as they trusted in God's promises. The coming Messiah would restore Israel.

Hopeful in the New Testament

Hopeful in Jesus. Just as Israel hoped in God in the Old Testament, Jesus brought hope to Christians in the New Testament: "In his name the nations will put their hope" (Matthew 12:21, in fulfillment of Isaiah

42:4). Jesus brought hope not only to Jews but also to Gentiles (Romans 15:12, in fulfillment of Isaiah 11:10). Christians can be hopeful because Jesus "loved us and by his grace gave us eternal encouragement and good hope" (2 Thessalonians 2:16). We can trust that God "does not lie" (Titus 1:2). Hope is easier when we see that God is trustworthy, fulfills his promises, and has our best interests at heart.

Hope in the midst of suffering. Even if we are confident about our future hope in heaven, it can be hard to remain hopeful because life is difficult and filled with temptations, trials, and suffering. Let's look at a few examples of people who remained hopeful despite difficulties: Jesus, Paul, and Martha.

Jesus' hope. Jesus showed how to remain hopeful when he continued to trust that God would deliver him despite an agonizing crucifixion (Psalm 22:8; Matthew 27:43). Because God is always faithful, Jesus fully trusted in his plan. We learn from Jesus to trust God's plan. Who would have guessed that the cross would turn out to be something good? Who would have guessed that the day of Jesus' death would be called "Good Friday"? We cannot know the end of our stories and how God may use our suffering for good. We can trust him.

Paul's hope. Paul also experienced vast suffering: "We were under great pressure, far beyond our ability to endure, so that we despaired of life itself. Indeed, we felt we had received the sentence of death" (2 Corinthians 1:8–9). Paul continued to be hopeful despite intense and continual suffering: prison, forty lashes, beatings, stonings, shipwrecks, danger, bandits, sleeplessness, hunger, thirst, cold, and nakedness (2 Corinthians 11:23–27).

How did Paul maintain hope in the Lord through all of these trials? Here is the key: Paul knew that God's "power is made perfect in weakness" (2 Corinthians 12:9). Paul saw Jesus' example of weakness and learned that God's strength is often displayed through weakness. So Paul remained hopeful in suffering, knowing he was suffering because of his ministry for Jesus. He was preaching the gospel and leading thousands to eternal life (Ephesians 3:13).

Martha's hope. Martha also understood what it meant to be hopeful in the midst of impossible circumstances. Her brother Lazarus had died. Since he may well have been Martha's primary source of stability and income, his death devastated her both emotionally and economically. Martha was convinced that Jesus could have saved him: "'Lord,' Martha said to Jesus, 'if you had been here, my brother would not have died'" (John 11:21). You can hear the disappointment in her voice. Have you ever been there—asking Jesus, "Where are you? Do you really care? Why haven't you done something"?

Jesus was not there, and Lazarus had died. But Martha clung to hope. She said, "But I know that even now God will give you whatever you ask" (John 11:22). I know we might read this verse and conclude that Martha was hopeful because she thought Jesus would raise her brother back to life. But here's the truth: She did *not* expect Jesus to raise him back to life. The text made it clear that she was not expecting Lazarus to come back to life (John 11:24, 39).

Jesus went to Lazarus's tomb and commanded that the stone be rolled away. If Martha were expecting him to come back to life, she would have run to the tomb and rolled the stone away herself, but she didn't. She told Jesus *not* to roll away the tomb because "by this time there is a bad odor, for he has been there four days" (John 11:39). It was too late.

Lazarus was dead, and Martha did not expect him to come back to life. There is no hope for someone to come back to life after being dead for *three* days, and Lazarus had been dead for *four* days. *Jesus came too late,* she thought. Yes, she believed Lazarus would be resurrected at the end of days, but she didn't believe he could be raised back to life in the here and now—an impossibility because four days had passed. In this hopeless situation, Martha continued to trust in Jesus and remained hopeful, despite not experiencing his rescue. Martha fully trusted Jesus in an impossible situation. She had hope despite her miserable reality.

Martha's example is one of the best examples in the Bible of continued trust despite impossible circumstances. From her perspective, Jesus had let her down, and yet she continued to hope.

Living Hopeful Today

I (John-Paul) received a phone call from the mother of a six-year-old boy asking me to make a hospital visit. The doctors told her there was nothing more they could do, and she would have to decide whether she wanted them to pull the plug on the ventilator that was keeping him alive. Because she was a woman of faith, she asked me to pray for her son. She called the nurses and doctors into the room and said, "I know what you told me, but this is my pastor. I am a woman of faith, and I'm going to trust God to revive my son."

I will never forget the response of one of the doctors. He said, "I don't mind standing in this room while you pray, but before you do, I need you to know the facts of your son's condition. There's nothing we can do." In that moment, I prayed and asked God to manifest his glory so that atheists, nonbelievers, and believers alike would know that God still provides hope to the hopeless. A few days later, I received a phone call that the son had been healed. In her hopelessness she was still able to trust God in the midst of impossible circumstances. I want you to know, though, that this woman had hope in God before her son was healed. She trusted him, regardless of the end result.

How to remain hopeful. Jesus, Paul, Martha, and many others in the New Testament teach us what it means to be hopeful and to expectantly trust in Jesus, despite suffering and seemingly impossible circumstances. How did they do it? They remained hopeful in God's promise to be with them: "Never will I leave you; never will I forsake you" (Hebrews 13:5). Jesus promised, "Surely I am with you always, to the very end of the age" (Matthew 28:20). God the Father is with us;

Jesus the Son is with us; and so is the Holy Spirit, whose power helps us to be hopeful in the midst of difficulties (Romans 15:13). The presence and power of the triune God allow us to wait patiently, joyfully, and calmly (Romans 8:25; 12:12; 15:13).

Perhaps knowing we are never alone in the midst of our suffering is the best way to remain hopeful. When I (Matt) was lying on a mattress for two months with dizziness and anxiety, the feeling of God's presence was what kept me going. I had hope as "an anchor for the soul" (Hebrews 6:19), and I tried my best to "hold unswervingly to the hope we profess, for he who promised is faithful" (Hebrews 10:23).

Our hope does not come from our wealth, our own abilities, or our positive wishful thinking. We are hopeful in Jesus' presence and faithfulness through the Holy Spirit's empowerment. The storms may not stop, but neither will the rainbows in the midst of the storms we face.

Hopeful in death. Hope even allows us to be encouraged as we face death: "Brothers and sisters, we do not want you to be uninformed about those who sleep in death, so that you do not grieve like the rest of mankind, who have no hope" (1 Thessalonians 4:13). Death is a dreadful enemy, but through Jesus, "Death has been swallowed up in victory" (1 Corinthians 15:54). Death is no longer the end of the story; its sting has been taken away. We can be hopeful because there is life after our physical life ends. Read this next statement carefully: We have life after life because Jesus' death destroyed death!

Heavenly hope. As we've declared throughout this book, only in heaven we will fully experience each of these terms. The promise of heaven changes everything. It provides hope in this life, even in the midst of seemingly impossible circumstances. If not for the promise of heaven, we are to be pitied: "If only for this life we have hope in Christ, we are of all people most to be pitied" (1 Corinthians 15:19).

Thankfully, God, who doesn't lie, has promised that there is a future "stored up for you in heaven" (Colossians 1:5). Christians have a lot to be hopeful for in the future, including the blessed hope of Jesus' return, the promise of eternal life, our resurrection from the dead, our becoming a new creation, and seeing Jesus face-to-face (Titus 2:13; 3:7; Acts 23:6; Romans 8:23; 1 John 3:2). All of these promises will be fulfilled in heaven. We won't experience any of them fully right now, but we are expectantly confident—that is, hopeful—because God has promised we will spend eternity in heaven with Jesus. Our future is secure. When we think about the brevity of life here in comparison to an eternity with Jesus in heaven, we can be hopeful because we know that things will get better.

Heaven is eternal, and knowing that truth provides motivation to be hopeful, as we live in the assurance that our present challenges will soon end. Hang in there because better things are ahead. The best is yet to come. All of our trials will end for all eternity. These aren't just empty words or clichés; they are the promises of a faithful, loving, and trustworthy God.

Final Biblical Thoughts on Hopeful

Hope is all about the future. We can trust that we will spend eternity in heaven because God is trustworthy and always fulfills his promises. Although we have a confident expectation about the future, it doesn't mean our lives are free from problems or suffering. The Old Testament tells of a multitude of people who were filled with hope despite difficult circumstances. Grab your Bible and take a few minutes to read Hebrews 11 to learn about Rahab, Gideon, Samson, David, Samuel, and many other men and women who underwent enormous suffering and persecution and yet remained hopeful in God's promises because God is trustworthy. May we do the same!

The Old Testament's promises and prophecies are fulfilled in Jesus, who remained hopeful even as he suffered horrific physical agony on the cross. Paul, Martha, and many other New Testament people also teach us how to remain faithful and hopeful in the midst of severe trials.

We Christians can be hopeful through the Holy Spirit's empowerment. Jesus' death on the cross provided the ultimate hope of eternal life—a better life here on earth and the promise of eternal life with Jesus forever. Despite our circumstances, we patiently hope, with confident expectancy and trust, because Jesus is faithful to his promises.

In one sentence, to be hopeful means that you have an expectant confidence and trust in Jesus, despite impossible circumstances, that God will fulfill his promises and that all will be made right for all eternity.

Finding Freedom in Jesus

We often get caught up in our present circumstances, don't we? When we talk with people who struggle with suffering, depression, or anxiety, they seem trapped in a small cage. Their trials allow them to see only a few moments right in front of them. They're stuck. They forget the hope they have for the future. What if we could see all of eternity from God's perspective? What if we could truly believe God's promises about the future? What if we lived confidently and with hope today, knowing that God's promises to make all things right are true, and that his promises about heaven are true? These truths would transform your life!

A glimpse of hope. We do have a glimpse of the future, don't we? The Bible reads, "The Lamb at the center of the throne will be their shepherd; 'he will lead them to springs of living water.' 'And God will wipe away every tear from their eyes'" (Revelation 7:17), and "'There will be no more death' or mourning or crying or pain, for the old order of things has passed away" (21:4). Those texts paint a picture of our future in heaven. We can confidently hope in our future because God is trustworthy. God said it, and I believe it.

Last week, Lauren, a former student of mine (Matt), posted on Instagram that her grandfather had died. She wrote about one of her final conversations with him, in which he said, "Someday soon I'm going to go to sleep, and I won't wake up here in this house with the smell of bacon cooking. I'll be in heaven. I'm going to wake up in Jesus' embrace. I'm going to see Jesus. He's going to know me . . . and I'm going to know him. How beautiful is that?" Her grandfather had no fear in death because he was filled with the hope of the truth of God's promises.

In a difficult, depressed, and anxious world, we need hope that there is more than what we can see with our physical eyes. We need hope for a better future. We need hope in the supernatural. We need hope that God has sent angels to serve and minister to us (Hebrews 1:14). We need hope that God is real.

Hope isn't always easy. We don't want to imply that being hopeful is easy. Life is difficult, isn't it? There is a tension between the already and the not yet, between the present and the future. It's crucial to remember that our hope is not based on our feelings. Did you hear that? Our hope is *not* based on our feelings, but on the completed work of Jesus. As the old hymn declares:

> *My hope is built on nothing less*
> *Than Jesus' blood and righteousness.*
> *I dare not trust the sweetest frame,*
> *But wholly lean on Jesus' name.*

> *On Christ, the solid rock, I stand,*
> *All other ground is sinking sand;*
> *All other ground is sinking sand.[1]*

We are hopeful *in Christ alone.* A bright future awaits us in heaven. Do you believe that?

How to be hopeful. All of these promises of a future and a hope are wonderful, but how can I become more hopeful? How can I have a confident expectation that my future will be better? We think the best way is to meditate on the character of God. He is trustworthy, loving, caring, and compassionate. God never lies and can bring good out of evil. Just as the cross turned into a triumph, our current suffering can lead to something beautiful. We don't yet know how our suffering will be used by God for good. If a loving God promises a future hope for all believers, we can believe him. Are you meditating on the truths of who God is?

Comforting the hopeless. Those who learn to believe in and cling to God's promises find hope and are comforted and confident. As a result of our hope, we can comfort others: "Praise be to the God and Father of our Lord Jesus Christ, the Father of compassion and the God of all comfort, who comforts us in all our troubles, so that we can comfort those in any trouble with the comfort we ourselves receive from God" (2 Corinthians 1:3–4). Is someone you know going through trials who seems hopeless? A text message, an email, a phone call, or a visit may be the only hope they experience today.

There's only one way to have hope in this world—through Jesus. Indeed, "All other ground is sinking sand."

Encouragement and Prayer by John-Paul and Matt: Point your phone's camera at the QR code and follow the link or go to youtube.com /@FindingFreedomInJesusBook.

Reflective Exercises for
Personal or Group Discussion to
Embrace That You Are Hopeful

1. Practice breathing exercises for three or four minutes each day. Breathe in: "in Christ alone"; breathe out: "I find hope." If you're in a small group, do the breathing together.

2. Go to YouTube, find a worship song with the theme of "hopeful," and listen to it several times each day. If you're in a small group, sing the song together.

3. Looking back at the chapter, what did you learn that you didn't know previously?

4. Take some time to ponder the biblical definition of *hopeful*: To be hopeful means that you have an expectant confidence and trust in Jesus, despite impossible circumstances, that God will fulfill his promises and that all will be made right for all eternity. What part of the definition really speaks to you?

5. *Living out hopeful*:
   a) Make a list of God's characteristics, such as loving, compassionate, and faithful. What else can you add to the list? Spend time meditating on God's character and his promises of a future and a hope for you. For extra credit, find biblical passages for each of these characteristics.
   b) Make a list of when God has been faithful to you in the past to encourage you to keep on hoping and

trusting God about your future. Take time to praise God for his faithfulness to you.

c) Because of the hope and comfort you have found in Jesus, think about the people in your life you can encourage and bring hope and comfort to amid their trials. Anyone come to mind?

6. Take time to meditate on and pray through Psalm 130:7–8; Isaiah 40:31; Romans 4:18; Colossians 1:5; and 1 Thessalonians 4:13. Allow the Lord to open your heart to the truth that you are hopeful in Christ. You may want to choose one of these passages to memorize.

Final Encouragement

It doesn't matter what your past is, as you've heard in the twenty-one video testimony stories at the beginning of each chapter. We are all damaged, bruised, or broken. We all have negative self-talk. Satan tries to use our past against us, but God sent Jesus to rescue us from Satan's lies and transform our lives into image-bearing women and men who walk in the power of the Holy Spirit and experience freedom in Jesus. What truly matters is your future, not your past. Why? Because God transforms your past to make you a new creation in Christ: "Therefore if anyone is in Christ, this person is a new creation; the old things passed away; behold, new things have come" (2 Corinthians 5:17 NASB).

God wants you to fully embrace your identity in Jesus so you can be transformed. He wants you to see the truth of who you are. Who are you in Jesus? What is your true identity in Christ?

I am . . .

Transformed	Rescued	Blessed
Loved	Forgiven	Alive
Known	Righteous	Empowered
Beautiful	Redeemed	Victorious
Image Bearer	Reconciled	Adopted
Free	Saved	Co-Heir
Shame-Free	Holy	Hopeful

God has transformed you from sinful and shameful to blameless and beautiful: "Christ loved the church and gave himself up for her to make her holy, cleansing her by the washing with water through the word, and to present her to himself as a radiant church, without stain or wrinkle or any other blemish, but holy and blameless" (Ephesians 5:25–27). God rejoices over you: "He will take great delight in you; in his love he will no longer rebuke you, but will rejoice over you with singing" (Zephaniah 3:17).

Transformed thinking. Have you embraced the truth of these terms? How has your self-talk and confidence in your identity changed as a result of reading what the Bible says about each term and doing the breathing, worshiping, and reflective exercises? When your mind wanders now, do you naturally think of your identity in Jesus? Are you able to speak truth to yourself about who you are in Christ, or are you still entangled in negative self-talk? Pay attention to your self-talk today and compare it to your self-talk when you began to read the book.

Transformed actions. God desires to transform and renew your thinking, as well as your actions. All these terms can be turned into actions: Those who are forgiven, forgive; those who are loved, love; those who are rescued, rescue; those who are reconciled, reconcile; those who are alive, bring life; and those who are saved, save.

I (Matt) gave an early draft of this book to a relative to read before it was published. This relative hadn't talked to her sister for months because of a problem between the two of them. As she read through the book and embraced her identity in Jesus, she was transformed in her thinking and actions. She called her sister on the phone and took the first step to reconcile with her.

We're hoping that all who read this book will embrace their identity in Jesus and live it out in their day-to-day lives—one small step at a time. What about you? Is your life becoming increasingly marked by love, care, and service to others? Jot down some of the actions you've taken (or could take in the coming weeks) as a result of reading the book.

Transforming others. God desires to transform your life, but he also desires to transform the lives of every man and woman on earth. God desires everyone to embrace the truth of their identity in Jesus. He often uses our transformation story to reach others. Who do you know that can be transformed by embracing the truth of their identity in Christ? Jot down in the margins of the book the people who come to mind. Consider meeting them for coffee and suggesting that you read through the book together. You may be able to play an important role in their transformation.

God sent Jesus to earth on a rescue mission—a mission we get to participate in. May each of us join God in reaching others with the truth of our identity in Jesus. One thing you can do to reach others is to write your transformation story, your testimony. You have watched twenty-one testimonies in this book. Now it's your turn. What were you like before meeting Jesus and how has he changed your life after coming to faith? Think of two people with whom you can share your story.

And may we also suggest that you find other people who can benefit from this book? Perhaps you can start a small group to work through the book together. You can play an important role in helping others embrace their true identity in Jesus and begin finding freedom in Jesus.

Final challenges. We urge you to write down all twenty-one definitions of the terms on note cards and meditate on one word each day before you get out of bed. There's no better way to start the day than with a reminder of your identity in Jesus.

God loves you so much that he sent Jesus to save you and transform your identity. May you rest in that truth.

Encouragement and Prayer by John-Paul and Matt: Point your phone's camera at the QR code and follow the link or go to youtube.com /@FindingFreedomInJesusBook.

Please check out our social media sites where many are posting testimonies of and praises for what God is doing in their lives as they find freedom in Jesus. Maybe you can share your story. #findingfreedominjesusbook

Challenges in Life Addressed in the Book

A nother way to use this book is to seek encouragement when struggling with a life issue. The following is a list of common issues or struggles in the left column. The chapters in this book that offer help are listed in the right column.

ABANDONMENT	Adopted, Shame-Free, Transformed
ADDICTION	Free
ALCOHOLISM	Free, Rescued, Saved, Shame-Free, Transformed
ANGER	Forgiven, Reconciled
BITTERNESS	Reconciled
BROKEN RELATIONSHIPS	Adopted, Forgiven, Loved, Reconciled, Shame-Free
LACK OF COURAGE	Empowered, Transformed
CULTURAL CHRISTIANITY	Holy
DEPRESSION	Co-Heir, Loved, Transformed, Victorious
DIVORCE	Shame-Free
DOUBTS	Alive, Blessed, Hopeful, Reconciled, Transformed
DRUGS	Rescued, Saved, Shame-Free, Transformed
EATING DISORDERS	Beautiful
EMPTINESS	Beautiful, Forgiven, Loved, Transformed
FATHERLESSNESS	Alive, Adopted, Co-Heir, Known, Saved
FEAR	Forgiven, Known, Transformed
FRIENDSHIPS	Known
GREED	Free
GRIEF	Co-Heir, Rescued
GUILT	Forgiven, Righteous, Redeemed, Shame-Free
LEGALISM	Righteous
LONELINESS	Alive, Adopted, Blessed, Known
LOST DREAMS	Hopeful, Known, Rescued, Transformed
LOW SELF-IMAGE	Beautiful, Introduction, Holy, Righteous, Shame-Free, Transformed
MARITAL ISSUES	Image Bearer, Shame-Free
MENTAL HEALTH	Alive, Forgiven, Known, Transformed
PORNOGRAPHY	Alive, Shame-Free
RACISM	Known, Image Bearer, Loved, Reconciled
SELF-HARM	Free, Known, Redeemed, Transformed
SELF-HATRED	Beautiful, Loved, Shame-Free

SEXUAL ASSAULT	Forgiven, Free, Victorious
SEXUAL PROMISCUITY	Co-Heir, Forgiven, Loved, Transformed
SHAME	Forgiven, Righteous, Redeemed, Shame-Free
SICKNESS	Hopeful, Loved, Saved
SORROW	Co-Heir, Rescued
SPIRITUAL WARFARE	Empowered, Forgiven, Introduction, Saved, Victorious
SUFFERING	Blessed, Hopeful, Rescued, Saved
TRIALS	Blessed, Hopeful, Reconciled, Rescued, Saved
FEELING UNLOVED	Loved
FEELING UNSEEN	Blessed, Image Bearer, Known

Notes

Chapter 1: Transformed

1. Blaise Pascal, *Pensées* (Penguin, 1966), 75.
2. James M. Kerr, "Can People Really Change Who They Are?," *Psychology Today*, June 20, 2023, www.psychologytoday.com/us/blog/indispensable -thinking/202306/can-people-really-change-who-they-are.

Chapter 3: Known

1. "Loneliness and the Workplace: 2020 U.S. Report," Cigna, January 2020, https://legacy.cigna.com/static/www-cigna-com/docs/about-us /newsroom/studies-and-reports/combatting-loneliness/cigna-2020 -loneliness-report.pdf.
2. Zara Abrams, "The Science of Why Friendships Keep Us Healthy," American Psychological Association, June 1, 2023, www.apa.org /monitor/2023/06/cover-story-science-friendship.

Chapter 4: Beautiful

1. Suzanne Moore, "One in 10 Men Think They Are Hot—Women Need That Confidence Too," *The Guardian*, September 17, 2019, www.theguardian .com/commentisfree/2019/sep/17/men-think-they-are-beautiful-women -need-that-confidence-too.

2. "Building the Perfect Body," Treadmill Reviews, accessed September 10, 2024, www.treadmillreviews.net/building-the-perfect-body/.

3. Jennifer S. Mills et al., "'Selfie' Harm: Effects on Mood and Body Image in Young Women," *Body Image* 27 (December 2018): 86–92, www.sciencedirect.com/science/article/pii/S1740144517305326.

4. "The Beauty Boom and Beyond: Can the Industry Maintain Its Growth?," McKinsey & Company, September 11, 2024, www.mckinsey.com/industries/consumer-packaged-goods/our-insights/the-beauty-boom-and-beyond-can-the-industry-maintain-its-growth.

Chapter 6: Free

1. "The Science-Backed Benefits That Random Acts of Kindness Have on Your Health," Life First, accessed January 3, 2025, www.lifefirstassessment.com.au/blog/2021/april/the-science-backed-benefits-that-random-acts-of-kindness-have-on-your-health/.

Chapter 7: Shame-Free

1. Brené Brown, "Shame vs. Guilt," BreneBrown.com, January 15, 2013, https://brenebrown.com/articles/2013/01/15/shame-v-guilt/.

2. "Brené Brown on Shame and Accountability," BreneBrown.com, July 1, 2020, https://brenebrown.com/podcast/brene-on-shame-and-accountability/.

Chapter 9: Forgiven

1. See Everett L. Worthington Jr., "The New Science of Forgiveness," *Greater Good Magazine*, September 1, 2004, https://greatergood.berkeley.edu/article/item/the_new_science_of_forgiveness.

Chapter 13: Saved

1. Jessica Martinez, "Biola University Replicates Iconic Los Angeles 'Jesus Saves' Sign," *Christian Post*, August 1, 2013, www.christianpost.com/news/biola-university-replicates-iconic-los-angeles-jesus-saves-sign.html.

Chapter 15: Blessed

1. Erika Stoerkel, "The Science and Research on Gratitude and Happiness,"

PositivePsychology.com, February 4, 2019, https://positivepsychology
.com/gratitude-happiness-research/.

Chapter 16: Alive

1. "Study: Americans Seek Soul-Mate Spouse," ABC News, June 13, 2001, https://abcnews.go.com/US/story?id=93078&page=1.
2. Cited in Robert McAllister, "Divorce Rates in US 2025: Current Trends and Analysis," NCH Stats, December 11, 2024, https://nchstats.com /divorce-rates-in-us/.
3. Ingrid Solano, Nicholas R. Eaton, and K. Daniel O'Leary, "Pornography Consumption, Modality and Function in a Large Internet Sample," *Journal of Sexual Research* 57, no. 1 (January 2020): 92–103, https:// pubmed.ncbi.nlm.nih.gov/30358432/.
4. "Suicide Data and Statistics," U.S. Centers for Disease Control and Prevention, accessed September 10, 2024, www.cdc.gov/suicide/facts /data.html.

Chapter 19: Adopted

1. "Statistics Tell the Story: Fathers Matter," National Fatherhood Initiative, accessed September 10, 2024, www.fatherhood.org/father -absence-statistic.
2. "About the Children," Adopt US Kids, accessed September 10, 2024, www.adoptuskids.org/meet-the-children/children-in-foster-care/about -the-children.
3. "Facts and Stats," Home for Every Child, accessed September 10, 2024, www.homeforeverychild.org/facts-and-stats.

Chapter 20: Co-Heir

1. See "Anxiety Statistics in the United States," Los Angeles Outpatient Center, October 20, 2024, https://laopcenter.com/mental-health/anxiety -statistics-in-the-united-states/.

Chapter 21: Hopeful

1. "My Hope Is Built on Nothing Less" (1834), words by Edward Mote.